Looking For America

Essays on Youth, Suburbia, and Other American Obsessions

Bennett M. Berger

University of California, Davis

Prentice-Hall, Inc., Englewood Cliffs, New Jersey

From their long haired father
this book is for Jane and for Nora,
who may read it someday;
and for my mother and father
from their son, the professor.

Neil Smelser, editor

Library of Congress Catalog Card Number: 70–127857

P: 13–540500–9
C: 13–540518–1

Current Printing (last digit):
10 9 8 7 6 5 4 3 2 1

Prentice-Hall International, Inc., London
Prentice-Hall of Australia, Pty., Ltd., Sydney
Prentice-Hall of Canada, Ltd., Toronto
Prentice-Hall of India Private Limited, New Dehli
Prentice-Hall of Japan, Inc., Tokyo

Contents

Foreword

On Cultural Resonance

Collecting a group of one's essays provides an occasion for raising questions about the meaning of one's work. But the occasion is probably not conducive to candid or conclusive answers to these questions because the prior decision to collect the essays and make a book of them constrains one to defend the decision: one's thinking is biased from the outset. When, for example, the traditional question is raised of whether the essays have that proverbial, and elusive, "unifying theme," no one really expects a negative answer and one is rarely provided. In this respect, I shall conform to prevailing practice; yet even though I believe that my work does have a common theme, I want to add that it is the prospect of seeing my scattered work collected, and the anticipation of holding the book, the *objet*, that motivates me to think in some detail about the character of that common theme, I am not, in short, collecting these essays *because* they have a common theme; I am constrained to think about and define that theme by the prospect of imposing coherence on a book.

This prospect is especially challenging to me because I have always been put a little uptight by questions, innocent as often as not, about what kind of sociologist I am, or what my "special field" (or fields) of interest is. Depending on my mood and/or the questioner,

I have usually evaded the questions, either with wisecracks like "I don't believe in premature specialization for young sociologists" or "I'm still trying to find myself as a sociologist"; or, if I think the ironies likely to be wasted, I answer simply and empirically, by reference to the things I have in fact researched or written on: youth, suburbia, generations, hippies, leisure, and so on. But I call these answers evasions because there are many things I not only don't know about these matters, but have no special wish to know. The fact is that I tend to get bored with (and more than a little sad about) a subject once I have satisfied my initial curiosity. I cannot, therefore, say that as a sociologist my professional interests lie in these "fields" because I believe that a scholarly interest in a "field" should imply at least *some* desire to become *exhaustively* familiar with it. But I am not a "dilettante" (although I do not regard the label as pejorative) because my curiosities do have a pattern; I think it is more accurate to say that my interests lie, not in the "fields" of youth, suburbia, etc., but in an abstracter something which they exemplify. I call that something "cultural resonance," and the sociological analysis of it is what I take to be my business.

Cultural Resonance

Let's try a definition. Events or images are culturally resonant when they evoke deep emotional response (positive or negative) from large numbers of people because they touch something vital or important (though perhaps not conscious) in the common life, which they affirm, challenge, modify, or (if it is not yet conscious) create. Babbitt was culturally resonant. Canny old New England codgers still are, and so too are crusty old Generals. Also Marlboro men and guitar-playing loners. But not accountants and dental technicians. Rich in symbolic content, culturally resonant images and events are the material of myth because they touch a people's sense of their past and anticipation of their future. Debutante cotillions and Homecoming weekends, Christmases and State fairs and "westerns" are culturally resonant. But so, it appears, is *The Graduate* (less a film than a Phenomenon), and so are sit-ins, be-ins. and love-ins; and, judging by the prime time and space they have commanded in the big media over the past few years, the Hippies are the most culturally resonant thing to have occurred in a long time.

The noun "resonance" suggests that, in going far beyond the people directly involved with them and the groups to whose interests they are directly relevant, such images and events mobilize widespread projective predispositions to reject or affirm them, and to identify with them or to render them alien. The adjective "cultural" is intended to signify that the power of resonant images and events to command these emotional responses is triggered not by economic self-interest, political expedience, or any other purely instrumental considerations (although these may in fact eventually be objectively affected), but by their direct appeal (or threat) to the "expressive" or "consummatory" values which presumably transcend immediate interests and characterize the cultural unity of a people.

But the common culture is continually contested in a pluralistic society like our own; and when the contest becomes politically acute (as it has in our own time, when previously submerged, voiceless, or barely tolerated groups are claiming not only power but legitimacy), the very institutions designed to cope "reasonably" with internal conflict are shaken. And as the values that define legitimacy are threatened, the fragility of social order itself is revealed. It is this kind of cultural resonance which reveals the dissolution of consensus and threatens the prevailing conception (or conceptions) of solidarity, that interests me as a sociologist.

Youth (and particularly youthful rebellion) is culturally resonant not simply because we almost all have children or because of the traditionally "child-centeredness" of our society and its belief in progress. Youth commands fascinated attention (1) because postindustrial development has spawned an enormous and concentrated cohort of young persons whose juvenile status has been prolonged beyond the capacity of the conventions of childhood to control them; (2) because many of their interests and aspirations cannot comfortably be accommodated in our social structure; (3) because in a society in which the structure of opportunity systematically loosens the young from parental influences, parents seem to make increasingly large sentimental investments in their children, and to continue looking to them for evidence affirming their own lives; and (4) because youth involves the problem of generational succession, and therefore of cultural continuity itself.

"Suburbia" is culturally resonant because, in promoting a homogeneous image of an undifferentiated America, it immediately evokes conflicting conceptions of the good life: the domestic enclave full of

plenty, or the dull, plastic, split-level trap. The whole topic of "leisure" is culturally resonant because the problem of overproduction and the endemic alienation from work which mass production technology brought with it have seriously weakened the ethic of work through which men were expected to find personal fulfillment, and made it necessary for them to find the activities that render life "meaningful" in leisure (our free-est time). Black culture is resonant because in claiming honor and authenticity as *American* culture, it threatens traditional conceptions of "the American" which have denied its reality by ignoring it. And finally, sociology itself is culturally resonant because in aiming at a science of human groups, it endangers human freedom by threatening to yield up to rational understanding matters traditionally regarded as *properly* and eternally mysterious.

Sociological Analysis of Cultural Resonance

When I was a graduate student, I used to think that I was interested in the sociology of knowledge because, like many radical students, I thought it could be used to "unmask" the establishment ideologies implicit in the conventional wisdoms, or for similar goals in the ideas-are-weapons game. But I found that beyond the fiery programmatics it could be used for, the sociology of knowledge was simply too demanding an empirical discipline for someone without comprehensive historiographic learning or any greater command of European languages than it took to pass Ph.D. examinations. Lacking the necessary tools (and insufficiently motivated to acquire them), I gradually lost interest in the sort of *Wissensoziologie* that American scholars had inherited from the great European (mostly German) macrosociologists, and turned to subject matter more suited to the poverty of my analytic equipment.

But the influence of my early interest in the sociology of knowledge seemed to rub off on virtually every intellectual task I subsequently undertook. For one thing, I was frequently more interested in images of and ideas about culturally resonant events than I was in the events themselves. Thus, for example, I was less interested in sociology's actual contribution to the understanding of men in groups than in the character of the discourse (particularly the stereotypes) generated among intellectuals by the possibility of such contribution; I was less interested in suburbanization as a major aspect of the more general

urbanization process than in the ideas about "suburbia" (particularly the myths about it) that were generated by the facts of population movement and the patterns of residential construction; I was less interested in the "problem of youth" than in ideas about the relevance of chronological age to social behavior (youth is radical, age conservative; youth is idealistic, age realistic, etc.)—ideas which, by *defining* "childhood," "adolescence," "adulthood," and "old age," *establish* a categorical age-grading system, *promote* behavior appropriate to each category, and therefore, in a sense, *create* "the problem of youth." Similarly, I was less interested in hippies and in what made them the way they are than in their ability to evoke such intense hatred from people not directly threatened by them and in the apparent inability of the mass media to leave them alone (confirming, in a way, the tendency of ecstatic youth to believe that "the movement" is the most important truly revolutionary thing that has ever happened in this country); I was less interested in differences between parents and children than in the magical, evocative qualities that the idea of "generations" (and generational conflict) seemed to possess in organizing the sentiments of groups whose character was defined less by age than by ideology; I was less interested in what people actually did with their free time than in the power of "the problem of leisure" to mobilize the latent punditry of the nation; and I was less interested in the politics of black power than in the mythic potential of ideas about black culture and black identity to legitimate Negro ethnicity and institutionalize it as an honorable part of the public life of the United States.

The subject matter, then, is mostly ideas, but the analysis is sociological in a manner not unrelated to familiar models of the sociology of knowledge. In most of the essays that follow, consistent attempts are made (1) to identify the specific groups that are most responsible for the development and promotion of the ideas, (2) to relate these ideas to the interests, aims, or needs of the groups promoting them by examining the kinds of action they facilitate or obstruct, and (3) to account for the cultural resonance of the ideas by revealing the ways in which they bear upon basic problems of solidarity and consensus in the society, and therefore evoke intense response from groups not directly concerned with them.

The satiric or resentful characterization of sociologists as jargon-ridden or Machiavellian or "reducing people to statistics," for example, was largely the work of journalists, philosophers, literati, and

other "humanists" who were threatened by the claims of sociologists to expertise in the kinds of social analysis traditionally regarded as a humanistic function. And these ideas were resonant because by suggesting that the efforts of "specialized" professionals at social analysis were heavy-handed, pretentious, and unilluminating, they touched the interests a democratic society has in maintaining the belief that the common sense of ordinary citizens is adequate for the solution of social problems. The power of the myth of suburbia lay in its unexpected ability to mobilize strong emotions in usually opposed groups, but for differing ideological ends. Main Street real estate interests could celebrate the wide distribution of comfort and affluence suburbia represented; urban intellectuals could attack its dullness and routine. The myth was resonant because, like "Our Town" and "Organization Man" and "The Melting Pot," it was another effort to create a homogeneous image of America. The celebration of black culture and of black identity ("soul," "black is beautiful," "naturals" dashikis, etc.) is obviously an attempt by black power militants to honor and affirm Negro ethnicity, and thus to combat the subtler forms of prejudice and discrimination which "disadvantage" blacks. The idea is resonant because, in aiming at the eventual integration of the group *through* the institutionalization of its ethnicity, it evokes the deepest sorts of racism which are endemic in America.

On Not Being One Thing

Cultural Resonance, then, is news. And the success of the gate-keepers of culture depends in large part upon the accuracy with which they estimate what large numbers of people will want to read about, see movies and TV about, what kinds of music they are willing to listen and dance to, what kinds of clothes they are ready to wear (and take off). Resonance is what makes editors decide that certain events are news while others are not worth reporting; it is what makes the *New York Times Book Review* decide that almost any work of fiction is worth reviewing but that very few scholarly books are (because novels are "of general interest" while research monographs are "for specialists"). Resonance is why there are sports pages and theater pages and "society" pages in newspapers, but not nursery school pages or pages reporting events in the worlds of optometry or dentistry (eyes and teeth are, after all, very important).

Although most of my subjects are news—and controversial—my hope is that in collecting these essays I go beyond journalism to sociological analysis. In doing so, I risk losing both of the audiences I want to reach. I want, first, to reach social scientists and their students. From them I need the indulgence that the *essay* requires—especially from those trained to look skeptically, if not disdainfully, at assertions unsupported by evidence systematically gathered to test them. What I want is the temporary suspension of disbelief that anyone who writes as I do could have anything of interest to say to someone who fancies himself an empirical scientist. Although there is very little systematic evidence here, I offer in return for indulgence not only a book which I venture to hope will be a pleasure to read, but also a conceptually disciplined, yet critical, perspective on the sociology of culture which can provide sociologists doing research on these problems with (1) a source of hypotheses, (2) a mode of interpreting findings, (3) a guide to the anticipation of error and the minimization of bias, and (4) a way of making their findings "relevant" through the conscious use of moral feelings to enrich analysis without violating the essential canons of science.

But I would be disappointed if my pretensions to social science were to put off the general reader who is looking for casual illumination of the issues I have called culturally resonant, because I want this audience too. When *Time* magazine decides to devote a new section of its "back of the book" to events in the social sciences, it suggests not only that social science has itself become culturally resonant but that *Time's* readers might be interested in some of what I have to say. From these readers I need the sort of indulgence that the occasional use of technical language requires. But the jargon is minimal; I do myself less an injustice, even, in calling it jargon, because most of what little technical language I use is well on its way into common usage. I need also from these readers some suspension of the impatience they may feel at the elusiveness of my "stand" on many of the issues I discuss. It is not my primary intention in these essays to praise and blame or to warn and exhort, although how I feel about these issues should be clear to a careful reader. In return for these indulgences I offer the kinds of analyses of persisting public issues whose relevance will survive tomorrow's news.

I want these essays to convey the sense of a whole man thinking with his full complexity and therefore not being merely one thing: not a scholar or a spokesman, not an academic or a demagogue, not

a specialist or a generalist, or an ivory towerer or a militant. These are the kinds of choices which an academic man writing on resonant and relevant public issues is continually constrained to make. I reject these choices in favor of an unsatisfactory and unstable attempt to be both at all times. I do not think that this is a veiled self-congratulation. I know that in affirming detachment I sacrifice something of the "human" in me; and I know that in affirming my own involvement with the materials of my essays, I sacrifice part of the scholar in me. I make these sacrifices consciously because although they diminish me as a "scholar" and as a "human being," what one actually "is" transcends these vain categories. If any justification for such transcendence is needed, it is because understanding American culture requires it. Hence, *Looking for America.*

Youth

Introduction

The essays in this part of the book express my interest in youth—
in everything from the systems of age-grading which define it, to
the specific nature of adolescence, to its prolongation under conditions of industrialization, to its alleged creation of a distinctive culture
or subculture of its own, to the more immediate preoccupations of
the moment with hippies and student rebellions. **How Long is a
Generation?** is my first published expression of this interest. It was
written in the winter of 1959 in response to the broad public discussion of the then-contemporary "Beat Generation," and was motivated by what I took to be very careless usage of the *idea* of generations by intellectuals who were educated to know better. With so
many sources of conflict among groups so readily apparent, it seemed
to me absurd that so flimsy a basis for conflict as age differences
should suddenly claim the attention of so many people. It was this
absurdity, too, that started me thinking about the cultural resonance
of certain ideas ("generations" is one of them) which provide intellectuals with conceptual vocabularies that, although precluding the
possibility of any solution to the problems to which they are applied,
allay anxieties about the problems by creating the impression that
we are "working on" them.

That year, the year after I finished my Ph.D. dissertation, I was giving a course on intellectuals at Berkeley, and the essay on generations contains some of the ideas I developed for lectures. Donald MacRae, who was Editor of *The British Journal of Sociology*, was Visiting Professor at Berkeley when I circulated a first draft of the essay among my colleagues for comment and criticism. Professor MacRae asked for it for his journal, and I was very pleased to have it published there, without substantial revision.

The Youth Business, is a review I did for *Commentary* of two scholarly journals that had devoted their entire issues to collections of articles on youth. The review emphasizes, as much of my work on youth does, two errors frequently made by scholarly as well as popular writers: the tendency to identify the experience of elite youth or deviant youth with youth in general, and the neglect by these writers (and the consequent misunderstandings) of the problem posed by discontinuities between the facts of chronological age (for example those revealed in survey data) and the phenomena of culture, (for example the issues that make their way into public discourse as "the youth problem").

Beyond this, the review taught me a little about the consequences of writing for prestigious general magazines, for example, the ambiguous attitudes of one's colleagues, combining envy and disdain (envy at having captured audiences of intellectuals outside of one's own "field," disdain for the price in conceptual simplifications one is presumed to have had to pay), and the gradual realization (via mail and other comment from readers) that one is actually being read by thoughtful people because one is an interesting writer rather than because what one has written is "in" somebody else's "field" and makes an "important contribution" to it. I was pleased, too, that with all I had heard about the heavy editing that went on at *Commentary*, the review appeared very much as I had originally written it—although the rumors turned out to be correct (and, I must admit, salutary) with respect to the article on Talcott Parsons, which appears later in this collection.

Adolescence and Beyond is also a review, written in 1962, when my thinking about youth was developing most rapidly under the influence of the several seminal books which had been published in the few years immediately preceding. Like thousands of others, I was enormously excited by Paul Goodman's *Growing Up Absurd* (even before its publication as a book, when it began appearing as essays

in *Commentary*), and found it, along with James Coleman's *The Adolescent Society* and Edgar Friedenberg's *The Vanishing Adolescent* very useful in developing my own ideas about youth. At the meetings of the Midwest Sociological Association in 1962 I discussed some of these ideas with Howard Becker, who was then Editor of *Social Problems*, which was initiating a policy of running long essay—reviews of groups of important books, and Becker asked me to do one on some of the recent books on youth. "Adolescence and Beyond" is the result, appearing more than a year later—which says something more about the slow pace at which I write than it does about the lag between finished manuscript and print.

If I seem excessively critical of these books, it is not because I regard them as pernicious or unimportant (I don't) but because I *used* them to help clarify my own ideas, and I could do this only by pinpointing as precisely as I could my grounds for disagreeing with much of what they said: with the thinness of Coleman's conception of adolescent culture and his neglect of some of its important functions, with the deliberately apocalyptic and flauntingly naive character of Goodman's utopianism, and with Friedenberg's unabashed love for certain features of some adolescents which alternately blurred his vision of what most of them were like and enraged him at the adult institutions which molded them in ways that offended his vision of what they might be.

On the Youthfulness of Youth Cultures was written in the same productive period as "The Youth Business" and "Adolescence and Beyond." I used the first draft for a lecture at Purdue University in the spring of 1961. It went through several writings, and I held on to it, partly because I was hoping to add some empirical material from a study of bohemian business men I was then planning (but never did because I decided to change jobs and move back to California). When I decided to commit it to print, I didn't quite know where to send it, because it seemed to me to be a model of that kind of article which is too "technical" for the general magazines, and too—what? discursive?—for the sociology journals. But because it contained my fullest statement on the relationship between age-grading and the development of subcultures I sent it to the *American Sociological Review*. It was returned with editors' remarks, many of them snide, about an article of this sort being more appropriate for a general magazine. Meanwhile, Dennis Wrong had taken over the editorship of *Social Research*, that oddly named theoretical journal

published by The New School, and it finally appeared there in the fall of 1963, without much change from the version completed about a year earlier.

The Identity Myth takes off from a point made in passing in "Adolescence and Beyond" about the fashionableness of the phrase "the search for identity." One of the continuing themes in my work is an attempt to discover the "functions" of (and hence, in a sense, to understand) successful ideas by attending to the problems they help solve (or perpetuate) for the groups promoting and receiving them. Ideas, especially when they touch sensitive spots in the culture, can become successful without much respect to the evidence on which they rest, and my interest in the problem of identity is less an interest in what "identity" actually is (if, indeed, it can be said to be "actually" anything) than in why "sensitive" young people (and their devoted following of sympathetic social scientists) seemed to take hold of the "problem" of identity as one that seemed "real" to them, as one with which they could "identify." In a seminar I was giving on youth culture in 1966 I took up the identity problem as one of the "typical" problems of adolescence and raised the question of what role the *idea* of identity as an adolescent problem played, how it became a familiar textbook problem, and how "who am I?" became the poignant question it is for "searching" young people as well as for those who study them. After exploring the problem with a second seminar group early in 1967, I prepared "The Identity Myth" as a lecture to a group of psychiatrists and psychologists and other staff people of a private mental hospital near Chicago. In it I used some material that I had previously used for an article in *The New York Times Magazine* in 1965.

The New York Times Magazine was also where my essay on **Student Unrest and the Crisis in the Universities** first appeared, although the Times' editors titled it "The New Stage of American Man—Almost Endless Adolescence." The flamboyance of this title reflects my emphasis on prolonged adolescence and the "idealism" consequent to it as important elements in the role students have played in antiwar and civil rights activism. Several readers interpreted the article as "conservative" and as a put-down of militant students. Rather than deny this by saying that my personal sympathy and identifications are with the militant students, it is more important that I note that the very character of my sociological *anaysis* leads to a "conservative" interpretation (despite my personal sympathies)

because the analysis "explains" the prominence of students in contemporary social movements by reference to the predispositions promoted by their social location rather than by reference to their nobility in transcending this location to oppose evil or misguided policies.

With such analysis I hope to emphasize the *ambiguity* of the fact that people whom we are pleased to call "kids" (and who are apparently not unpleased by such reference) may, under the right conditions, transform the "disadvantages" of their less-than-adult status and their ghettoization in university-warehouses into a "children's crusade" sufficient to bring down a President and bring the country to the edge of paralysis. I write this as four Kent State University students lie dead, as hundreds of colleges and universities remain closed or on strike, as thousands of students march on state and national capitals, as the New York Stock Exchange is nearly brought to a halt by riots in the street outside, and as Administration officials resign, consider resigning, or admit to being "deeply troubled," while surviving spokesmen take to the TV tubes or scurry about hastily arranging audiences with outraged citizens to defend administration policy or to accommodate the outpouring of feeling whose magnitude they clearly did not anticipate.

There are other ambiguities in the article, some of which I did not anticipate. The closing of the universities, for example, is something militant students have repeatedly tried to accomplish, but they hardly expected it to be done at the order of a Governor yielding not to their demands but trying to cool their passions by urging them to go home and talk with their families. But in anticipating the closing of the universities, I minimized the importance of its effects upon the national economy without realizing that it would free millions of university students to take to the streets. However, I did foresee that keeping the universities open was significant more for the warehousing function it would perform than for any educational benefits that might accrue. Similarly, I expected student anger to turn from the universities to more crucial institutions, like the stock exchange and the Bank of America, although when I anticipated attacks on the Bank of America more than a year before its Isla Vista branch near the University of California, Santa Barbara was burned down, I did not anticipate attacks of such violence.

This section of the book concludes with three shorter pieces I have collectively called **Ecstatic Youth** in order to suggest that they

cover both hippies and some sectors of the "New Left." "*Hippie Morality*" was a new departure for me in the sense that it is the first essay I didn't agonize over for a long time. Early in the summer of 1967 I was invited to prepare a paper for delivery at the Plenary Session of the annual meetings of the Society for the Study of Social Problems. Although the assignment was something on "the new morality," I knew that this was code for something on the hippies—in whom I, like thousands of others during that "summer of love," was not exactly uninterested. I was thinking much that year about what seemed to me an incipient revolution in the spoken language—more than incipient, really, because it seemed to me that the institutionalization of "obscenity" was sufficiently far along that its use on public occasions, in official circumstances, even in ceremonial situations, was becoming more acceptable. I had, at the very least, *heard* it so used, and it tittilated me to imagine myself rising before the plenary session of the SSSP in the Grand Ballroom of the San Francisco Hilton, and not only making this point, but *demonstrating* it before the distinguished assemblage. Once motivated by this vision, I took about a week to write the paper. It was very well received, and several magazine representatives asked for it on the spot. It appeared in *Trans-action* (December 1967), in a special issue of that magazine devoted to hippies. The only problem arose when one of the editors suggested to me, in a memorable telephone conversation, that he might substitute the appropriate Latin phrase for one of the "obscenities" I used. It is the only time in my life that I threatened to withdraw an article unless it were printed as I wished. I have included in the version printed here a short introduction which was eliminated in the *Trans-action* version.

Self-Hatred and the Politics of Kicks began as a letter to Daniel Bell who, as a member of the "Committee on the Year 2000," had written to me asking for my thoughts on what he called "the enragés." Shortly after I replied to his letter, I was invited to participate in a conference on intellectuals at Oakland University in Michigan, and my long letter to Professor Bell became my contribution to that conference. One of the participants, Lewis Coser, is an editor of *Dissent*, and he suggested that I publish it there. I agreed, as long as the printed version contained a note explaining its origin as a personal letter and preserved the informal tone of that genre. It was printed in *Dissent* in the summer of 1966.

There is a story, too, behind my review of Lewis Yablonsky's book,

The Hippie Trip. The review was requested by *Psychiatry and Social Science Review*, a journal that deals exclusively in essay-reviews of current books. I read the book, wrote the review, and sent it to the editor. Shortly thereafter, it was returned with a note from the editor that he and his staff were resigning from the journal, and suggesting that it would probably not continue publication. So I sent the review to the Book Review Editor of *Trans-action*, who said that he liked it but would send it on to the Editor-in-Chief for final approval. I heard nothing further for a few months. I then got a letter from the *new* editor of *Psychiatry and Social Science Review* asking what had happened to the review I had agreed to do. In the meantime, I had reread my review several times, and decided it was a little harsh, so I toned it down somewhat and, having heard nothing final from *Trans-action*, resent it to the journal which had originally requested it. That very week, *Trans-action* (February 1969) appeared with my original review as the lead item in its book review section.

How Long Is a Generation?

1960

All of the recent talk in the United States about the "beat generation" and its meaning for our "age" may prove to have been worthwhile after all if it provokes, among British and American sociologists, serious interest in the study of the problem of generations—a problem which, from Comte down to Mannheim and Ortega y Gasset, has consistently interested serious continental thinkers.[1] For Mannheim and most other European students of the subject, the sociological importance of generations lies in the assumption that they are the

From *The British Journal of Sociology* 11, no. 1 (March 1960); reprinted with the permission of Routledge & Kegan Paul Ltd.

I would like to thank Reinhard Bendix, Leonard Cain, Erving Goffman, Robert Merton, and David Riesman for critical readings of an earlier draft of this article.

[1] That this interest may in fact be developing is indicated by three recent treatments of the problem which have just come to my attention. See Anselm Strauss' discussion in *Mirrors and Masks* (Glencoe, Ill.: Free Press, 1959), pp. 132–41; see also Herbert Hyman's comprehensive and disciplined analysis of data on generations in his *Political Socialization* (Glencoe, Ill.: Free Press, 1959), ch. VI, especially pp. 129–32; see also the paper by Norman Ryder, "The Cohort as a concept in the Theory of Social Change," delivered at the 1959 meetings of the American Sociological Society in Chicago.

agents or "carriers" of major cultural changes; changes in the "spirit of the age" or the formulation of a new *Zeitgeist* are in large part the work (in Ortega's fateful view, the "mission") of rising generations.[2] While British and American sociologists have in general neglected the problem of generations so conceived, survey researchers frequently use age-groups as one of the basic variables in terms of which they interpret their data. This essay is an attempt to analyze the peculiar place the generation concept has come to occupy in the vocabulary of American cultural discourse, and by so doing, to render the concept more useful for the purposes of empirical sociological analysis.

Webster following Herodotus, defines a generation as the period of time it takes for father to be succeeded by son, "usually taken to be about thirty-three years," and Mannheim says that most students of the problem of generations agree that a generation "lasts" about thirty years.[3] Presumably, then, if one begins at some arbitrary point, one would expect there to be roughly three "ages" in a century— but only if a change in the spirit of the age follows the rising of each new generation.[4] Clearly, however, this has not consistently been the case. In England it is commonly held that the last age of the nineteenth century (the one we call "Victorian") "lasted" for some sixty years. But regarding the sixty years of our own century in the United States, it is now usual to suggest that there have been at least four distinct cultural "periods," or "ages." Before World War I there was the "age" of tycoons and moguls. The war was followed by the period known simply but eloquently as "the twenties," or, in its roaring version, as the "jazz age." October 1929 ushered in the "proletarian decade" and the collective cultural experience with Marxism that

[2]Generations, according to Ortega, create changes in "vital sensibility"; he sees generations as a "compromise" between Marxist and Heroic theories of historical change. See ch. I of *The Modern Theme* (London: C. W. Daniel, 1931).

[3]See Karl Mannheim, "The Problem of Generations," in his *Essays on the Sociology of Knowledge* (New York: Oxford, 1952), p. 278. Mannheim says that some Europeans have taken a generation to mean a period of about fifteen years. Among these is Ortega. See Ortega's overly dogmatic statement in *Man and Crisis* (New York: Norton, 1958), ch. 4.

[4]To say even this, of course, assumes that there is *some* ultility in abstracting generational age-groups for analysis—that there is something more than an infinite succession of persons being born and dying at every moment.

American intellectuals have still not fully exorcized. The second world war marked the "transition" (all ages, of course, are "ages of transition") to this "age of conformity" which is said to be characterized by a generation of Organization Men and "suburbanites." And if, as some have remarked, the recent summit conferences, U.S. Supreme Court decisions, the passing of Senator McCarthy and the waning of his ism symbolize yet another turning point, then perhaps the emergence of still another "age" is imminent. From a "Victorian age" spanning about sixty years, we seem to have reached a point where a change in *Zeitgeist* may be expected at approximately ten-year intervals.

I say seem. Are generations shrinking? Is the character of our "age" so ephemeral that it is gone almost before it has had time to take shape? Certainly the aplomb with which intellectuals play the game of naming the age and the generation would lead one to think so. Certainly, too, the view has been cogently argued. The apparent tendency for the time period referred to by the term "generation" to shrink, and the corresponding tendency for the duration of an age to contract have been explained as the cultural consequences of the increased pace of technological change and the repeated cataclysmic social upheavals to which our century has been witness—upheavals which create sudden discontinuities between the age groups upon which they have had a sharp impact and the age groups to which they are only history.[5] When C. S. Lewis says that Dr. Johnson is closer to Seneca than he is to us, he is suggesting that the changes wrought by the past two hundred years are more profound than the changes in the previous two thousand. Neumann, in a shorter historical view, says that "The Cavalcade of thirty years nowadays includes more changes than three centuries before did," and Lionel Trilling has called attention to the "enormous acceleration in the rate at which the present is superannuated as the past." If we accept these views for the moment, it may certainly seem sensible to expect the concept of the generation to telescope—as critical events and

[5]The clearest expression of this view is in Sigmund Neumann, "The Conflict of Generations in Contemporary Europe," *Vital Speeches* (August 1, 1939), which begins, "Modern European politics from Versailles to Munich can be largely explained in terms of a conflict of generation." Neumann conjures up an image of Hitler and Chamberlain at Munich: Hitler, the young warrior of World War I (age 48) and Chamberlain, the late Victorian gentleman (age 68).

experiences crystallize at an accelerated pace to create new "generational mentalities" which are subsequently manifested as "the spirit of the age."[6]

But even putting aside the circular logic that usually lies behind this kind of formulation, there is really very little evidence to suggest that recent generations are coming to maturity in quicker succession than in previous centuries. At the same time, however, one cannot avoid being struck by the rapidity with which intellectual "movements" are given generational identities; intellectuals seem to crouch ready and waiting to spring upon each political and cultural event with interpretations suggesting imminent and momentous changes in the temper of the time, and magazines both big and little, stand ready to print them. But to imply, as I have, that this is not a generational phenomenon is not to suggest that it has nothing to do with age-groups and conceptions of age; it has: the length of adolescence is increasing in the United States. And along with this "stretching" of youth have come great increases in the numbers of intellectuals, and in the specialization, decentralization, and bureaucratization of intellectual life.

1. Youth in America

Far from generations coming to maturity more rapidly today than in previous centuries, what little evidence there is seems to suggest the opposite. The age at which one enters adolescence appears in general to be getting lower, whereas the age at which one becomes a "mature" adult appears in general to be getting higher; the period of adolescence is thus expanded. Children dance, drink, date, go steady, become sexually aware and variously delinquent earlier today than thirty years ago.[7] At the other extreme, the increasing educa-

[6]Most students of the generation (in the sense of *Kultur*) agree that the source of the 'unity' of its outlook is its common exposure to decisive politically and culturally relevant experiences in the formative stages of its members' development—usually conceived of as late adolescence. See, for example, Rudolph Heberle's chapter on political generations in *Social Movements* (New York: Appleton-Century-Crofts, 1951).

[7]Increases in juvenile delinquency in recent years have come more notably in the 11–14 year old group than in the 15–21 group. On the developing group-consciousness of teen-agers, see Dwight McDonald's interesting profile of youth pollster Eugene Gilbert, *The New Yorker* (November 22 and 29, 1958).

tional requirements for occupational mobility upward lengthen the years spent in school, and to that extent postpone the assumption to full adult responsibilities by students. And even when students marry early and take on some responsibilities, there is a sense in which a student, no matter what his age, is not quite completely an adult. Mannheim calls attention to the "youthful" functions of student life when he remarks that evidence shows that late exposure of mature persons to a broad, liberal education precipitates an apparent seizure by "adolescent" traits; they pass through stages of tumult, vehemence, exhilaration, doubt, confusion, despair and so on.[8]

Evidence from novels (that first and last resort of the sociologist in search of data) suggests that for intellectuals especially, the resolution of moral and political perplexities into a mature and lasting *Weltanschauung* takes a longer time to formulate. If we compare nineteenth century European novels with contemporary American novels that deal with groups of young people struggling to "find themselves," a modern reader is rather startled to discover inadvertently and perhaps rather late in, say, a George Eliot or Dostoevski novel that some marvellously mature, articulate, and aware character is twenty or twenty-one years old. Their counterparts in contemporary American novels are usually in their late twenties and frequently as "old" as their late thirties.

This extension of "youthfulness" is rife in American culture. Youth groups today usually include members in their middle and late thirties; the junior chamber of commerce includes thirty-five year old business men; and our young writers—as Seymour Krim has shown—are as often as not middle-aged.[9] An English actress, generalizing lightly about American men recently, no doubt exaggerates but makes her point clearly when she says

[8]See "The Problem of the Intelligentsia," *Essays on the Sociology of Culture* (New York: Oxford, 1956), p. 164. Certainly there is some evidence to the contrary—especially regarding young people who are not students. Early marriage certainly dampens the irresponsibility and adventurousness of young people, and the whole complex of Organization Men with their ideology of "responsibility" suggests that maturity may come early to some. The cultural problem posed by this heterogeneity is discussed below, but it seems to me that the extension of youth is most visible among those intellectuals engaged in the creation and discussion of culture, that is, in the formulation of the spirit of the age.
[9]"Our Middle-Aged 'Young Writers'," *Commentary* (October 1952).

I find it difficult to separate the men from the boys. American men always look seven or eight years younger than they really are. When an Englishman is thirty years old, he looks thirty. And he's pretty well settled in his ways. When I meet a young American, I sort of pat him on the hand thinking he's a college lad. Then I find he's married and has four children.

What all this suggests is that Americans are members of the "younger generation" from the time they begin to stay out at night to the time they begin to grow bald and arthritic, and find the stairs steeper, and the coeds younger looking. The ease with which high school sub-bohemians mix with their thirty-five year old mentors in the same cool coffee shop milieu symbolizes the extended duration of "youth" in America—a period prone to cultural pronouncements, movements, "statements," rebellious outbursts, revolutionary flurries, and so on. In a public debate not long ago, Philip Selznick argued the view that the radical behavior of students is largely a function of their *temporary* alienation—temporary because it is their youth and immaturity which alienate them from participation in the major adult institutions, and not something permanent in their psychological make-up. What I am suggesting is that the extension of cultural definitions of "youth" to a period covering at least twenty years and sometimes longer, extends the period in which "youthful" (i.e. "irresponsible") behavior is positively sanctioned. Understanding this may help explain the apparent proliferation of "new" *Zeitgeist* and "new" generation "movements," which, if not the creations of precisely "young" men, are the creations of youthful men with a longer time to be young. It may also, for example, help explain the notorious failure of perpetually "promising" American novelists to "fulfill their promise" simply because acceptable *models* of intellectual "maturity" become difficult to find: as the chronological age associated with "maturity" goes up it becomes only too easy to identify maturity with loss of vigor, idealism, and principle—in short, with compromise.[10]

[10]The psychological crisis experienced by many American women who are passing into middle age may be the result of the lack of an ideal model of female middle-agedness. David Riesman has suggested to me that middle-aged men (or at any rate, rich, middle-aged men) are enabled to be vicariously young by surrounding themselves with young women—as one can see in the ads for Cadillacs and other elegant products—although this can have, too, the unanticipated consequence of increasing the poignance of aging.

And besides, the generation that students of culture trends are interested in is usually the "younger" generation—which may encourage intellectuals and other creative people to identify themselves with the "rising" group.

It may, of course, be that the extension of "youth" is related on the one hand to the demographic fact of increased life expectancy in industrialized societies, and on the other hand to the political fact that bureaucratization and party control of democratic processes in industrialized parliamentary societies subject young men to long periods of training, that is, waiting, for positions of power and responsibility. Over a hundred years ago, Comte believed that increases in life span would slow down the rate of social change because the period of dominance of any single generation would increase with increasing length of life; as the generation grew older its increased conservatism would, according to Comte, dampen the forces making for change inherent in the "rising" generation. What Comte failed to foresee was that the gerontocracies of Western Europe and the United States (how many more fatal attacks of the degenerative diseases. can our political elite sustain?) would, apparently, not only result in the extension of the definition of youth, but intensify the "youthfulness" and the resentments of the already balding "younger" generation.

2. Intellectuals: Numbers, Decentralization, Specialization

Clearly, if the concept of the generation, which is a *temporal* abstraction, is to have any utility for the empirical analysis of cultural phenomena, it must be kept analytically distinct from *structural* or *locational* (income, occupation, religion, ethnic status, etc.) concepts which also affect perspective or point of view.[11] Thus, although the extension of the period of time in which youthfulness is culturally defined as appropriate helps explain the apparent proliferation of divergent *Zeitgeist*, there are other social processes bearing upon the structure of intellectual life which also help foster this heterogeneity.

The rapidly increasing *numbers*, both absolute and proportionate, of intellectuals in the United States comes to mind first. S. M. Lipset

[11] It goes without saying, of course, that the current tendency to identify "my generation . . ." with "my school of thought . . ." obscures this distinction.

has recently called attention to this fact in an attempt to explain the relative isolation of American intellectuals (vis-à-vis Europeans and others) from the sources of power.[12] But the fact is relevant to the point under discussion here; for if it is too much to expect American economists to be able to formulate a joint statement of economic policy, it would be even more arrogant to expect American intellectuals, who must number in the hundreds of thousands, to be able to formulate a "spirit" common enough for all or even most to subscribe to. And it is surely more difficult for Americans to do this than English or French or German—or Australian intellectuals, whose numbers are so much fewer. And even in countries with relatively few intellectuals, the problem is by no means a simple one. The multiparty political system of the continent represents, perhaps, only the crudest dimension of experience which may fragment a single generation, and Mannheim's labored discussion of "generation units" is testimony to the difficulty in which analysts of generations find themselves the moment they attempt to comprehend not only the "unity" of a generation but its diversity also: The "age" of the tycoons and moguls was also the "age" of the muck-rakers; the "roaring twenties" was also the "age" of Harding, Coolidge, Babbitt and the "Booboisie."

In addition to the increase in the numbers of intellectuals, the cultural life of the United States is much less centralized than that of most European nations. French culture means Parisian culture; the revolt of England's Angry Young Men has been a revolt against the cultural domination of England by the London–Cambridge–Oxford "axis" and the classes it represents. New York does not come near to dominating the cultural life of the United States in the sense that London and Paris dominate the cultural life of England and France.

While New York may be said to be the intellectual capital of the United States, there are important groups of intellectuals scattered round the country whose combined number is far greater than those in or adjacent to New York. Important schools of writers and painters

---

[12]". . . in 1929 *all ten* professors of economics in Australia met and told the government they believed it would be disastrous for the country to go off the gold standard. The Labour government of the day was not happy about this but felt it should not move against the 'experts'. There are far too many such experts in America for them to have such corporate 'influence'. S. M. Lipset, "American Intellectuals: Their Politics and Status," *Daedalus*, (Summer 1959), 470.

exist in various parts of the country . . . [and] The two leading universities in the country . . . are located in Metropolitan Boston and San Francisco.[13]

One consequence of this, as Lipset himself observes, is to limit the extent to which American intellectuals are acquainted with each other —even when they happen to be in the same "field." Not only size, then, but the geographical dispersion of American intellectual communities, fosters the development of simultaneous multiple "generations" and "ages" based both upon the multiplicity of intellectual cliques and the influence of regionalism: the "proletarian decade" dates also the public emergence of the Southern Agrarian movement, conservative and anti-industrial; and, of course, Organization Men and "suburbanites" coexist, indeed, even interact with the "beat generation."[14]

But perhaps more important than the size and decentralization of American intellectual communities for the heterogeneous cultural character of the "age" and "the generation" is the bearing of occupation upon chronological age. Differences in the meaning of age in terms of occupation are probably most clear in athletics; a prize-fighter is an old man at thirty, a baseball player at thirty-five, but a presidential candidate is young at fifty. Factory workers begin losing their hopes for the future (such as they are) at around thirty-five. The thirty year old Ph.D. student is indeed an "old" student, but one successful year later, this thirty-one year old professor is a *young* professor. These are only the most striking examples, but instances could be multiplied of the difference in average age at which the incumbents of different social and occupational roles are considered "young," "mature," "old," etc., that is, differences in the age-range within which they tend to or are expected to produce their best or most representative work. Novelists, for example, often produce their best work in their twenties or early thirties. Musicians and painters, on the other hand, usually "mature" much later—painters, for example, are still "young" in their forties.[15]

---

[13]Lipset, ibid., 470–71.
[14]See Eugene Burdick's discussion of week-end bohemians in "Innocent Nihilists Adrift in Squaresville," *The Reporter* (April 3, 1958). See also, "Beatniks in Business," *Mademoiselle* (March 1959).
[15]In a book called *Young Painters of Promise* (London and New York: Studio Publications, 1957), of the 118 "young" artists whose birth dates are listed,

What this means is not only that members of the same age-groups may experience their most productive or representative period in different decades, but also that what they produce may be affected by different series of events. For these reasons it is essential, when using the concept of the generation in a cultural sense, to specify generations of *what*, because it is only in a demographic sense that people in the same age-group constitute a homogeneous unit, and because the character of any cultural generation depends in part upon the relationship of "youth" to years, and upon the average length of its vital or effective period—which differs according to occupational milieu.[16] There are, in short, literary generations, political generations, musical generations, etc.; the length of each fluctuates, and the age-range which constitutes the "younger" generation in one may be considerably older (or younger) than the age-range constituting the "younger" generation in another, to say nothing of the internal differentiations which may fragment a single cultural generation however defined.

What I am suggesting, then, is that if the concept of the generation is to be rendered useful for the sociology of culture, the temporal location of a group must first be kept analytically distinct from its structural location; second, when considering them together, we should be aware that the impact of structural (e.g. occupational) factors on the nature of the temporal location may, under some conditions, be such as to fragment the cultural "unity" of a generation beyond recognition just as under other conditions the unity of a generation may be such as to withstand the divisive influence of, say, class factors.

These tendencies toward divisiveness and heterogeneity do not, of course, go unopposed. The increasing *numbers* of intellectuals is accompanied by their increasing *organization* (for example, into professional associations), which restrains the tendencies toward heterogeneity. The increasing decentralization of intellectuals is accompanied by better *communications* among them, which acts as a brake on the tendency toward ideological fragmentation which geographical

---

45 are 35 years of age or older, 18 are over 40, 4 are over 50, including one young artist born in 1894.
[16]With some sarcasm, Harold Rosenberg, observes, ". . . one may, especially today, call any age-group he chooses a 'generation'—among ensigns or ballet dancers a generation is replaced every three or four years." *The Tradition of the New* (New York: Horizon Press, 1959), p. 247.

dispersion often encourages. (A remarkable feature of Jack Kerouac's novel *On the Road* is its suggestion that a network of bohemian communities exists between San Francisco, Denver, Chicago, and New York, each ready to accept to its bosom the bohemian travellers of the Road.) Finally, the tendency to specialization, which encourages the *ordering* of common bodies of data into increasingly different theoretical frames of concepts and meanings, is countered both by interdisciplinary tendencies (such as those represented in universities by comparative literature departments, integrated social sciences departments, and the new hybird physical and natural science disciplines) and by the processes of mass culture which act to break down the divisiveness of specialization. But to note that these counter-tendencies exist is not to attribute to them equal importance; it seems to me that at the present time, for reasons which will be made apparent below, that the divisive influences are stronger than the integrative ones.

In any case, it must seem odd that American intellectuals should be so preoccupied with the naming and fixing of "generations" and "ages" in a culture which is apparently so ill suited to being characterized in this way. Mannheim gives us the beginning of an explanation when he writes

. . . the mentality of a period does not pervade the whole society at a given time. The mentality which is commonly attributed to an epoch has its proper seat in one (homogeneous of heterogeneous) social group which acquires special significance at a particular time, and is able to put its intellectual stamp on all other groups. . . .[17]

I call it only a beginning because Mannheim goes on to explain *Zeitgeist* essentially as a function of the antagonisms *between* generations, and writes off the frequently polar responses of what he calls "units" of the *same* generation as an example of the dialectical principle which is synthesized by a common "generational mentality."[18] Indeed, Mannheim ignores the implications of his own specific insight when he raises (in a footnote) the question, "why have generations become so conscious of their unity today?"—and then drops it.

[17]"The Problem of Generations," op. cit., p. 313.
[18]In this respect, Mannheim comes close to Ortega, who believes that no difference between members of the same generation is as profound as the difference between persons of different generations.

One is tempted to be ill-mannered enough to answer the rhetorical question: for the obvious propensity of intellectual groups to identify themselves as generations (something that has grown even more pronounced since Mannheim noted it in the twenties) suggests that other modes of identification may have become less viable or, at the very least, less fashionable. Structural identifications such as those of class, party, ideology, race, etc., belong, in industrial societies, to a milieu of *conflict* in which the *function* of their identification is to foster the solidarity of the group so identified *against* other classes, parties, ideologies, etc. Generational identifications, on the other hand, although usually incapable of eliminating the structural sources of conflict, belong to a milieu of *integration,* and foster the structuring of conflict in terms of age-groups rather than in terms of other kinds of interest.[19] Such a mode of identification, by implying that age is a more significant source of disagreements among men than party or ideology, suggests that in due course these disagreements may disappear; that, for example, the "radicalism" of youth is more youthful than ideological, and that as the age-basis of commitment wanes, so will the commitment itself. This view permits one the luxury of *managing* one's opposition rather than *combating* it; political problems become administrative ones, conflicts over leadership become problems of succession; victory and defeat become questions of who co-opts and who is co-opted.

But that generational identifications are apt to be spurious (Harold Rosenberg states tartly that "belonging to a generation is one of the lowest forms of solidarity,"[20] in a complex industrialized society is indicated not only by the inherent structural heterogeneities of any age-groups in such a society (which I have discussed above), but by the interesting fact that the very *characterization* of "the age" and "the generation" has itself become an object of conflict. The "spirit of the age" is no longer merely something that "emerges" naturally (if indeed it ever did) out of the work of a generation's intellectual elite (as Ortega would have it) or even something that is formulated retrospectively by historians of later generations; the character of

[19]Neumann argues that the revolt of the Nazi elite was a revolt by young men against the pre-World War I generation of German leaders, and cites figures to show that the leaders of political and economic life in Weimar Germany were, in fact, a gerontocracy. Reinhard Bendix and others have argued that the early electoral successes of the Nazis was due in part to their winning the votes of young people.
[20]Op. cit., p. 244.

the contemporary "generation" and the "spirit" presumably created by it have become *ideological* questions *for its own members*. The problem of assessing the "spirit of the age" becomes not only a question of analyzing the works of its creators; a struggle ensues between different groups of intellectuals of the same generation (each conscious of itself not as a structurally defined group, but as a temporally located "generation") for the right *deliberately to define*, indeed to *name* the spirit of the age. For "naming" the age is not only a diagnostic function, it is an ideological one too; and to belong to a beat generation in an age of Organization Men is, like being a classicist in a romantic age, or an analyst of *Zeitgeist* in an age of logical empiricism, to be fated to live in a historical limbo, that is, to have been born too late (or too early) for "one's time."

Clearly, age-groups are important in the analysis of cultural phenomena, but their full significance is likely to remain elusive unless supplemented by the structural variables which not only give a cultural meaning to age but which locate one in a "school of thought," give one a distinct "perspective," and a place within an intellectual tradition which began neither in a North Beach bistro in San Francisco nor in a New York conference room high above Madison Avenue, nor, for that matter in a panelled salon in Bloomsbury. Viewing the matter this way, one is enabled conceptually to handle multiple continuities of thought between generations, and at the same time to distinguish between structurally defined groups of the contemporary generation who carry on the continuing struggle for the right to "represent" the age.[21]

It should be obvious, however, that all formulations of the nature of "the age" and "the generation" are essentially mythic in character; no "age" is wholly romantic, classic, anxious, or conformist, and no "generation" is wholly lost, found, beat—and certainly not silent.

[21]It is really to no one's benefit that the concept of the generation and the related concept of spirit of the age refer primarily to activity in the arts. The phenomena these concepts attempt to deal with occur in every field of intellectual endeavour—although probably with decreasing sharpness as one moves from the humanities through the social sciences to the natural sciences, the physical sciences and mathematics. Allen Ginsberg and Jack Kerouac on the one hand, and Truman Capote and William Styron on the other, belong to the same generation but to different intellectual and esthetic traditions. One could cite similar examples in music, painting—and sociology too. The work of C. Wright Mills is clearly an attempt to influence what the character of sociology shall be like in the twentieth century; but so is the work of David Riesman—and Paul Lazarsfeld—and Talcott Parsons.

Nevertheless, cultural struggles go on *as if* possession of the myth of the age were at stake; and in a sense it is, for those who win the struggle for the right to be considered "representative" of their age, in Weber's striking phrase, "usurp status,"[22] and their contributions are preserved in the large print of intellectual history, while those who lose are relegated to the always significantly smaller print of footnotes. Yielding, however, to the almost irresistible temptation to find something new and unprecedented in the contemporary situation, Harold Rosenberg has observed that "what is remarkable about the manufacture of myths in the twentieth century is that it takes place under the noses of living witnesses of the actual events and, in fact, cannot dispense with their collaboration."[23] Rosenberg's observation summarizes the apparent belief of intellectuals that their historical sophistication is great enough to permit them to anticipate the historian's function; understanding that the characterization of the past is in large part a function of contemporary documents, intellectuals are tempted to treat the present as history, for by doing so they weight the future's characterization of the present. It is almost as if a contest were being waged to see which of the contending intellectual groups could leave the largest and most convincing body of contemporary documents for the historian of the future to assess. Sometimes they don't even wait:

> . . . to the young people educated in the late forties and early fifties it seemed that a war was being fought in American culture between two styles of asserting one's seriousness as an intellectual: the old style of "alienation" . . . and . . . the new style of "maturity."[24]

Regardless of the merits of the substantive assertion, I would call attention to the historical mood of this writer's prose; he is writing the history of his generation—no more than a few years after they've received their bachelors' degrees. This is anticipatory socialization or other-directedness of a peculiarly ghostly sort; oriented toward history, intellectuals collapse the historical process in their attempts

---

[22]That this usurpation may be a precarious one is suggested by Dean Inge's warning that the man who marries the spirit of his own age is likely to be a widower in the next. One need go no further for an example of Inge's prophecy than the present experience of those who captured "the myth of the thirties."
[23]Rosenberg, op. cit., p. 221.
[24]Quoted from Norman Podhoretz by Rosenberg, op. cit., p. 248.

to find their place in it; and by attempting to write the history of their time before it is actually made, intellectuals create the myth of their time. Attempts like these to structure one's experience so as to make it public, and thus historical, have probably always been with us but David Riesman suggests that

they have been speeded up in recent years by the enormous industry of the mass media which must constantly find new ideas to purvey, and which have short circuited the traditional filtering down of ideas from academic and intellectual centres. We can follow an interpretation of the suburbs from an article in The *American Journal of Sociology to an article in* Harper's *to a best selling book to an article in* Life *or a TV drama—all in the matter of a couple of years—much in the way in which a . . . 'beat generation' . . . [is] imitated almost before [it] exists.*[25]

Surely, this is the cultural dimension of what Weber meant by "rationalization": the increasing numbers, decentralization, and specialization of intellectuals, the availability of print, the respectability of almost any scheme of values (as long as they are logically articulated), and our predilection to think that by naming something we understand it, all contribute to the helter-skelter rush with which we hasten to confer the status of "trend," "movement," "spirit," etc., on a series of events which, with some historical distance, we might recognize as a minor cultural quiver. This is not intended as a defense of Olympian detachment or as a recommendation that intellectuals abdicate their responsibility to comment on and interpret the direction of contemporary culture. We always see the present and immediate past more critically and in more complex detail than we see more distant times, and many of the results of the impulse to record and identify the temper of one's time while it is happening or to make coherent sense of contemporary events perhaps before any coher-

---

[25]"Flight and Search in the New Suburbs," in *Abundance for What?* (Garden-City, N.Y.: Doubleday, 1964), p. 259. Riesman also points to the tendency for intellectuals to create myths of themselves by writing autobiographies while still relatively quite young. Presumably, Stephen Spender, Mary McCarthy, Phillip O'Connor and a number of others still have a good part of their lives ahead of them. Riesman says, "It is as if the principle of buying on credit and living now rather than later was extended into all spheres of intellectual life."

ence or pattern has appeared, may be invaluable as ethnography to future historians and social scientists.[26] At the same time, they may be seriously misleading or puzzling to future researchers who find a five-year period labeled an "age of conformity" (at precisely the time that a "beat generation" is flourishing undiscovered by the mass media) or who read of three different "post-war" generations within a period of fifteen years.

This discussion of the relationship of the concept of the generation to the concept of *Zeitgeist* can be extended to the somewhat firmer scientific ground upon which survey research stands. If Lipset *et al.* are correct in saying "there has been no attempt to apply systematically the concept of generation to modern survey research techniques,"[27] then survey research is probably the poorer for it. Shed of its philosophic overtones, the German tradition of generation analysis would simply argue that culturally defined generations may be as important an explanatory variable as class, income, religion, ethnic status, or any other structural variable. This is a simple and reasonable enough assertion, and Lipset *et al.* have cited a few studies of political behavior in which the generation idea illuminated the data quite markedly. More recently, William Evan, in outlining a procedure for studying long-term opinion change, has emphasized the importance of analyzing survey data in terms of generation cohorts.[28] Both Evan and Lipset *et al.*, however, suggest that aging, as such, may have less effect upon opinions and attitudes than the impact of certain historical situations. They say, for example:

If, in fact, it is the case that generations tend to vote left or right depending on which group was in the ascendency during their coming of age, then it may be necessary to reconsider the popularly held idea that conservatism is associated with increasing age. . . . If a society should move from prolonged instability to stability, it may

[26]Paul Lazarsfeld has commented on the responsibility of today's public opinion pollsters to the future's historians. "The obligations of the 1950 Pollster to the 1984 Historian," *Public Opinion Quarterly* (Winter 1950–51).
[27]S. M. Lipset et al., "The Psychology of Voting," in G. Lindsey, *Handbook of Social Psychology* (Cambridge: Addison-Wesley Press, 1954), vol. II, p. 1148. Hyman's work (op. cit.) is certainly a major effort in this direction.
[28]William Evan, "Cohort Analysis of Survey Data," *Public Opinion Quarterly*, (Spring 1959), 68.

well be that older people would retain the leftist ideas of their youth, while the younger generation would adopt conservative policies.[29]

Certainly, this observation is readily applicable to the many university teachers (come of age in the thirties) who may be frequently heard remarking in a melancholy vein on the cautiousness, conservatism, and generally restricted horizons of their students. But at the same time, if what I have previously suggested makes sense, one would expect the definition of "coming of age" to vary depending upon the structural factors affecting conceptions of "youth" and "maturity." The possibility that Lipset et al. envision does not make a mere stereotype out of the apparent association of conservatism with aging; it suggests only that this is one tendency among others, and Hyman has carefully analyzed some of them; it seems clear enough that differences in "mentalities" due to the differing historical circumstances under which they are formed may frequently persist over time strongly enough to remain only slightly affected by the conservative tendencies of aging. Evan, this time with data (however scanty), suggests, in fact, that the historical situation has a greater effect upon opinion change than aging does. What he and other students of the problem do not take into account, however, is *relative* (or occupational) age; that is, that the forty year old painter may be responding to historical circumstances as a young man, whereas the forty year old editor of a mass-circulation magazine may respond to the same circumstances as a member of the "older generation." One may not be as old as one feels, but one can be as young as the age-norms of one's status and reference groups permit one to be. To be sure, this factor may considerably complicate the practicability of applying the generation variable, but not, it seems to me, to such an extent as to preclude its usefulness—especially where occupation and education are already known.

But the idea of the generation can be effectively used not only in conventional survey work; there seems to be good reason for survey methods to be used to cast light on the larger cultural problems with which the Germans concerned themselves. If survey methods can inquire into political attitudes, sexual behavior, child rearing practices, and such elusive topics as apprehensiveness among professors, then those methods may be used to elicit the attitudes of intellectuals

[29]Lipset et al., op. cit., p. 1148.

toward questions of style and taste, optimism and pessimism, "responsibility" and alienation, atmosphere and temper—in short, toward components of the *Zeitgeist*. A survey can be no better than the subtlety of the relationships it hypothesizes and the ingenuity of the questions it asks to measure them. Such work will probably show, in empirical terms, that the concept of the generation is a structural variable of major and statistically identifiable significance and not merely a sentimental projection of aging retrospective philosophers.

The Youth Business

1962

Business is booming in the study of youth. Most of the recent books and articles on youth and adolescence have addressed themselves to such practical problems as juvenile delinquency, the not-quite-delinquent "wildness" of teen-agers, the impact (or lack of impact) on students of academic values, and, somewhat more generally, the special tensions attendant upon adolescence as a "transitional stage." But beyond this concern with relatively practical problems, there lies a body of recent work whose preoccupations with youth are intended to tell us as much about adults as about children. I have in mind, for example, Edgar Friedenberg's fine book *The Vanishing Adolescent*, Paul Goodman's much discussed *Growing Up Absurd*, Kenneth Keniston's long article last year (1961) in *The American Scholar*, Eric Erikson's work on adolescence and identity, and James Coleman's carefully researched but disappointing *The Adolescent Society*. The

A review of *The Annals of the American Academy of Political and Social Science*, November 1961 ("Teen-Age Culture," edited by Jessie Bernard) and *Daedalus*, Winter 1962 ("Youth: Change and Challenge," edited by Stephen Graubard. Reprinted by permission from *Commentary* Spring 1962 (© 1962 by the American Jewish Committee) where it appeared under the title "The Youth Field."

latest additions to this literature are the two present symposia, which contain a total of twenty-two articles.

The major preoccupation of the contributions to *The Annals* is a quasi-ethnographic fascination with something called "the teen-age culture" or "youth culture," or sometimes "the adolescent subculture." These terms summarize the belief of many that adolescents are a species of exotica—that they move in a hedonistic, irresponsible, and "expressive" milieu, distinctive enough to qualify for the sociological classification "subculture." Adolescents, in any case, seem mysterious enough that their parents require manuals on how to understand them.

The central theme of *The Annals*, however, is that the rebellious, anti-adult, Dionysian features of "teen-age culture" have been grossly exaggerated. One article, it is true, uses teen-age magazines to document the major preoccupations of teen-agers (sex appeal, Hollywood, TV, records, popularity, and so on) and a second discusses the spread of these motifs to Britain and the Continent. But the substance of most of the other selections suggests that the character of adolescent peer groups should not seriously obstruct young people from eventually becoming responsible adults—which is, after all, what most official worriers about youth are worrying about when they worry. For example, Kirk Dansereau sees adolescent behavior as a prototype of the adult world of the near future, in which life will be organized around leisure, not work. Again, a study of rural youth concludes that these young people are fully as traditional and conservative as their parents. Ira Reiss argues that while the sexual codes of adolescents are more liberal than traditional norms allow, for the most part they are quite in accord with the "permissiveness" that actually governs sexual behavior today. And so on. In her editorial summary of the entire issue, Jessie Bernard concludes: "The volume might well be viewed, therefore, as a picture of adult culture today as reflected in the teen-age culture which it fosters." But adults know that the distorted reflection is temporary ("they'll grow out of it"), and this knowledge in large measure accounts for the chuckling benignity with which many adults regard the "excesses" of adolescents. Genuine subcultures are never taken so lightly.

But if *The Annals* succeeds in making its rather bland point that the adolescent society is far from being beyond the pale of respectability, far from worshipping at the feet of Dionysius, this success ought not to deceive us into believing that "youth culture" is merely

a myth. Though genuine subcultures of youth involve only minorities of young persons and, indeed, spill over the usual barriers of age-grading, they do flourish. In what is far and away the best and most interesting paper in *The Annals'* collection, David Matza introduces the idea of "subterranean tradition," which is adhered to by a small part of the population, tolerated by somewhat broader segments of it, and, although officially denounced, regarded by the public "with ambivalence in the privacy of contemplation." He argues very persuasively that in the U.S. subterranean traditions of youth take three major forms—radicalism, bohemianism, and delinquency. He maintains that these rebellious traditions do not attract more young adherents than they do because each has a "conventionalized version" which serves to drain the original of its most significant content. Thus radicalism competes with the tradition of "doing good," of social reform and community service; the conventionalized version of delinquency, on the other hand, is "teen-age culture"; and certain aspects of fraternity life (though Matza admits that this is the most questionable of his parallels) provide a conventionalized version of bohemianism. If you can't squelch 'em, co-opt 'em, seems to be the great American principle of civil order.

One of the many virtues of Matza's paper is that it enables us to distinguish between the routine, ephemeral, essentially transitional features of adolescence—which can be understood as an attempt by adolescents to cope with the specific temporary pressures our system of age-grading imposes on them—and genuine subterranean (i.e. subcultural) styles—which tend to leave a relatively permanent mark on those who have been extensively involved in them. Ex-delinquents, ex-radicals, and ex-bohemians tend to be permanently visible; ex-swooners, ex-hot-rodders, and ex-basketball players do not. I think that an important source of much of the confusion and contradictory noises one hears about youth is the failure to distinguish between youth or adolescence as a chronological age-grade with its distinctly transitional pressures and problems, and youth or "youthfulness" as a configuration of cultural qualities or psychological predispositions, which, although concentrated among the young, are neither exclusive to it nor necessarily temporary. Everybody knows (or says) that some adults are more youthful than others. What they often do not observe is that the tendency to maintain youthfulness in later years is not just randomly distributed. Certain adult milieux are especially receptive to or tolerant of hedonistic, flamboyant, irresponsible, sponta-

neous, and expressive kinds of behavior; and it is toward these milieux that those youngsters who have been most deeply involved in genuine "youth" cultures tend to gravitate as they get older. Some never "grow out of it," and as adults they contribute to the maintenance of subterranean traditions from which succeeding generations of youth can draw sustenance.

In *Daedalus*, only Bruno Bettelheim devotes his entire article to "The Problems of Generations," but it troubles virtually all the contributors. While Talcott Parsons sees traditional American values as fundamentally unchanged and believes that youth shares in the widespread consensus regarding these values, most of the other authors are deeply concerned about "the search for identity," the conflict of generations, the difficulties of finding anything worth believing in, and the impact of accelerated social change which alienates youth both from the obsolete past and from the engimatic, unanticipatable future.

A schematic summary of topics like this cannot begin to do justice to the richness and complexity of the *Daedalus* discussions, which contain some of the very best thinking on youth that I have encountered. Although I do not have space to praise each of the articles individually (and all ten deserve a great deal of praise), I do not think it a quibble to point out that the *Daedalus* symposium is not, as its title suggests, about "Youth: Change and Challenge." The symposium is about elite youth, or college youth: the kind of people about whom the myth of "generations" is created. We deceive ourselves, though, if we think that our diagnoses of cultural "generations" tell us much about the actual statistical distribution of experience in age groups. "Youth" is not James Dean rebelling with plenty of cause and choking us up with poignance, just as "age" is not snow-white Robert Frost barking his eccentric wisdom to students in search of a Sage. My father was a young man in the 1920s, but he never drank bathtub gin, nor leapt into the fountain at the Plaza, nor Charlestoned to jazz, and he certainly was not beautiful and gay and damned. But my bet is that his experience, such as it was, was actually more representative than that of those who captured the myth of the twenties. Culturally speaking, however, it is as if he never lived; history as myth ignores him. Until we free ourselves from this myth of homogeneous generations, we shall continue to be innocently surprised and troubled when surveys of adolescents reveal lots of young people to be quite ordi-

nary reflections of their parental milieux—good, pimply-faced kids with a host of ordinary problems, who'd be at home in any Y, 4-H club, or Boy Scout troop, and will later be at home in the Methodist church, the Lions Club, and the Republican party.

This, of course, may change as one moves from high school to college and beyond—bohemianism and radicalism are very rare in high schools; they begin to emerge clearly only in college and then by no means equally in every college. But what evidence there is suggests that even most elite youth move rather smoothly through their college years into lifelong commitments to family, community, and career. They do not pay terribly much conscious attention to the search for identity, which, whatever else it is, is not cause for disapprobation of intellectuals. In spite of the clinical concerns of social psychiatrists, "growing up" in our society is perceived not as the gradual development of a firm, stable ego-identity, but as a sobering process of increasing responsibility, deferred gratifications, irreversible roles, and an instrumental approach to the world. And it is this attitude which, from the point of view of a utopian or a Dionysian, renders growing up "absurd," and which predisposes many of us to see reluctance and lack of enthusiasm among those who opt for "maturity." Thus Bettelheim:

If manhood, if the good life in the good community, is the goal of adolescence, then the goal is clear, and with it the direction and the path. But what if existing manhood is viewed as empty, static, obsolescent? Then becoming a man is death, and manhood marks the death of adolescence, not its fulfillment.

With more emotional power than either Goodman or Keniston, Bettelheim is suggesting in this passage that although puberty provides us with a good objective criterion of the beginning of adolescence, we have no objective mark of its end; "maturity" remains *essentially* a matter of opinion. Several of the *Daedalus* writers apparently agree with Dostoevsky that "to live beyond forty is bad taste." Kaspar Naegele refers to the Greek wish that youth should not be spoiled by age, and Erik Erikson remarks that the cumulative experience of childhood and adolescence "bequeaths to all methodical pursuits a quality of grandiose delusion." Under these conditions, then, growing up is indeed absurd. But *Daedalus* chickens out at the end. Having convinced us that "we" have given "them" a rotten world full of

bleak prospects to grow up into, *Daedalus* turns right around and, like the forced, affirmative Hollywod ending in which the logic of dramatic necessity is blithely discarded in favor of "upbeat" requirements, recommends to the young that they carry on, *engagé*, heads high.

But if the world of youth, as so many of these writers suggest, really is a truer, wholer, more authentic kind of existence, on what basis do we recommend that it be left behind in favor of the mixed blessings of "maturity"? Because there's no choice? Because one "has to" grow up? Well, not really; one doesn't have to. Henry Miller hasn't. Bertie Russell never grew up. Ernest Hemingway didn't. Norman Mailer is probably a superior kid today to what he was in 1948. Kenneth Rexroth isn't grown up. Dylan Thomas died adolescent and so did Charlie Parker. They remain, as the song says, Like Young, and quite unlike those who drink Pepsi. I do not sentimentalize, I do not make heroes of these men, and I do not recommend to anybody their modes of staying young. But it is a fact that these lives are available as models, and plenty of young bohemians and radicals dedicate themselves in this manner to perpetual youth. And who will say that they contribute less to our civilization than the thousands who get up off the couch, bristling with ego-identity, to return, strengthened, to the grim combat of family, community, and career?

Adolescence and Beyond

An Essay Review of Three Books   **1963**
on the Problems of Growing Up

Few social problems have enlisted the attention of a wider variety of writers than the problems of youth. There are good reasons for this. Few sections of the population exemplify so clearly Louis Wirth's dictum that every statement of fact about the social world touches someone's personal or group interests: as teachers, as parents, as molders of the world which our children will inherit, we are *involved* in what is said about youth. Moreover, social scientists for purposes of research, and social critics for purpose of comment, find adolescents very strategically located in the social structure, for an initial

A review of *The Adolescent Society*, by James Coleman (Glencoe, Ill.: The Free Press, 1961); *Growing Up Absurd*, by Paul Goodman (New York: Random House, 1960); and *The Vanishing Adolescent*, by Edgar Z. Friedenberg (New York: Dell Laurel Editions, 1962). Reprinted from *Social Problems* 10, no. 4 (Spring 1963) with the permission of the journal and the Society for the Study of Social Problems.

I want to acknowledge the help of Barbara Williams. Several of the ideas discussed here emerged out of extended conversations with her regarding her research on adolescents.

curiosity about adolescents tends to direct attention out into the society in ever widening circles, like the proverbial pebble in a pool. Finally, under conditions of rapid social change, the position of youth is particularly poignant because so much of the past is rendered obsolete—that is, provides, no viable models for future orientations—and because the turbulence of the present makes so much of the future unanticipatable.

It is not surprising, then, that youth or adolescents and their allegedly arcane social life have come in for so much recent attention. Nor is it surprising that the issues explored should be controversial, since a comprehensive characterization of the position of youth in the social structure and their response to it almost always implies a judgment about the world their fathers have bequeathed them. This is one of the reasons why books on youth are so rarely detached, and why they frequently reveal as much about their authors as they do about the situation of youth.

These remarks are prompted by the publication in the early sixties of three specially notable books on youth. Not the least part of their interest is that although they arrange themselves neatly on a continuum from dispassionate to polemical, they demonstrate that dispassion is no insurance against distortion and that a polemic is not, by virtue of that fact, mere ideology useless for social scientists. James Coleman's *The Adolescent Society*, for example, is the very model of sophisticated design and execution of a scientific sociological survey, but it is not without distortion. Paul Goodman's *Growing Up Absurd*, on the other hand, as its very title suggests, is the polemic of a radical utopian against the system of social institutions which, says Goodman, engenders a wide variety of pathologies among the young by rendering absurd the process of growing up. But sociologists might well profit from giving it their attention. Edgar Friedenberg's *The Vanishing Adolescent*, the most important of the three books, occupies a tonal middle ground between these extremes. Friedenberg observes the academic rules against stridency and uses interview data—albeit illustratively—but he does not attempt to disguise either his sympathy—even love—for his subjects or his anger at high school educators who, in his view, are robbing students (at great eventual cost to the society) of their right to the experience of adolescence. In their different ways, however, all three books—and it is this which makes them comparable—deal with the relation of adolescent experience to future adulthood.

The Adolescent Society is a report of research in ten Illinois high schools, selected in order to represent a wide range of types of communities from small rural towns to Chicago and its suburbs. The book has two major points to make: first, that a distinctive adolescent society exists (with, to be sure, some variation from school to school), having a correspondingly distinctive subculture and status system—although Coleman is less than clear in his analytic distinctions among these basic concepts. Second, the distinctive cluster of values and interests which characterize the adolescent subculture systematically diverts the energies of students away from the academic goals of the schools.

The strength of Coleman's book comes from the technical skills of its author. The design of the study, the representativeness of the samples, and the care with which the data were apparently gathered are of such high quality that it is not likely this kind of fundamental adolescent ethnography will soon have to be done again. Moreover, Coleman's virtuoso's abilities at the statistical analysis of survey data are genuinely impressive. The inventiveness and the skill, for example, with which he traces the influence of social background variables, sociometric popularity, athletic prowess, and extracurricular participation on being or not being a member of student elites, and on the self images and the scholarship of adolescents, can evoke only the highest admiration. But although the bulk of *The Adolescent Society* is devoted to such analysis of data, and interesting as these data are, it is not the patterned ways in which adolescent societies vary from school to school and group to group within schools that constitute the most important findings of the study. By Coleman's own admission the ten schools are more alike than they are different, and it is these relatively gross data that constitute the book's major claim to attention.

Is there an adolescent subculture? Coleman says there is, and here are some of its major features: adolescents care a great deal about the search for status and popularity, but academic achievement counts for very little in this search. Boys care a great deal about cars and sports and athletic prowess; girls care about beauty and glamour and attractiveness. Both regard dating and extracurricular "activities" as very important, and members of high school elites confer even greater importance on these things than do other students. Brains and good grades, however, bring few if any tangible rewards from adolescent peer groups. Coleman, in short, gives us a very detailed

picture of an adolescent milieu not at all inconsistent with the "glamour" and "rah rah" images that come from the mass media, and which should surprise no one familiar with Sunday Supplement discussions of "teen-agers."

Do such descriptive data warrant conceptualization as a "subculture"?[1] I think not. The idea of an adolescent subculture or "youth culture" is getting to be one of the most frequently encountered concepts in sociology. Yet there is absolutely no good body of data on adolescents, Coleman's included, which indicates the existence of a really deviant system of norms. Adolescents, no doubt, have a rather unique set of artifacts, and they may even have a somewhat distinctive system of social relations, but so probably do most groups marked by a special location in the social structure. If one chooses to designate as a "subculture" all of the distinctive patterns of normative differentiation which the peculiar location of social groups helps engender, then "American culture" dissolves as a concept before one's very eyes; it becomes an empty abstraction hiding the countless number of more or less systematic variations contained in it. In order to distinguish the concept of subculture from the rather wide variations that the parent culture permits, one must look not only for relatively distinctive styles of life, but styles of life which are to a great extent self-generated, autonomous, having institutional and territorial resources capable of sustaining them in crisis and insulating them from pressures from without. If it is not to be confused with passing fads and fashions, a subculture needs a certain durability too, a continuity over time sufficient to enable it to draw upon a stock of tradition which previous groups who have borne the subculture have left behind. The Amish, for example, have a subculture; ghetto Jews have a subculture; bohemians maintain a precarious subculture; delinquent gangs in urban slums frequently have a subculture. But

[1]Perhaps the major item in Coleman's questionnaire which he regards as an empirical indicator of the existence of an adolescent subculture is an item that measures parental or peer-group orientation. Coleman asks, "Which ones of these things would be hardest for you to take—your parents' disapproval, your teacher's disapproval, or breaking with your friend?" Why was the wording of the question biased in this way? Certainly "breaking with" is a much more severe sanction than "disapproval." Even so, a slight majority of the respondents answered that their parents' disapproval would be hardest to take. Unfortunately, this is only one of several instances in which the data are distorted by the way in which questions were asked. In spite of these distortions, however, the ethnography is in general quite good— good enough, as is indicated below, to sustain interpretation quite different from that which Coleman imposes on it.

there is little in Coleman's excellent ethnography to suggest the existence of an adolescent subculture.

Quite to the contrary, almost all of the values and interests of adolescent revealed by Coleman's data seem to be derived from and shared by the great majority of their parents; the kids even preferred Pat Boone to Elvis Presley better than two to one—as good an indicator as any of tendencies to utter respectability. The strength and importance of high school football and basketball in Illinois and throughout much of the Midwest is sustained at least as much by parents and local booster organizations as it is by the students themselves. Their parents, too, care a great deal about prestige and popularity, and they engage in the search for these important illusions using criteria much more akin to those of their adolescent children than to the scholarly criteria that Coleman would espouse. From Coleman's treatment of the *adolescent* "subculture" one might think that cars and masculine prowess and feminine glamour and social "activities" and sex and dating and wearing the right clothes and being from the right family were concerns entirely alien to American adults.

In attempting to account for the "frivolous," leisure-oriented values of adolescents, Coleman tells us that good grades and concentration on academic work are seen by adolescents as acquiescence and conformity to adult pressures, whereas social affairs, extracurricular activities, and athletics are seen as "their own." But these activities do not "belong" to adolescents nearly so much as Coleman imagines. How could they when they are initiated and supported by the schools, sponsored and run by faculty advisors, coaches, and local advisory groups, and considered by grown-ups to be organized training grounds for the assumption of adult responsibilities? Such activities are apparently considered by educators to be so important to the overall purposes of the schools that many high schools force student participation in them by building an "activities" period into the regular curriculum. Indeed, if one were looking for evidence of subcultural tendencies among adolescents, one might do worse than to look to the students who had a strong commitment to intellectual values rather than to the students who carry the very American patterns of culture that Coleman found.

Is all this merely a quibble over terminology? Does it make a difference whether or not one regards adolescent values as "subcultural?" I think it does. It is no doubt true, as Coleman says, that

*"Whether or not there is an adolescent subculture is partly a matter of definition . . .," but every sociologist knows that matters of definition, especially where they concern basic concepts, are not inconsequential matters; they affect research and they color the interpretation of data. This is specially relevant in Coleman's case, for he makes no secret of the fact that he does not like what he found: the adolescent "subculture" sabotages the formal academic aims of the schools. If this is true, and I think there can be little doubt that it is, it becomes a very crucial question whether the anti-intellectual character of adolescent life is attributed primarily to autonomous social processes *within* the adolescent groups, or primarily to the larger culture which adolescents simply "reflect." For if the normative content of adolescent life *is* a reflection of or a selection from the larger society's major values, and if one regards this normative content as subversive of the academic aims of education, then one is logically led to be critical of adult institutions. But if one conceives the normative data of adolescent life as genuinely subcultural, as deviant from or evasive of adult goals, then one can assume that parents may want this altered, and one's skills as a sociologist can be offered in the capacity of an expert, to advise the adult authorities in charge of the schools as to how they may capture or co-opt the adolescent society and use it to redirect adolescent energies toward the academic aims of education.

Coleman chooses this latter course.[2] His analysis of the strength of the adolescent subculture is essentially functional: the importance of the cluster of student values and interests which focus around the athletic complex (prowess in sports, winning teams, cheerleading, and other sports-related activities) rests in the functions they perform for the high school society; they promote solidarity. They bring credit and honor not only to the individuals who participate but to

[2]But not without ambivalence, an ambivalence due in part, I think, to the fact that Coleman wants the attention of both his colleagues and school boards. Early in the book, in round, PTA rhetoric, Coleman writes, "In our modern world of mass communication and rapid diffusion of ideas and knowledge, it is hard to realize that separate subcultures can exist right under the very noses of adults. . . ." Is it? Certainly not for sociologists. But apparently not for parents either, for not much later Coleman writes, "But parents also want their children to be successful in the . . . things that count in the eyes of other adolescents. And parents know what things count." Unable to have it both ways, he finally compromises and says . . . "it is as if the adolescent culture is a Coney Island mirror, which throws back a reflecting adult society in a distorted but recognizable image."

the school as a whole. Rewards, consequently, are commensurate with the contribution. Those students who play an important role in enhancing the cohesion of the collective by bringing credit to it are rewarded with prestige; in this way, motivation is built into the social structure. Because this is a legitimate need of organizations, and because scholastic achievement as presently structured brings credit only to the individual who achieves, Coleman proposes what is essentially a "functional alternative" for athletics and "activities": the institution of interscholastic intellectual games and other scholarly competitions in which the academic excellence of students will bring not only prizes to the individual, but glory to the school and pride of membership to the student body. Such measures, in Coleman's view, may be expected to redirect student motivation into academic channels because they will be serving the same functional requisites that athletics and activities presently do.

This reasoning makes sense only if we assume that these are the major, or the *only* functions performed by the adolescent "subculture," and Coleman's proposals are practical only if we assume that adolescent norms, being genuinely "subcultural" are disturbing to adults who, consequently, would support attempts to manipulate them. Neither of these assumptions can be easily granted. For one thing, academic excellence already does bring considerable credit to schools. Some schools take great pride in the depth and breadth of their academic curricula, in the proportions of their graduates going on to college, the number of scholarships they win, and their performance in college when they get there. It is true, however, that neither very many students nor adult members of the *community* seem to care much about these accomplishments. I have not, for example, heard of a triumphant *College Bowl* team, fresh from a TV victory in New York, being welcomed back at the home town airport by a crowd of 10,000 wildly cheering supporters. That intellectual competitions apparently do not produce such evidence of solidarity is due less, I think, to the lack of institutionalization of more enterprises like the *College Bowl* on a high school level, than it is to the *unsuitability* of academic pursuits to the local *community* functions actually performed by the adolescent "subculture."

The achievement of such solidarity requires activities capable of enlisting the traditional loyalties, the vicarious identifications, and the half-unconscious yearnings of most members of the community. The dominant features of the adolescent "subculture" are eminently

well suited to these functions; academic excellence, unfortunately, is not. Relatively few can realistically expect to be brilliant students— few are bright. But many can aspire to be sociable, popular, and well liked through the kinds of activities in which anyone can participate and with which, therefore, any adult can empathize. High school athletics receives the support it does at least partly because it is an important source of spectator–leisure in small towns, and in many communities an important focus of *community* spirit. Athletics is not only an activity in which most boys have at least some minimum competence and experience, and not only an activity which the adult world endows with heroic models of wealth and celebrity; it also involves adolescents in the use of faculties which are clearly superior to those of their parents. Athletic competition demonstrates the beauty, the strength, and the vigor of young bodies, which gives to the adolescent athletes a sense of their own incipient manhood, and to their fathers a mixture of nostalgic regret at their own declining physical powers and vicarious pride in the powers of the coming generation. Vis-à-vis their mothers, something of the same sort is probably true for girls, with their emphasis on sexuality and attractiveness. Add to this the well known fact that most high school teachers prefer average students to brilliant ones, and one begins to understand the sources in the *adult* world of resistance and indifference to the academic goals of the schools. That Coleman should have failed to see all this is a direct consequence of his decision to treat the adolescent society as a relatively autonomous social system, and his utter neglect of the forces impinging on it from without.

In a sense, it is the wholesomeness of Coleman's intentions that render his analysis so misleading. So dedicated is he to documenting the trivial and superficial character of adolescent life and to emphasizing the obstacles it places in the way of academic achievement, that he fails to understand it as *culture* rooted in the parental soil. It was not, after all, an adolescent who had America singing "you don't have to know how to read and write/When you're out with a feller in the pale moonlight." It may not come as "natchurly" as Senior Citizen Irving Berlin believed—Coleman would no doubt be correct in admonishing us that the moonlight fades and that literacy is a requirement of advanced industrial societies; but this is no reason for not understanding that the whole romantic complex that pervades adolescent life is a very important part of the culture and traditions of the United States—something which, in this time of revolutionary

technological change, is one of the *few* features of the culture which link the generations together in whatever semblance of cultural continuity we have.

In Coleman's hands, adolescent life does not receive the respect that culture warrants. To him, adolescent romanticism seems like a nasty bit of arbitrary trivia obstructing the kinds of accomplishments that really count, like A's in math and physics and cooking. These things count, presumably, because they are positively functional for the kinds of futures that actually await adolescents, and the adolescents' subculture is "superficial" because it contributes nothing to their later adaptation, indeed subverts it. There is no doubt that this is true if one conceives futures, as Coleman apparently does, exclusively in terms of specialized occupational and kinship roles. But these do not, of course, exhaust the futures that adolescents imagine for themselves—which are to an ever greater extent leisure-oriented. As a matter of fact, I find something meanly puritanical in Coleman's apparent aversion to the frivolous and erotic character of adolescent life, especially where it concerns girls. He seems to recoil somewhat from the girls' heavy emphasis on beauty, clothes, and "an enticing manner," although he regards these simply as dysfunctional. Dysfunctional for what? Well, for the futures as wives and mothers and nurses and secretaries and receptionists that actually await them. "The adult women in which (sic) such attributes (beauty, allure, etc.) *are* important . . . are chorus girls, models, movie and television actresses, and call girls. . . ."[3] These (attributes) are quite different from the attributes of a good wife, which involve less superficial qualities." Frankly, I find this schoolmarmish. I think there is nothing at all superficial about sex or the desire to be alluring or about the romantic images which grip the fantasies of a population; and Coleman's own data tell him that the girls *want* to be models and actresses, and the boys *want* to be star professional athletes. Coleman, I suppose, is entitled to look askance at such romantic and "foolish" aspirations, but he would be very hard pressed to argue that such fantasies are autonomously generated within the peer groups of adolescents or that such fantasies are not widespread among adults.

[3]Notice the association of the, so far as I know, respectable occupations of model, actress, and chorus girl, with that of call girl. No doubt they require some similar "attributes"; but they require rather different talents too.

Athletics, extracurricular activities, dating, popularity, cliques, cars, dances, the mass media—the whole paraphernalia of adolescent life is surely not nearly as irrelevant to adult futures as Coleman appears to think. For most students (the half that will never get to college, and the more than half who won't finish) qualities like popularity, charm, sociability, and attractiveness will be very valuable in later life. Indeed, where Coleman suggests that it is the content of the adolescent "subculture" which *separates* adolescents from adults, we might seriously ask if the reverse is not closer to the truth. For the *one* activity which sharply *differentiates* most adolescents from most adults is that the former have to go to school and pay at least *some* attention to academic matters. But of course this is not *all* they do, and the content of the so-called adolescent subculture may well provide a universe of discourse between adolescents and adults, a community of nostalgia and barely repressed yearning more meaningful than the latest material learned in math or physics class. In this light, the adolescent subculture may easily be regarded as a milieu marked by the dominance of plenty of mechanisms of anticipatory socialization for adulthood. To see the matter this way would, of course, very nearly reverse the main point of Coleman's book, but this is the sort of ambiguous interpretation to which a study of a "subculture" is subject if it does not consider *critically* the way that subculture is implicated in the society and culture which surround it.

If what weakens Coleman's book is its uncritical view of the adult society and its neglect of the relation of adolescents to it, it is at least to some extent redeemed by the wealth of reliable information it imparts. Paul Goodman's *Growing Up Absurd* contains no such redeeming feature. It does, however, contain what Coleman's book lacks. Where Coleman locates the adolescent problem in the adolescent subculture which obstructs access to adult futures, Goodman locates the adolescent problem in the unattractiveness of those futures, which makes growing up absurd. Goodman, indeed, is almost exclusively preoccupied with a polemic, in the great tradition of radical social criticism, against the system of corrupt institutions which precludes and subverts the healthy processes of growing up.

"My purpose is a simple one," writes Goodman rather preciously (for it is not simple at all): "to show how it is desperately hard these

days for an average child to grow up to be a man, for our present organized system of society does not want men. They are not safe. They do not suit." In what I find a rather annoying style which vacillates between the bitter irony of a man who knows he can't win and the deliberate innocence of a naif, Goodman spends his considerable polemical talent striking out in all directions at a society best characterized by the metaphor of an enormous rat race inside "a closed room." In chapter after chapter, Goodman attempts to convince us that our society is

lacking in enough man's work. It is lacking in honest public speech, and people are not taken seriously. It is lacking in the opportunity to be useful. It thwarts aptitude and creates stupidity. It corrupts ingenuous patriotism. It corrupts the fine arts. It shackles science. It dampens animal ardor. It discourages the religious convictions of Justification and Vocation and it dims the sense that there is a Creation. It has no Honor. It has no Community.

"Just look at that list," he tells us in wide-eyed mock disbelief at the seriousness of his own indictment, and quite a serious indictment it is. In Goodman's view, these "facts" constitute a system of conditions whose burden falls very heavily on the young. Then, as if to validate the debilitating effects of these conditions, Goodman turns to some of the more publicized groups of young men, and discusses the beat generation ("the early resigned"), juvenile delinquents ("the early fatalistic"), and Young Organization Men as case studies of the pathological extremes to which potentially wholesome, decent, young persons are systematically driven by the huge institutional betrayal perpetrated upon them.

The worst thing that can be said about Goodman's book is that it will convince no one who is not already predisposed to agree with him, and even some of these may be repelled by his posturings and overstatements.[4] The book makes no claim to being a detached

---

[4]The following is typical: "For the first time in recorded history, the mention of country, community, place, has lost its power to animate. Nobody but a scoundrel even tries it." Leaving aside the fact that it is usually people who do not study history who preface their assertions with "for the first time in recorded history . . .," I want to point out that Goodman's statement is no truer today than it was two hundred years ago when Dr. Johnson defined patriotism as the last refuge of the scoundrel. Evocations of American places

objective treatise, nor to having discovered anything new or interestingly subtle about youth; it is an argument, a howl of pain, full of sympathy for embattled youth and righteous anger at what it regards as their betrayal. A conventional sociological critique, therefore, which emphasized such things as Goodman's naive conception of social class or his failures to observe the niceties of rigorous method, would be largely beside the point. But aiming, as it clearly does, to be one of the 'books that changed our minds," it invites criticism which goes beyond the criteria of those who may usually be expected to respond with acclaim to any book that heaps withering scorn on institutions and gentle sympathies on the innocent children victimized by them.

I happen to agree with a good deal of what Goodman says. I frequently find public life rather disgraceful. I think that the numbing clichés of public rhetoric disfigure the language and emasculate its vigor.[5] I think that many of the most important and useful jobs are the least publicly rewarded and honored, that many of the most cynical and meretricious occupational skills are the most rewarded and celebrated, that popular religion has shown itself unequal to moral crisis, and that the economy is trapped in its inability to cope with the problem of abundance. But I have seen no very persuasive evidence that enormous numbers of adolescents see this; or that of those who do see it, very many are seriously troubled by it; or that of those who are very troubled by it, very many have their lives necessarily blighted by it. We all discover that the world is not quite as we would have made it, but this discovery does not relentlessly lead to the youthful pathologies that Goodman prefers to emphasize. Until evidence to the contrary is provided, we have good reason to go on believing that there are millions of ordinary kids who continue to go to church and make moral resolutions on the basis of sermons

---

still move a great many people. Whatever else he may be, Robert Frost was no scoundrel; yet he found it quite possible to read a quite creditable patriotic poem at President Kennedy's inauguration.

[5] In a foreign policy speech some years ago, President Eisenhower made reference to the U.S. commitment to a "last and justing peace." This is the kind of "slip" which a speaker, having made it, usually "hears" and then corrects. Ike did not hear it and so far as I know, the press did not either. I like to think the effort went unnoticed because "a last and justing peace" is fully as meaningful, that is, meaningless, a phrase as is "a just and lasting peace." So that which way one says it does not make much difference after all.

they hear, who applaud and are moved by political speeches, who write essays on Americanism for the Legion's contest, who take the Boy Scout oath with a straight face, whose hearts go pit-a-pat when the flag passes by, and who, with considerable application and some dedication, prepare themselves to be doctors, lawyers, engineers, advertising men, accountants, salesmen, and electricians. And who with a grim sense of moral right will, when ordered, loose the missiles against Moscow. As for the disaffected, bohemians and delinquents have been with us for a very long time, much too long, certainly, for us to be able to find the source of their disaffection in institutional conditions that are of relatively recent vintage. And even if we could, it is not exactly a compelling argument to condemn a whole society because a small segment of its population demonstrably think it a fraud.

But such matters do not disturb Goodman who, it turns out, is not really interested in establishing any causal relationships; he argues mostly by definition. The "resignation" of beatniks and the "fatalism" of delinquents are by definition pathological; the society is by definition immoral for its institutional practices systematically degrade the cultural values it professes. Goodman, that is, *can't* be wrong: the "maladjusted" are blamed on a society which makes adjustment absurd, and the adjusted, of course, are even worse, for what they adjust to is beneath contempt. Curiously enough, though, beyond a little more than stereotyped understanding of the problems of Organization Man, Goodman devotes precious little attention to the apparently well adjusted. Why this is so is revealed, I think, in a remark that Goodman attributes to Jean Genet, who says that when he tries to write about the Bourgeoisie, his "pen sticks," but when he writes about delinquents his thoughts "take wing"—and this makes him *know* that delinquents are superior, more heroic people. Genet's bias is clearly Goodman's for the "excesses" of youth provide him with excellent ground for flaying the institutions that engender them. "Where everything has become property and order, it is quite impossible to be vivacious, aggressive, undeliberate, exploratory, and venturesome (i.e., "youthful") without being out of order and sometimes smashing things." So goes the defense of delinquency: adolescent truancy is the fault of the schools; if the schools were better, the teachers more interesting, and the curriculum more vital, the kids would truant less. Kids steal cars because adults have made them symbols of power, manliness, and the freedom to go, go, go—

to which the kids have a right.[6] Adolescent sexuality is harmless and healthy; the harm comes only from the stigma and guilt adults attach to it. What kids need is not less but more sex of the unguilty variety. To Goodman, then, the "natural" is the good: ". . . to do the forbidden, in order to transgress limits that *seem* unnatural is normal and innocent; and if the limits *are* unnatural it is often necessary and admirable."

One need not quarrel with such Rousseauian sentiments; they have much to commend them. But to some extent every man is his own judge of what is natural, and most men cease to praise the natural when it begins to offend their judgment. The facts remain, though, that most kids are not habitual truants, most kids do not steal cars, and there is no evidence that most kids' sexual capabilities are ruined by puritanical inhibition; quite the contrary. Research on adolescents suggests that the norms governing sexual behavior are growing ever more permissive. It is even now quite clear, for example, that the semiofficial sexual morality portrayed in the mass media defines premarital intercourse as morally OK as long as one is in love; in the movies, on television, good girls sleep with the men they love and are neither punished for it nor cease to be good because of it. Moreover, bohemians are not all sick, Organization Men are not all psychopathic, and public officials are not all cynical. The persistent survival of Bohemias in the cities of Western Europe and the United States suggests that they are viable subcultures capable of providing important services for the human beings who inhabit them and for the cities which harbor them. Many Organization Men struggle mightily with the problem of developing and preserving individuality within bureaucratic contexts, and many public officials *probably* try to do their conscientious best under very severe and usually conflicting pressures. Some of us do find manly work in which we can take loving pride; and even if one grants that most men probably do not love their work, I know of no evidence that would suggest that most men ever have. Moreover, those who find neither pleasure nor honor in their work are not necessarily, therefore, ruined human beings— especially in an age oriented more and more toward leisure.

But I have no interest, really, in finding grounds to be hopeful about, or reason to praise the society that Goodman condemns. No

[6] In an attempt to minimize the seriousness of auto theft, Goodman comments that it is regarded as an important crime merely because cars are expensive —which may be rather like saying that murder is serious merely because life is precious.

real society, no *complex* society, that is would satisfy Goodman, for he is a Utopian, a revolutionary, in love with visions of apocalypse that would bring about a just and pure, a candid and forthright moral order. But I doubt that a culturally pluralist nation can afford very much candor on moral issues that people care a great deal about. In a society in which Arkansas Baptists must live in peace and civil order with Greenwich Village bohemians, it is perhaps fortunate that their opportunities for candid dialogue with one another are not great. Candor and forthrightness are admirable where we have reason to believe that the parties to a dispute really share an underlying moral consensus which candor would help reveal. But where candor and forthrightness will only polarize irreconcilable positions on a fundamental moral issue, duplicity, evasiveness, and perhaps even fatuity may take on a perplexingly moral character. Thus, for example, it may be wiser and in the long run more humane to leave the moribund laws against fornication as they are, and at the same time to provide opportunities for those who wish to fornicate to do so discreetly and with impunity, rather than engage in a totally open, honest, candid national debate on the merits of free love, which might set group against group in a basic moral conflict which our society might not survive. The pure of heart, no doubt, will find such duplicity offensive, but Innocence is neither the sturdiest nor the most durable of virtues.

And yet, *Growing Up Absurd* is an admirable book because it contains a core of basic good sense that survives even its author's exaggerations, and because it points to problems to which sociologists might do well to devote their attention. I am impressed when Goodman quotes what is presumably a television commercial, "Juicily glubbily/Blubber is dubbily/Delicious and nutritious/eat it, kitty, it's good," and comments: ". . . what I want to call attention to in this advertising is not the economic problem of synthetic demand, not the cultural problem of Popular Culture, but the human problem that these are human beings working as clowns; that the writers and designers of it are human beings thinking like idiots." Sociologists, though, know very little about what it does to a grown man to earn his living by babbling nonsense in the voice of an imbecile child, while under the supervision of a director who will order retakes until the proper degree of imbecile frenzy is achieved on tape. I am impressed when Goodman cries Shame! at the fact that in the same year that the West makes a cultural *cause célèbre* out of the suppression of Pasternak's *Dr. Zhivago*, it is discreetly silent as the

Archbishop of Dublin effectively bans a theater festival because of the presence on the program of plays by Joyce and O'Casey. Sociologists, however, know very little about the conditions under which censorship is likely to be perceived as unjust suppression or about the conditions under which it is likely to be perceived as the defense of public morality. I am impressed especially by Goodman's final chapter in which he discusses more than twenty of the "missed" or "compromised" revolutions of our time, whose partial or only incomplete successes have destroyed the communities that were, without having been able to provide any viable substitutes.

Finally, I am impressed when, in chapter after chapter, Goodman cites cases illustrating the fact, as I would put it, that our culture does not yet contain the moral vocabularies and the myths that might confer honor on much of the behavior and many of the social roles to which our transformed technology and social organization commit us. But instead of coming to grips with this problem, a problem to which no one has an adequate solution (not even the Soviets, who have the advantage of being able at will to mobilize their cultural resources to this end), Goodman chooses to point the accusing finger at a society that does not complete its revolutions as quickly as he wishes. The problems of youth, he tells us, "test and criticize the societies in which they occur. The burden of proof rests with the society." Perhaps. But in writing a book, the burden of proof rests with the author. Goodman proves little since for most of the arguments he makes from selective evidence, effective counter arguments can be made from other selective evidence. And this blunts the power of his polemic.

Edgar Friedenberg's *The Vanishing Adolescent*, the slimmest and most modest of the three books considered here, is also by far the best of the three. Friedenberg believes that adolescence, as a stormy decade of identity-seeking, is disappearing in the United States, due largely to the premature co-optation of the young by adult authorities, primarily in the high schools. Friedenberg points to the elaborate structure of pseudo-and quasi-adult organizations and activities, student participation in which is either encouraged or made compulsory by the schools. These student councils and courts and governments, the world affairs clubs, the psychiatric counseling and advising , the encouragement to plan careers early tend, in Friedenberg's view of the matter, to impose upon adolescents the trappings

of an adult milieu, to absorb them in rationalistic and bureaucratic thinking, in collective and "adjustive" modes of adaptation before they have had the opportunity to bring to fruition what he, like Erik Erikson, calls "the main developmental task of adolescence"; that is, the formation of a stable, clear ego-identity which, he says, is acquired in the process of the young individual's necessary conflicts with a recalcitrant society which has more to do than cater to the needs of children. In his terms, then, adolescence "vanishes" as a distinct developmental stage when the storminess of the identity-seeking period is replaced by an adult-in-training program, none too beneficently supervised by a high school staff trained in deceptively bland methods of administrative control.

Friedenberg's argument, then, is virtually the opposite of Coleman's. For Coleman, what is wrong with youth is that the subcultural processes within adolescent peer groups subvert the aims of education which are functional for the kind of society they must eventually enter. For Friedenberg, what is wrong with youth is that the schools systematically subvert the humanizing potentialities of adolescent growth in the interests of early socialization. Where Coleman finds the source of the trouble in the failure of the schools to cope with the adolescent subculture, Friedenberg finds the source of the trouble in their premature success, or in the debilitating consequences of that success. Like *Growing Up Absurd*, then, Friedenberg's book becomes a criticism of institutions, but it is also a much better book than Goodman's. For one thing, Friedenberg does not dissipate his argument by indiscriminately flailing at institutions all over the sociological map; he sticks close to what he knows most intimately, the schools and their students. Second, Friedenberg writes from the coherent theoretical framework of Neo-Freudian social psychology which gives to his book, as it seems to give to many Neo-Freudian writers, a wholeness and a consistency that eludes the more eclectic Goodman. Third, Friedenberg's is a book to *read;*[7] he writes with

[7]By which I mean that *The Vanishing Adolescent* is a *book*. Unlike *The Adolescent Society* which, if I may adumbrate a distinction, is a *report of a study*, I think that many sociological works belong to a higher form of what *Time* magazine sometime ago called "non-books." When sociologists ask each other what they've been doing lately, the answer usually goes "I'm doing a study of . . ."—almost never "I'm writing a book on . . ." Even when they *are* writing, sociologists are likely to say, "I'm writing up my study of . . ." Of many sociological works, that is, it is almost impossible to imagine a human being sitting over a typewriter struggling to shape sentences into forms that will communicate ideas, present evidence, come to conclusions,

truly astonishing grace and feeling, and with a firm command of metaphor that never allows the rich texture of his prose to smother the force of his argument.

That argument has a freshness which is almost stunning. Where many students of youth emphasize the prolongation of adolescence, he tells us simply that adolescence is disappearing, that we are reverting to the situation of primitive societies or backwashes of modern societies—social structures, that is, which have no room to tolerate Erik Erikson's "psycho-social moratorium": a period of years relatively free from adult pressures and responsibilities in which young persons may engage in "identity play" and other forms of interpersonal experiment in an attempt to find out who and what they are. Arresting as it is, however, the argument does not contradict the view that adolescence is being prolonged. It is quite clear that adolescence is being lengthened in the plain-facts sense that its beginning is pushed back by the earlier onset of puberty and by processes of anticipatory socialization which constrain preadolescents to begin rehearsing their adolescent roles long before the show's opening night. [8] At its later stages, adolescence is prolonged by additional in-school years, which postpone the ability to be self-supporting and the "maturity" that implies, and which, says David Riesman in his Introduction to *The Vanishing Adolescent*, is "caricatured by the psychoanalyst-in-training who at 40 is still his supervisor's 'boy,' dependent on his approval for certification, self-esteem, and patronage."

When Friedenberg speaks of a *vanishing* adolescence, he is speaking of the pressures put into teen-age years by adult authorities who, youth culture theorists to the contrary notwithstanding, continue to remain in control. The specifically bureaucratic, manipulative character of these pressures, argues Friedenberg, interferes with the naturally benign processes of adolescent growth, and by obstructing the adolescents' search for identity, which is the major psychological *function* of adolescence, *robs* them of their adolescence. In this

---

and hold the attention of a reader. Many sociological works are written to be used, consulted, referred to, quoted from, browsed in, and tested on, but very seldom to be read as books. Sociology may not yet have found its proper form of publication.

[8] Note the advertisements of bras for preadolescent girls. Mothers are encouraged to buy them for their daughters even if they don't need them yet, for having one will make the daughters feel more grown up, that is, more adolescent.

search, adolescents are naturally preoccupied with their developing capacities for intimacy and tenderness and intense subjective experience, and by their needs for sources of self-esteem and the clarification of experience. But these incipient capacities and desires are met by a manipulative educational bureaucracy which confuses and humiliates where it should clarify and support, and by teachers and counselors who, with the "anxious passivity of petty civil servants," mete out guilt and anxiety to indications of adolescent tenderness and intensity, and whose own repressed or declining sexuality is panicked by the all too obviously burgeoning sexuality of the kids, which they meet with fear and hostility. Under conditions, then, in which the schools regard the pains of adolescent growth as something to be ashamed of or to be "treated," rather than nurtured and lovingly cared for, adolescent anxieties, grown too great to bear, bring on a premature "adjustment" which means the defeat of adolescence, the cessation of the search for identity, and the redefinition of maturity as "adjustment."

Homo sapiens is undergoing a fundamental model change. . . . The change can be described as a weakening of the relationship between maturity on the one hand, and stability of identity on the other. . . . As the conditions of life alter in such a way as to provide less scope for self-direction, autonomy itself either becomes suspect or must be redefined as a kind of considered acquiescence in the demands of group living. The persistence of the older ideal of maturity, then, becomes a source of conflict and anomie, burdening those who try to live up to it with additional self-doubt. Maturation itself, then becomes a source of anxiety from which the adult must seek refuge.

The new model of man that Friedenberg sees being manufactured is one engineered to fit the Organization society. Such a society, in his view, needs other-directed men with weak, diffuse identities, and the high schools are helping to create them by abolishing adolescence. There is an irony here because, as Friedenberg suggests, it is only in relatively advanced societies that a genuine adolescence is possible, since it is only in such societies that less-than-adult statuses can be imposed for a long time on persons biologically quite capable of filling adult roles. The strains so engendered are more than compensated for, however, by the humanizing fact that genuine adolescence encourages a high degree of personality differentiation: the

conflict of young persons with institutions that deny them adult status engenders the growth of distinctive individualities. The blunting of this conflict in the interests of a bland harmony, and the consequent sacrifice of adolescence to the requirements of bureaucracy is for Friedenberg a bad bargain. He blames this subversion of adolescence for a variety of widely deplored conditions, from the "conformity" that social critics see so ubiquitously, to the reported high rates of collaboration with the enemy by American captives in the POW camps in Korea: conformists and collaborators lack the ego resources to sustain them when the going gets rough, and with which a genuine adolescence would have provided them.

Friedenberg's thesis is splendidly set forth, and the few doubts and demurrers I have about *The Vanishing Adolescent* are in large measure evoked by the force and the clarity of this very fine book. I have no doubt that much of what Friedenberg says about the betrayal of adolescence in the schools is true, but to indict the schools for not nurturing the search for identity is to ask of them something which may not be possible for them to give. Publicly supported educational systems are for the most part aimed at producing the skills society wants, and local school systems can only rarely go beyond the values of the communities that support them. Where there are great demands for organization men, one ought not be very surprised to find the bureaucratic virtues being cultivated in the schools. Nor need one be terribly upset by it. The schools do not exercise total control over adolescents, and those who undertake the search for identity can still, fortunately, find ways of evading the tightening bureaucratic grip of institutions. Surely, it is not easy, but it probably never has been easy to develop a firm sense of self, and there is no evidence to suggest that the number of lives led in quiet desperation or selfless acquiescence is any greater today than at some time in the past, nor that any fewer dedicate themselves today to the search for identity. And if the popularity of the phrase "the search for identity" is any indication, it is possible that many more are so dedicated. In any case, it may not be the proper role of the schools, nor of any other major institution for that matter, to cater to identity-seeking. Identity, as Freud said of happiness, is of no apparent cultural value; it seems to me to be a rather elite preoccupation and task which goes on in the interstices of institutions and which a society does enough to encourage so long as it permits those interstices to remain open and accessible.

Moreover, I am not quite convinced that the bureaucratic virtues, such as impersonality, adaptability, flexibility, and other-directedness, are as unambiguously inhuman as Friedenberg seems to think. Certainly, adaptability may seem like spinelessness, flexibility like duplicity, and other-directedness like characterlessness, but a firm identity may often manifest itself as pig-headed, stubborn rigidity, and a clear, stable ego-identity might well become an intolerable burden in a rapidly changing society where social and geographic mobility put enormous pressures on larger and larger numbers of people who must anticipate the new demands that unfamiliar life situations will make on them tomorrow. In a too neglected article some years ago, Daniel Lerner, rather courageously I thought, played devil's advocate, and had the temerity to suggest that the real significance of the apparent spread of other-directedness might well be that a net increase in the imaginative and projective capacities of the population was occurring; that, indeed, other-directedness required an inordinate talent for role-taking, which is, of course, at root an imaginative talent, a sensitivity to others.[9]

A more serious problem, however, is the image of adolescents which lies behind Friedenberg's whole book. Stated as simply as possible, *Edgar Friedenberg loves adolescents*. One wants to shout it in the streets, carve it into a tree, etch it in concrete. Where he sees adults as mean, narrow, repressed, and manipulative, he sees adolescents as noble and full of fine potential:

Adolescents often behave much like members of an old fashioned aristocracy. . . . They can be extravagantly generous and extravagantly cruel, but rarely petty and conniving. Their virtues are courage and loyalty. . . . They are honest on occasions when even a stupid adult would have better sense. . . . Adolescents insult us by quietly flaunting their authenticity. They behave as if they did not even know that passion and fidelity are expensive. . . . This, certainly, is inexcusably valorous; and it is not excused.

Whose adolescents are these? Where might we validate that these are, in fact, the qualities of an uncorrupted adolescence that we would do well to nourish? Certainly not from Coleman's data, nor

---

[9]"Comfort and Fun: Morality in a Nice Society," *The American Scholar* (Spring 1958).

from Hollingshead's *Elmtown's Youth* nor from Remers' *The American Teenager* and certainly not from Eugene Gilbert's youth polls; not from any large scale study of youth that I know. Who, then, are these adolescents? I think they are a figment of Friedenberg's loving imagination, a composite image drawn from what is absolutely best and rarest in adolescence (as it is in adulthood), from Huckleberry Finn to Holden Caulfield. We do adolescents no favor when we impose on them a burden of heroism that is rare in any stage of life. Friedenberg's own chapter in which he brilliantly reports and interprets interviews with "five exemplary boys," shows not only the way in which the humanity of adolescents is betrayed and corrupted; it shows also a couple of ways in which young persons can succeed in coping adequately with the difficult pressures of adolescence. These interviews illustrate that not only maturity, but youth too, is a kind of hell, but that with the cooperation of nature and fortune, one's humanity can be preserved in a hot climate.

On the Youthfulness
of Youth Cultures

1963

For more than twenty years now, sociologists have increasingly concerned themselves with the study of "youth culture." Talcott Parsons' very influential article, published in 1942, with its much quoted characterization of youth culture as "more or less specifically irresponsible" has become a point of departure for an enormous amount of research and discussion on youth.[1] Parsons' characterization of youth culture, however, inadvertently suggests that whatever it is that constitutes the "youthfulness" of youth culture may have less to do with chronology than with culture. To characterize youth culture as "irresponsible," to describe its "dominant note" as "having a good time," or to say that it has "a strong tendency to develop in directions which are on the borderline of parental approval or beyond the pale . . ." clearly excludes those large numbers of adolescents who have had no important experiences in anything remotely resembling such a milieu. Many, and probably most young persons, while they experience the classic problems of adolescent psychology described in the textbooks, seem to make their way through to full

A revised version of a talk given at the annual banquet of Alpha Kappa Delta, Purdue University, May 19, 1961. Reprinted from *Social Research* 30, no. 3 (Autumn 1963).
[1]"Age and Sex in the Social Structure of the United States," *American Sociological Review* (October 1942).

adult status without grave cultural damage, without getting into serious trouble, without a dominating hedonism, and without generalized attitudes of rebellion toward parents and the world.

These introductory remarks are not intended as a preface to a "defense" of adolescents against the bad press they have been getting in recent years. I intend, rather, to suggest (1) that "youth culture" should refer to the normative systems of *youthful* persons, not necessarily of young ones; (2) that whatever it is that normatively distinctive about youth culture is probably not characteristic of all or even most adolescents, and therefore is not attributable solely or even primarily to chronological age; and hence (3) that the definitive characteristics of youth culture are relevant to groups other than the age-grade we call adolescence.

While Frederick Elkin and William A. Westley believe they have exploded "The Myth of Adolescent Culture"[2] with survey data showing that a sample of middle-class adolescents comply with the norms of deferred gratification and get along well with their parents, without hostility or resentful feelings that "they don't understand us," what they have actually done is present evidence that certain adolescents do not share the norms of youth culture. By thus implicitly distinguishing the facts of chronological age from the phenomena of culture, they invite us to consider the hypothesis that what we are in the habit of calling "youth culture" is the creature of some young and some not so young persons. If hedonism or irresponsibility or rebelliousness are essential features of youth culture, then it may be unwise as well as unnecessary to restrict the consideration of youth culture to adolescent groups, for These qualities are dominant in several adult groups as well—and the fact that this is so is probably not fortuitous. I am suggesting, in short, that youthfulness, like fertility, is unequally distributed in society, and that it cannot be explained satisfactorily by reference to chronological age. This essay is an attempt to explore theoretically some of the conceptual problems that an investigation of the structure and dynamics of youth culture will encounter.

Youth Cultures of the Young

Two Images of the Young: "Teen-agers" and "American Youth"[3]
To begin, let us note a recurrent ambiguity in the images with which

[2]*American Sociological Review* (December 1955).
[3]I am indebted to Barbara Williams for the terms of this distinction.

American adolescents are usually conceived. The "teen-agers" are those who, in Dwight McDonald's apt ethnography,[4] spend an hour a day on the phone and two hours a day listening to disc jockeys; they are the most assiduous moviegoers in the nation, preferring especially films about monsters, rock and roll music, and teenagers like themselves. More than half of them "go steady" and practice the sexual or protosexual intimacies implied by that phrase. The boys are very car-conscious, and spend a good deal of their leisure reading about, talking about, and working on hot rods. They read *Mad*, and its imitators *Frenzy* and *Thimk*; they don't read the Bible, don't go to church regularly, are bored by politics, ignorant of the Bill of Rights, and so on.

If one shifts one's perspective for a moment, and begins to think of the adolescents who populate Boy Scouts, Youth for Christ, 4-H clubs, Future Farmers of America, and other groups of this sort, McDonald's characterization (based in part upon the results of Remmers' work[5] and Eugene Gilbert's youth polls) has a rather jarring effect. These doers of good deeds and raisers of prize pigs and winners of essay contests on Americanism are clearly not the adolescents who have seemingly become a permanent "problem" on the American scene.

"Teen-agers" and "American youth" are, of course, images, and as such, they may be little more than stereotypes; we may, and likely will, find rock and rollers belonging to the FFA. But it is also likely that these distinctive images express differences in social and demographic variables like class, region, ethnicity, and religion. In any case, the initial distinction between "teen-agers" (the adolescents publicly worried about) and "American youth" (the adolescents publicly praised) does suggest the useful banality that some adolescents engage in ways of life essentially at odds with or indifferent to the official desires and expectations of "responsible" adults, whereas other adolescents comply with or actively pursue the aims and expectations set down for youth by adult authorities.

Transitional Stage and Subculture

One way of extending this distinction between types of adolescents

---

[4]See his two-part "profile" of Eugent Gilbert in *The New Yorker* (November 22 and 29, 1958).
[5]H. H. Remmers and D. H. Radler, *The American Teenager* (Indianapolis, Ind., Bobbs-Merrill, 1957).

is to contrast two ideas that are frequently used in psychological and sociological discussions of youth. Most standard works on the social psychology of adolescence speak of it as a "transitional stage" between childhood and adulthood, a period ridden with conflicts and tensions stemming partly from an acceleration in the individual's physical and cultural growth but also from the age-grading norms of our society that withhold from adolescents most of the opportunities, rights, and responsibilities of adults. When sexual desires are more powerful than they will ever again be, sexual opportunities are fewest; obedience and submission are asked of adolescents at precisely the time when their strength, energy, and desire for autonomy are ascendant; responsible participation in the major institutions are denied them at the moment when their interest in the world has been poignantly awakened.[6] Such tensions, generated by our age-grading system and exacerbated by a decline in parental control and a world in a state of permanent crisis, are frequently cited as the major source of adolescent difficulty. Conceived as a "transitional stage," adolescence is a very difficult period: it is described (and caricatured) as a time of awkwardness and embarrassment and trouble and pain—something to be got out of as soon as possible by orienting oneself primarily toward eventual membership in "the" adult community.

For many years, apparently, this conception of adolescence as a difficult transitional stage was the dominant framework in which adolescent problems were discussed. In 1944, Caroline Tryon could write, "we have a tendency to disregard or to minimize the educational significance of the child's experience in his peer group."[7] Today this statement strikes the eye as incredible; certainly it is no longer true. Very few contemporary discussions of youth fail to mention the significance of the involvement of young persons in their own age-graded peer groups. The emphasis in these discussions, is quite different from that in discussions of adolescence as a transitional stage; the stress is on the orientation of adolescents to their peers. From this perspective emerged the idea of an adolescent sub-

[6]These are a few of the "discontinuities" made famous by Ruth Benedict in her celebrated article "Continuities and Discontinuities in Cultural Condi- ticning," Psychiatry (May 1938). See also Kingsley Davis' related discussions: "Adolescence and the Social Structure," The Annals (November 1944) and "The Sociology of Parent-Youth Conflict," American Sociological Review (August 1940).
[7]"The Adolescent Peer Culture," 43rd Yearbook of the National Society for the Study of Education (Chicago, Ill.: University of Chicago Press, 1944).

culture[8] as a relatively autonomous "way of life", controlled internally by a system of norms and sanctions largely antithetical or indifferent to that offered by parents, teachers, and clergymen—the official representatives of the adult world.

By itself, the subcultural view of adolescence suggests nothing *inherently* transitional, except in the sense that all experience is transitional, representing, as it does, the passage from what one was to what one is about to become. But oddly enough, it is precisely the concern for consequences that is missing from the conventional usage of the concept of "transitional stage." To suggest that adolescence is a "stage they go through"—something that adolescents "grow out of"—is to violate much of what we know about the permanent effects of socialized experience. It is as if adolescence, frequently designated "the formative years," formed nothing, but was simply a rather uncomfortable period of biding one's time until the advent of one's twenty-first birthday or until one's graduation from school induced the adult world to extend a symbolic invitation to join it. But if the transitional view of adolescence minimizes the permanent influences of adolescent experience, the subcultural view exaggerates the degree to which adolescents create an insulated, autonomous milieu in which they may with impunity practice their alleged antiadult rites. *No large scale study of high school youth, for example, has successfully demonstrated the existence of a really deviant system of norms which governs adolescent life.*[9]

The point I wish to stress here, however, is that our understanding of the varieties of adolescent experience depends heavily upon whether adolescent group life is primarily conceived in the vocabulary of developmental psychology as a transitional stage, or in the sociological vocabulary of subcultures. Conceived as a transitional stage, adolescence is typically described in ways which make its termination devoutly to be wished by adolescents as well as adults.[10] When

[8]This is not the place to go into the problems of applying the concept of "subculture," developed on ethnic models, to age groups. See J. Milton Yinger, "Contraculture and Subculture," *American Sociological Review* (October 1960) and my own comments in "Adolescence and Beyond" (p. 43).

[9]The most ambitious attempts to demonstrate this is James Coleman's *The Adolescent Society* (Glencoe, Ill.: The Free Press, 1961).

[10]The characterization of adolescence as "the awkward age" full of pimples and embarrassment has validity only for the very early teen years. It may merely be a survival from a period when adolescents were completely dependent and completely subordinate. Today, high school students, free and

adolescence is discussed in subcultural terms, no such implication is carried with it. The literature on youth culture most consistently describes it in terms of hedonistic, irresponsible, and "expressive" behavior. Although most adults may believe that this behavior and the norms that constrain it *ought* to be terminated at the threshold of adulthood, it is by no means self-evident that a group which can "get away with" a life of hedonism (read: fun, kicks), irresponsibility (read: freedom, license), and expressiveness (read: immediate gratification, ego enhancement) may be expected to terminate this life easily in exchange for the mixed blessings of recognition as adults, and the sometimes baleful responsibilities that this entails. Objectively—and at the very least, adolescence is a portion of a life lived—*formative* attitudes and orientations, talents and commitments, capacities *and incapacities* develop that affect adolescents' various modes of adaptation into adult worlds, which more or less facilitate or obstruct their eventual recruitment into a specific adult milieu. If the child is father to the man, an understanding of the varieties of experience adolescents undergo, the varieties of milieux they touch, should contribute to the understanding of the kind of adults they are likely to become—and *not* become.

Chronological Age and Youthfulness

Before attempting to describe the groups that might fit the categories of "teen-agers" and "American youth," and the groups that might be usefully analyzed with the concepts of "transitional stage" and "subculture," I wish to make explicit one more distinction alluded to earlier which is conceptually parallel to the two sets of distinctions I have already made. To say that youthfulness is far from perfectly correlated with chronological age is to imply that some adolescents are more youthful than others. Once the distinction is made, we can speak categorically of youthful young men, unyouthful young men, youthful old men, and unyouthful old men. This fourfold classification suggests, perhaps oversharply, that chronological age and the culture—personality variables associated with it may be analytically separated. To render the distinction fruitful, however, it is necessary to specify what is meant by youthfulness. It seems wise

relatively affluent, frequently feel that they are currently living what they expect will be the best years of their lives.

to approach this problem indirectly, by contrasting youthfulness with the relative lack of it in "American youth."

In this connection, let me again draw attention to *The Vanishing Adolescent* in which Edgar Friedenberg argues that adolescence as a stormy decade of identity-seeking and as a distinctive stage of human development is disappearing in the United States largely as a result of premature socialization primarily in the high schools. Without replacing my earlier discussion of Friedenberg's thesis, we *can* say that we have all known adolescents of the kind about which he is concerned. They do well enough in school, are "well adjusted," popular with their peers, have few great conflicts with their parents or other authorities, and in general have few if any serious quarrels with the value system into which they are being socialized or with the institutions representing these values. Grant this image some validity; then let us ask, in what sense are these young persons youthful? Certainly they are young and probably inexperienced in the affairs of the world. But adolescents who respond docilely to the expectations of school authorities, who accept as legitimate the limits imposed on them by their parents,[11] who engage in the activities that are deemed appropriate by adult authorities, are more aptly described as going through the final phase of their preadult socialization, as junior grown-ups, rather than as incarnations of youthfulness. For when, in common usage, we describe persons as "youthful," we mean not primarily that they are obviously young, and hence relatively naive and inexperienced; we mean that they tend to manifest certain qualities in their behavior, and that although these qualities do seem to be empirically *associated* with tender years, they are not *exclusively* age-graded.

Regardless of chronological age, youthful persons tend to be impulsive, spontaneous, energetic, exploratory, venturesome, and vivacious; they tend to be candid, colorful, blunt in speech (having not acquired the skill and habit of dissimulation); they are often irreverent, frequently disrespectful, extreme, immoderate, they know no golden mean; they are "action seekers"[12] rather than seekers of stable routine. They joke a lot; the play motif dominates much of

---

[11] There actually are many adolescents who respond to questionnaires with the opinion that teenagers are not really old enough to smoke or drink or in general to know what is good for them.

[12] The term "action seeker" is taken from Herbert Gans' characterization of some working-class Bostonians. See his *The Urban Villagers* (New York: The Free Press of Glencoe, 1962).

their activity, which they tend to transform into games, even in the most apparently unpropitious of circumstances. Lacking caution and judiciousness, they tend to throw themselves with full passion and sexually alert intensity into those activities that promise thrills and excitement, which they tend to pursue with little regard for consequences.

Notice that these are primarly the qualities of persons, not roles, and certainly not rationalized bureaucratic roles—although they may become quasi-institutionalized as "deviant" roles. Notice too that they are all very active—one might say erotic. When abstracted from behavior and made conscious, qualities such as these assert themselves on *ideological* grounds. When, that is, they take on the character of moral imperatives, we can properly speak of a system of subcultural norms.[13] Such norms underlie the content of youth culture. Clearly, they are dangerous. From the perspective of the major institutions of social order, youthfulness is excess; it is implicit or incipient disorder; for society, it is a "problem" that requires handling, control, cooperation, or channeling in socially approved directions.

Society has at its disposal a great armory of means to control this implicit threat of disorder. I mean not the police and the courts or the more informal sanctions wielded by parents and other authorities; I mean the community youth center, the chaperoned dance, organized sports, school-sponsored extracurricular clubs, and the junior auxiliaries of business, religious, fraternal and veterans' associations —for adults have learned that adolescents will frequently accept from their peers the same norms they may reject from adults. But the effectivenes of these organizational weapons in coping with youth varies with the location of particular youths in the social structure. Where, for example, adult leadership is poor and community facilities limited, as in urban slums and certain new suburbs; or where sudden discontinuities in style of life create inter-generation tensions and anxieties, and disqualify parents as models worthy of emulation and respect, as frequently occurs in immigrant or highly mobile families; or where failure or anticipated failure in academic competition leaves the failed with the perception of a bleak future and with no approved

---

[13]For modern formulations of this theology, see Norman Brown, *Life Against Death* (New York: Random House, 1960); Herbert Marcuse, *Eros and Civilization* (Boston, Mass.: Beacon, 1959) and Paul Goodman, *Growing up Absurd*, (New York: Random House, 1960).

alternative sources of self-respect, as frequently occurs among ethnic and working-class boys in schools dominated by middle-class norms —where these and other early experiences of incipient social disaffection can mobilize ideological supports and some degree of structural insulation from the major institutions, there we are likely to find fertile ground in which the seeds of youthful excess and disorder can grow, and, eventually, bear the exotic flower called "youth culture."

Varieties of Youth Culture

The flower has many blooms; the varieties of youth culture are as wide as the variety of cultural contexts and opportunity systems offered by a pluralistic society. At its broadest and most innocuous, the youth cultures of the young touch the fringes of what is called "teen-age culture": popular songs, rock and roll, disc jockeys, juke boxes, portable phonographs, movie stars, dating, and romantic love; hot rods, motorcycles, drag racing, and sports cars, panty raids and water fights, drive-in hamburgers and clandestine drinking, football games, basketball games, dances and parties, and clubs and cliques, and lovers' lanes. At its delinquent extreme, youth culture is black leather jackets, gang rumbles and switch blades, malicious mischief, and joy riding in stolen cars. Politically, it is expressed in sit-ins, freedom rides, peace marches, and folk songs; it is jazz at Newport, vacations at Fort Lauderdale—and their attendant riots. And it is also bohemians and beatniks and beards and hipsters, and coffee house desperadoes plotting everything from literary magazines to assaults on the House Committee on Un-American Activities.[14]

I intend by this apparently formless catalogue of symbols to suggest how wide a variety of group styles and expressions the youth cultures of the young include. Intimations[15] of youth culture will be found more frequently among "teen-agers" than among "American youth," more frequently among "conflict" and "retreatist" delinquent gangs than among the "rational" criminal delinquents,[16] more among

[14]For a very similar formulation, see David Matza, "Subterranean Traditions of Youth," *The Annals* (November 1961) in which Matza argues that radicalism, bohemianism, and delinquency are the three basic forms which subterranean traditions (that is, subcultures) of youth take.
[15]I say "intimations" because "teen-age culture" is what David Matza calls a "conventionalized version" of what I would call a genuine youth culture.
[16]See Richard Cloward and Lloyd Ohlin, *Delinquency and Opportunity*, (Glencoe, Ill.: The Free Press, 1960) for a discussion of these types of gangs.

"bohemian" and "collegiate" undergraduates than among academically or vocationally oriented college students,[17] and more among politically militant and extreme student groups than among the student adherents of "moderate" sentiment within the two major political parties. The wide social spectrum represented by these groups should reassure the skeptic that I have no ideological axes to grind; few of those prone to moral judgments of youth could unambiguously approve or disapprove of *all* of these groups at the same time. But what delinquents and bohemians and campus radicals and even some high school hot rodders and college fraternity boys have in common is, I am suggesting, their youthfulness, that is, their tendency to behave in patterned ways normatively hedonistic, irresponsible, and expressive.

In spite of the wide variety of dissimilar forms in which it is expressed, it seems reasonable and useful—and also more objective—initially to designate this normative behavior as "youthful" (rather than, say, "deviant" or "delinquent" or "alienated," although it may *become* these) because it is in large part the autonomous creature of subsocieties of the recalcitrant young. However, as I have suggested above and will argue at some length below, it is also selected from, supported by, and modeled after a long cultural tradition, nourished by several contemporary subcultures of adults, and is hence in principle viable into adulthood and beyond. The youth cultures of the young man are an adaptive response by *some* adolescents to problems presented to them by their parent society and culture (for example, contradictions or imbalances in norms, blockage of opportunity, inadequately defined roles, ambiguities of age-grading, the prospect of meaningless work), and *the forms they take in specific groups reflect a choice from traditions available to them.* To see the matter this way takes account of both the autonomous character of the subculture and its linkage to important traditions which antedate it. The significance of the adjective in the term "youth culture," however, rests not in the fact that many of its participants are young, but in the fact that their selective interaction with one another, under the difficult conditions generated by our age-grading norms and in contexts that limit the exercise of adult supervision and control, may sustain a set of more or less counter-

[17]See the typology of college student orientations in Martin A. Trow and Burton Clark, "The Organizational Context," in *College Peer Groups*, T. M. Newcomb and E. K. Wilson, eds. (Chicago, Ill.: Aldine, 1966).

norms which encourage and support, however ambivalently, a pattern of behavior at odds with the official norms of the culture in which it is located, but *adaptive* in the sense that it can provide—not just temporarily—a more or less viable way of life.

Adult Youth Cultures

The Preservation of Youth Culture: Its Links with the Adult World

Earlier, I criticized the usage of the concept of "transitional stage" because it did not sufficiently specify the differential impact of adolescent experience upon subsequent careers. We already know that adolescents eventually become adults; but we do not know much about the ways in which variations in adolescent experience affect subsequent adult adaptations. The concept of "transitional stage" is often employed largely as a palliative for society's functional problems of recruiting and integrating youth into adult worlds: if it's merely "a stage they're going through," then adults need not frankly confront the problems their behavior raises, because, after all, "they'll grow out of it."

Most of them, it is true, do grow out of it, and the fact that they do is testimony not only to the power of adult agencies of socialization but to the vulnerability to co-optation of "teen-age culture"—to its lack of resources to sustain it in crisis and insulate it from attack.[18] But some do not or cannot grow out of it. What becomes of those young persons whose "youthful rebelliousness" turns out to be not "a stage they're going through," but a series of subculturally rewarding experiences that subjectively validate their initial opposition to or irritation with the official demands of adults? And what becomes of those whose participation in political, delinquent, and bohemian forms of youth culture leaves permanent stigmata that render them permanently visible to a henceforth skeptical and suspicious world? Delin-

---

[18]It is this lack which distinguishes "teen-age culture" from more genuine subcultures such as ethnic communities, delinquent gangs in urban slums, and bohemias. Ethnic communities frequently have a full blown institutional structures to shield its members from the society's encroachments; delinquent gangs emphasize the inviolability of "turf" for good sociological reason; bohemias are usually ecological communities as well as subcultures; and even political radicals have, at the very least, a strong ideology to sustain them. Teen-agers have very little.

quency statistics, the beatnik craze (and its successor, the hippie movement), student militance and riots suggest that for substantial numbers (how many, no one knows) adolescence is not simply an awkward but benign transitional stage, and it is these facts to which we refer when we speak of youth and their growing up as a "social problem." To the extent that we can conceive of growing up as a *career* (and in this psychoanalytical age it is not difficult to do so), *"not* growing up" (that is, the preservation of the essential features of youth culture in later life) can also be considered as a career. Although there is a certain joylessness in the idea of "maturity" (identified, as it is, with sober responsibilities and solemn commitments), there are relatively few niches in the adult social structure where "youthfulness" does not receive severe negative sanctions, and those adolescents whose peer group experience has developed in them incapacities for growing up or perhaps even conscientious objections to it may be expected to gravitate toward those niches.

Those adolescents whose youthful attributes are weakest—for example, those studied by Elkin and Westley, the prematurely socialized type described by Friedenberg, and the bulk of adolescents only superficially involved in teenage culture—will probably have the least difficulty in making the transition to the typical adult careers offered in a highly industrialized, bureaucratized society. On the other hand, those in whom youthful attributes are strong will have the greatest difficulty in making those sacrifices of youthfulness that most executive and professional and other prestigious adult careers require.

What kinds of adult occupations and milieu are likely to reward or at least tolerate youthfulness, and thus normatively support an attempt not to grow up or an inability to grow up? If it is true that some adolescents are more youthful than others, it is also true that some adults are more youthful than others, and it is likely that some of the important forces that sustain youthfulnes in those who are no longer young may be found in the norms of the occupations they choose (or which choose them) and in the milieu that those norms help create.[19] What are some of these types of occupations?

---

[19]Statuses other than occupational ones, of course, may also help sustain youthfulness: bachelor, divorcé(e), student, for example. Periodicals such as *Esquire* and *Playboy* are apparently directed at youthful adult audiences, and an analysis of their readers might provide evidence of youthful adult statuses.

Youthful Careers

I submit the following short list for illustrative purposes. My best hope is that it will be taken as suggestive of one way of theoretically linking the content of adolescent youth cultures with important subterranean or deviant traditions in the adult world, and hence of linking certain kinds of youthful experience in the adolescent milieu with the subsequent taking up of adult careers.

Bohemian business: By bohemian businessmen, I mean the proprietors or managers of small enterprises that cater to the needs, tastes, and desires of bohemians. These enterprises range all the way from those that are central to bohemian subcultures (*espresso* coffee houses, small art galleries, sandal and leather shops, pottery shops, jewelry shops, and so on) to other marginal busineses serving other markets as well ("art" theaters, paperback bookstores, small night clubs specializing in modern jazz, accessory and specialty shops for women, and so on). Wherever a "deviant" community exists (in this case a bohemian community), a business community is likely to exist to supply the wants that symbolize and define its deviance—in a sense analogous to that in which organized crime is symbiotically interrelated with government, law enforcement agencies, and parts of the legitimate business community. Bohemian business enterprise is one of the relatively few types of careers available to persons who, having had their basic orientations to the world shaped by experience in an adolescent subculture, have developed trained incapacities for pursuing more conventional kinds of business or professional or "bourgeois" careers—although the ironic and economically "reactionary" character of bohemian enterprise is that it gives its entrepreneurs the status of shopkeeper.

But their status as shopkeepers is less important and less revealing than the fact that they are likely to be bohemians. Bohemian businessmen, that is, are more like their customers than like other small businessmen. Even in their strictly economic capacities, bohemian businessmen are likely to reflect the habits of their customers. They may, for example, be expected to keep irregular hours, to open their shops late in the day and remain open late in the evening. Located primarily in the "Latin quarter" of large cities or near university campuses, they frequently take long summer vacations or move their shops to summer resorts of the "art colony" type. They are not likely

to keep rigorous books and their prices are frequently not standardized—sometimes because their wares are not. Often, they do not have a primarily commercial or instrumental orientation to what they sell, but rather an expressive one.[20] Dealing mainly in beauty—in esthetic objects or experience—they are not likely to think of themselves primarily as businessmen, but either as craftsmen or as esthetic functionaries performing services for the community of avant-garde good taste. However they think of themselves, bohemian businessmen (recruited largely from the student bohemian world of craftsmen, failed or insufficiently talented artists, and hangers-on and camp followers of the cultural avant-garde) live in a milieu that tolerates and rewards a youthful adaptation to the world. Bohemian business offers a moderately viable niche in the adult world for those unable or unwilling to grow out of youth culture.

Perhaps an *image* of a viable niche in the world would be a more accurate statement. For it is, of course, true that the actual opportunities for a successful career in bohemian business are probably not very good. Although it is a theoretically open milieu, the rate of business failure is high, and the population of bohemia is probably not large enough to support the commercial enterprises of very many of those young persons who are more or less successfully resisting or evading middle-class socialization. Nevertheless, the image of an adult bohemian life is culturally fertile and ambiguously seductive to many. Bohemia is always newsworthy; its consistent coverage in the mass media, its consistent status as a"tourist attraction" means that it is of great interest to the vicarious lives of large numbers of people. For every core bohemian there are probably five fringe bohemians; for every fringe bohemian there are probably five "weekend bohemians"; and for every weekend bohemian there are probably scores of Walter Mittys each of whom might be secretly flattered to have one of his perhaps idiosyncratic habits labeled "bohemian" by a suspicious and surly neighbor. My point is simply that although full-time bohemianism as a career may not be viable very long for very many, its part-time or fantasy appeal is apparently much stronger than the actual opportunities it offers. But it is the existence of this appeal and the ambiguous possibilities represented by it that enable

[20]An example: a customer walks into an "art mart" to purchase a teapot that goes with a set of china that the customer knows the shop stocks. With some hauteur, the proprietress informs the customer that she does not sell the teapot (although she sells all the other pieces in the set) because it is "poorly designed."

it to serve for the youthful as a *milieu of orientation* tolerant of their behavior and to which they may look for permanent sustenance.

Show business: Many actors, singers, dancers, musicians, comedians, and other entertainers inhabit a world suffused by the myth of youth—a world in which grandmothers and grandfathers are noted for their sex appeal. The professional milieu of jazz musicians interpenetrates with the hip and bohemian varieties of youth culture, bonded by a common antipathy to "squares." Much like the jazz milieu, the world of the off-Broadway theater is heavily populated with aspiring actors and actresses, committed to their expressive art, who live on the fringe of bohemia. The celebrity world of Hollywood stars is, for public consumption at least, "La Dolce Vita," with its dominating motifs of sex, speed, alcohol, drugs, and perversion set in a context of luxury. Most of the "new" American comedians have come up from the dark basement clubs catering to bohemian-intellectual audiences into the bright glare of the legitimate stage and the TV studio to continue, somewhat diluted, their savage satires of the routine, the usual, the ordinary (that is, the "adult")—but now to the masochistic audience upon whose lives and opinions their material is based. Finally, teen-age pop singers, despite their ritual affirmation of God, Home, and Mother, and their pious promises to "continue their education" (directed, one supposes, at the parents of their admirers), create a professional image compounded of thinly disguised erotica and forlorn adolescent alienation, and, with the help of publicity, transform their slum or otherwise poverty-stricken backgrounds into a romantic determination to "be somebody." ("I want to become a really good actor instead of just a teen-age singer.")

That show business careers and similar occupations are in fact subject to much the same economic circumstances and bureaucratic controls as are other occupations, and that many show folk in fact live model middle-class lives are less important than the carefully nurtured Dionysian images of show business life, the persistent myth that careers are made" overnight," that its durable stars are ageless, and that "expressive" opportunities are offered by the public spotlight. Like other "creative" occupations, show business tends to be tolerant of irregular, spontaneous, unpredictable, exhibitionistic behavior—indeed, these are sometimes built into the very conditions of employment; more, show business expects this kind of behavior, and some-

times rewards it (in publicity, if nothing else—and publicity is seldom nothing else), at least among its stars. The hedonism and public irresponsibility of show business celebrities is disingenuously mythologized as "artistic temperament," suggesting that in those industries in which "creativity" is a basic commodity, perversities of other sorts must also be accepted: great beauty, great talent, great acclaim imply great vices. Thus Ava Gardner (a living Lady Brett) leaves a trail of discarded lovers across the bull rings of Spain; thus Maria Callas sails the Mediterranean in her Greek billionaire's yacht, telling the press at Riviera ports that they are "just friends"; thus Ingrid Bergman conceives an illegitimate child on a volcanic Aegean island to the merely temporary dismay of her fans; thus Lana Turner rears a daughter who becomes the killer of her mother's gangster–lover; thus Eddie leaves Debbie for Liz and Liz leaves Eddie for Richard to a breathless watching world of column readers. Billie Holiday, the greatest jazz singer of the era, wasted from years of addiction to heroin, dies under guard in a hospital; idols of teenage girls get picked up for homosexuality; Dean Martin nurtures a lucrative public image built on a reputation for alcoholism, and the Frank Sinatra clique spread across the night life of the country their money, their liquor, their arrogance, and their talent to delight the press.

With this newsreel, I intended neither a documentation of the lurid nor a righteous cry of decadence but only a vivid suggestion that, manufactured or not, the image of show business careers exists in a milieu in which Dionysian excess has a long tradition and an honored place—a cautious and implicit honor (given its dependence on the whims of public opinion), but a milieu in which one neither loses face nor gets fired for scandalous behavior, a milieu in which the only bad publicity is no publicity at all. The extremes to which the public behavior of show business celebrities is constrained are, like that of gang delinquents, justified by the "rep" it engenders; the Dionysian comings and goings of middle-aged Frank Sinatra and his middle-aged friends are apparently regarded by the public with the same mock severity reserved for the pranks of teenagers. There is a normative kinship between the Dionysian motifs of the celebrity world of show biz and the hedonistic, expressive values of youth culture. A substantial part of the material content of youth culture is provided and sustained by the industries of mass entertainment and a large part of the entertainment business depends upon youth for its markets. Notice also that show business careers (and satellite show

business careers such as disc jockeying and modeling) are virtually the *only* occupations or occupational images offered to adolescents in the pages of the "teen-age magazines." Like bohemian business, show business offers the image of a career to talented young people with trained incapacities for business or the bureaucratized professions. People with "artistic talent" have, according to legend, no "business sense," and show business careers are often said to require the kind of single-minded dedication that is unable even to imagine another kind of future. Like bohemian business, show business tolerates or rewards a youthful orientation to the world and offers the inducement of "romantic" or "glamorous" careers to those unable or unwilling to "grow up."[21]

Like bohemian business too, show business has an important component of vicarious appeal: there is a sense in which show business is everyman's vicarious business; there are probably thousands of Americans who sit in front of their TV sets quietly confident that they can sing as well, dance as well, tell jokes as well, ride a horse and sling a gun as well as those merely lucky ones on the screen. Show business not only involves the audience in the imaginary worlds its creates, it involves them vicariously in show business itself. This may be one of the reasons for the proverbial interest of Americans in the private lives of celebrities, and why professional, in-group banter and jokes about show business is virtually the only kind of esoteric humor of interest to out-groups. So that in addition to the promise of an actual career, show business, again like bohemia, offers an abundance of vicarious careers to the imperfectly socialized, and is thus, in an oddly perverse sense, functional to the extent that, by mollifying largely unfulfilled yearnings for a freer, more spontaneous that is, more youthful life, it softens the tensions and frustrations engendered by socialization without internalization. Like the Horatio Alger myth, which told us that we too could succeed, the myths of the adult milieux which combine the exciting with the unsavory tell us that our lives need not be routine and colorless. The Alger myth succored an age of economic growth preoccupied with

---

[21]Moss Hart, who should know, writes, "I would hazard a guess . . . that the temperament, the tantrums, and the utter childishness of theater people in general, is neither accidental nor a necessary weapon of their profession. It has nothing to do with so-called 'artistic temperament.' The explanation, I think, is a far simpler one. For the most part they are impaled in childhood like a fly in amber." *Act One* (New York: Random House, 1959).

objective success; the youthfulness myth succors an age of psychology preoccupied with subjective "fulfillment."

Working-class occupations: Many of the adolescents whom I have called "youthful"—the high school rebels, the flouters of adult authority, the claimers of autonomy for adolescents—are likely to be of working-class background, especially ethnics, culturally "deprived," without much talent, who drop out of high school or do poorly in it, and are probably headed not for the glamorous careers I have mentioned but for the lower reaches of the manual labor force. Nevertheless, there are good reasons for believing that many working-class occupations and the subcultural norms associated with some of them are more supportive of youthful orientations than most middle-class occupations.

Several otherwise disparate intellectual traditions converge in their characterizations of working-class life in terms akin to my conception of youthfulness. The Marxist tradition, for example, confers upon labor the innocent dignity of useful work, the tragedy of exploitation and alienation, and the heroic mission of carrying within it the seeds of a bright and revolutionary future. Having nothing else to lose but their chains, the proletariat can take dramatic and passionate steps in its own interest. Sabotage, walk-outs, general strikes, the Marxist myth of a militant working class—bold, defiant, resentful of its oppressors, impatient to bring down the system of authority which victimizes it—strikingly partake of much the same spirit and imagery as rebellious adolescents vis-á-vis the world of adults. Both groups claim for themselves, in the strident tones characteristic of those without a parliamentary voice, autonomy: freedom from their illegitimate subordination to an authority they never chose, from consignment to a future they do not want.

There is also a literary tradition more than 150 years old that bestows upon laborers—especially rural laborers—greater energy, vitality, and sexuality than it does to the pale, thin, beardless, repressed pencil pushers who inhabit the offices of the world. In this literary tradition, workers are impulsive, strong, intuitive, passionate —capable of great anger and great tenderness; above all, they are, like adolescents, *personal*, largely alienated from and disgusted with the rationales and rationalizing of the impersonal bureaucratic world.

Paralleling these two romanticisms of working-class life is a third intellectual tradition that emphasizes the common values and long

history of both the highest and the lowest classes of traditional Europe, which the despised, calculating minds of the *arriviste* middle class could never share: aristocrats and peasants share a tendency to violence, to alcoholic excesses, and to blood sports. This kinship between the highest and the lowest may be rather forced, but the peculiar combination of aristocratic and vulgar motifs, or élite and egalitarian themes which crystallize around a disdain for middle-class life has persisted for nearly 200 years.[22] The intellectual core of this tradition is the belief that the powers, privileges, and immunities of aristocratic life, and the passion, desperation, and anarchy of life in the depths are both preferable to the calculated moderation and mediocrity inherent in burgeois definitions of maturity and responsibility. Each extreme is, in its different way, transcendent; the middle class is forever earthbound. Translating this tradition into my own terms, the lower classes and the upper classes are more youthful than the middle classes.

Finally, recent empirical descriptions of working-class culture by sociologists lend considerable support to these romanticized versions of working-class life. These studies show a highly remarkable but generally unremarked upon similarity to standard descriptions of youth culture. Thus workers tend to be hedonistic, unable or unwilling to plan ahead or defer gratification; they are highly expressive rather than instrumental in their basic orientations, given to violent and extreme views, irrational, anti-intellectual, "person-centered" (rather than "role-centered"), and generally indifferent to their civic responsibilities.[23] Certain working-class occupations, then, especially *lower* ones, are likely to require much less in the way of sacrifice of youthfulness than most other occupations, and it should come as no sur-

[22]Especially strongly in the bohemian tradition from, say, Diderot to Norman Mailer. One is reminded that "teddy boys" affect the garments of Edwardian gentlemen and the manners of hoodlums. Leslie Fiedler has argued at some length that "highbrow" and "lowbrow' culture have more in common than either has with "middlebrow" culture. See his, "Both Ends Against the Middle," reprinted in *Mass Culture*, Rosenberg and White, eds. (Glencoe, Ill.: The Free Press, 1957).

[23]See, for example, William F. Whyte, *Street Corner Society*, (Chicago, Ill.: University of Chicago Press, 1943); S. M. Miller and Frank Riessman, "The Working Class Subculture," *Social Problems* (Summer 1961); Richard Hoggart, *The Uses of Literacy*, (London: Chatto and Windus, 1957); A. K. Cohen and H. M. Hodges, "Characteristics of the Lower-Blue-Collar Class," *Social Problems* (Spring 1963); Herbert J. Gans (note 13); and Seymour Martin Lipset, "Working Class Authoritarianism," in *Social Controversy*, W. Petersen and D. Matza, eds. (Belmont, Calif.: Wadsworth Publishing Co., 1963).

prise that recalcitrant youth without academic ability or usable deviant talents should gravitate toward these jobs.

Conclusion

What I have offered here is in a sense a conceptual model for the analysis of adolescent behavior and the youthful adult milieu to which, under certain conditions, it may lead. There are youthful occupations and milieu other than those I have described. I have not, for example, mentioned free lance art or the military or professional sports, nor have I mentioned several niches in the academic and intellectual worlds that support youthful orientations. But I think that by now my major point should be clear. I have tried to suggest that the successful socialization of children into the dominant value system is always problematic especially in pluralistic societies; that recalcitrance can be spotted early; and that what I have called youth culture begins when adolescent rebellion against dominant adult norms takes on ideological supports from existing deviant adult traditions. For many adolescents, of course, this is only "a stage they go through," and most of them eventually internalize or at least comply with the norms constrained on them by the major agencies of socialization. At the same time, it is important to recognize that many adolescents do not, that the experience of many in adolescent subcultures shapes their futures by incapacitating them for bureaucratic roles. Most of these, it is true, wind up at the lower end of the occupational hierarchy, especially those who are unable to survive high school. But those who do survive and who are fortunate enough to discover the other face of their trained incapacities—in college or elsewhere—are uniquely enabled to take advantage of the few sheltered places a pluralistic society offers in its occupational structure which will permit them, as adults, to sustain that normative variation without which pluralism is emptied of its cultural meaning, leaving a society highly differentiated on the level of social structure but homogeneous on the level of culture.

With this analysis, I am not offering only a more differentiated view of socialization—substituting a frame of reference emphasizing conformity to milieu rather than to general cultural norms. I mean also to emphasize that groups differ in the extent to which they tolerate or encourage normative dissension, and the extent to which this is true is directly relevant to the *roles* that inveterate dissenters

can find in the social structure. In groups which require a high degree of uniformity, dissenters are constrained to yield or to withdraw from active participation; but in groups that place a high value on innovation—and many youthful groups are prominent among these—dissenters are much more likely to be able to retain the privileges of active association.[24]

This analysis also bears upon the problem of adaptation to failure, and casts a little light on the ingenious way in which society provides for the comfort of its failures, while using its own failure to socialize some of its members as a way of easing the tensions engendered by its excessive success with others: those who are relegated to the bottom of the occupational heap, for example, are heir to a ready-made ideology, a myth that invidiously contrasts their own vigor, vitality, and authentic humanity with the repressions, the desk-boundness, and the futile status-seeking of the successful. Society uses the luckier ones too—those who are able to find loftier, more glamorous, youthful adult niches. These feed the vicarious appetites of the nation, and are living testimony to the bored, the alienated from work, and the otherwise vaguely dissatisfied that exciting careers *do* exist. And the definition of these careers as newsworthy by the mass media peculiarly fits them for the strategic role they play in the vicarious lives of others.

[24]For empirical data on this point, see Yrjo Littunen, "Deviance and Passivity in Radio Listener Groups," *Acta Sociologia* vol. 4, no. 3 (1959), pp. 17–26.

The Identity Myth

1968

I call this essay the Identity Myth because I want to discuss the concept of identity (or ego-identity) as a sociologist of knowledge might: as an item of ideology rather than as a feature of personality or developmental psychology. The ideological form of the identity idea is mythic in the sense that its popularity in the intellectual discourse of the educated and the semieducated suggests that its cogency may rest less on its contribution to the understanding of personality than on the important social functions the widespread acceptance of the idea implies.

I take this perspective with some fear and trembling for two reasons. First, because among some psychiatrists, psychologists, and sociologists (as well as certain other kinds of intellectuals), the identity idea comes as near to being a sacred receptacle as any concept in the intellectual baggage of social science. Experts may disagree over precise definitions of the concept, but like "culture" and "maturity" and a number of other ideas, whatever they may contain, we are strongly constrained to believe that the contents are *good* things. Second, because in analyzing the idea sociologically

A lecture delivered at Forest Hospital in Des Plaines, Ill., January 1968.

(in this case by concerning myself with its ideological rather than its quasi-medical or scientific dimensions) I run the risk of providing aid and comfort to the enemy: I mean those anti-intellectuals and other pooh-poohers who regard a preoccupation with anything they can't see or touch as weak, effeminate, and probably un-American— although I must confess that I sense a touch of that philistinism in myself whenever I find it useful to apply gross or coarse criteria or even a naive phenomenology to those ideas whose fashionableness or whose too ready acceptance may obscure their lack of objective substance or felt reality. I want, then, to adopt here a sort of Devil's Advocate role—not only because I enjoy the risk of stepping on the sacred, but also because I am not quite sure of where those steps lead. An *essay* should help find out. In any case, I wish to put before you a sociological analysis of the idea of identity, with particular reference to the so-called identity crisis of adolescence.

Erik Erikson: "I have called the major crisis of adolescence the *identity crisis*; it occurs in that period of the life cycle when each youth must forge for himself some central perspective and direction, some working unity, out of the effective remnants of his childhood and the hopes of his anticipated adulthood; he must detect some meaningful resemblance between what he has come to see in himself and what his sharpened awareness tell him others judge and expect him to be."

Edgar Friedenberg: "Adolescence is the period during which a *young person learns who he is, and what he really feels. It is the time during which he differentiates himself from his culture. . . .*"

Allen Wheelis: "Identity is a coherent sense of self . . . the awareness that one's endeavors and one's life make sense."

In each of these and many other attempts to come to grips with defining the idea, the emphasis is on the sense of wholeness or integration. Presumably, a clear and stable identity should enable one to provide a straight and satisfying answer to the straight question "who am I?"—an answer which presumably transcends or comprehends the roles, occupied or anticipated, which characterize one as a social being at any given moment. Yet I know of no vocabulary sufficiently deep and comprehensive (yet part of the language

of public discourse) to make such an answer possible—particularly for adolescents, the people presumably most affected by the problems posed in the question. The terms in which the question is posed, in short, preclude the possibility of a satisfying answer.

When I was a much younger and crueler professor than I am now, I used to begin my introductory lectures on roles and self by asking sharply "who are you?" and arbitrarily picking on students to provide an answer. But the embarrassment, the sense of threat, even panic, among them became so heavy in the air that I soon abandoned the practice. Students would say I am a student or I am a boy or I am a housewife taking a sociology course or I am a sophomore, and on and on, the room almost invariably burdened with the sense of unsatisfactoriness: these are merely roles; what I *am*, my *self*, the *real* me is something elusive, difficult, indescribable.

I think it is no great mystery why an answer seems inaccessible to many young people in modern societies. In stable, traditional societies, the most comprehensive source of identity is kinship—a fact which, when known, indicates not only one's past but can often predict nearly one's entire future, and which is hence an excellent source of an integrated or coherent identity. In modern societies, where the control exercised by ascriptive categories like race, sex, and kinship has declined, occupation and ethnicity are important sources of the sense of who one is, but sanctions against ethnic identities are prevalent in doctrinally equalitarian societies (or were until the recent upsurge in "ethnic pride"), and adolescents don't have occupations (certainly not "professions")—which is precisely one of the sources of the major problems of adolescence. Yet the students in my class seemed to feel threatened by the inaccessibility of a satisfactory answer to the identity question, as if the inaccessibility were evidence of some inadequacy of their own, as if "who am I?" was a question one was *morally* obligated to be able to answer satisfactorily.

How come? My answer is because we (psychiatrists, psychologists, sociologists—and the media which mold what Philip Rieff has called "psychological man") have taught the educated young to conceptualize as an "identity problem" their quite understandable anxieties about an uncertain future. An "identity," they learn, is something one is obligated to "search for" or "create" (particularly if one comes from an upper middle-class family and is in college majoring in the humanities or social sciences). But although one is constrained to

search, one is constrained not to find (who would be so fatuous as to announce that he had found his identity?), but rather to continue searching until one's commitments to and immersion in family, community, and career result in the disappearance of the identity problem—whereupon one may be told that the identity crisis has been resolved.

The psychoanalytic answer is part of the theory of ego-development which suggests, in Erikson's terms, that "each youth must forge for himself some central perspective . . ." and so on. *"Must"* or else what? Well, or else a healthy personality capable of intimacy will be prevented from developing, and the rest of his life will be emotionally impoverished. Or, in Friedenberg's terms, he will feel a certain lack of emotional vividness, an insufficiently delineated character, an overvaluation of "adjustment" as a criterion of maturity. Or in Wheelis' terms (terms shared by many other thinkers), the absence of a clear sense of coherent identity will lead to a sense of estrangement, the feeling of being an alien in his own body and hence vulnerable to all sorts of anomic disorders.

These *ideas are* of course emotionally vivid—although there is far less than conclusive evidence to support them. But I am concerned less with the problem of evidence (lots of good ideas have less than conclusive evidence to support them) than I am with the fact that the wealth of emotional resonance in these ideas rests first, upon an insufficiently sociological theory of adolescence, and second, on a certain moral absolutism regarding the relationship of self to the constraints of a changing social structure, as is suggested by the implicit *moral* threat contained in the psychological diagnosis.

One of the difficulties with the theory of identity crisis as it bears upon adolescence is in what I regard as the excessively naturalistic conception of adolescence it implies—a conception in which adolescence is typically thought of as primarily a natural or psycho-biological category, rather than a social one, whose problems are therefore primarily set by nature rather than culture. Children everywhere, of course, pass through the sudden crisis of puberty, and the more gradual maturation of their sexual and other physical powers. But whereas in many societies the onset of puberty and the strength to do a man's or woman's work qualify a young person for membership in adult society (at a low status, perhaps, but at a low *adult* status), industrial societies like our own introduce into the culture a special *age-grade* we call adolescence—a social category

which *defines* that part of the population that fits it as not children, exactly, but not quite adults either, that is, not quite fully competent citizens. From a sociological view (or *this* sociologist's view) adolescence is one of the ways in which culture violates nature by insisting that, for an increasing number of years, young persons postpone pressing their claims for the privileges and responsibilities of common citizenship, and no less importantly, by persuading young and old alike of the justice of that postponement. Persuasion is always partly a matter of ideology, and, as I hope to make clear, one element of the persuasive rhetoric is the theory of identity crisis.

Since the early nineteenth century in England, and probably the middle of the century in the United States, the postponement of adulthood has been gradually institutionalized and increasingly prolonged, as more and more occupations required higher levels of skill, as lengthened life expectancy prolonged the tenure in power of older generations, and as the increasing complexity of society enabled its caretakers to allege with apparent reason that longer periods of preparation were needed for adequate adult functioning in it. Whereas at one point in the not too distant past, adolescence could be said to have lasted for a period of three or four years, that is, from the onset of puberty (say, age 13–14), to the time one was "ready" to take up one's full adult responsibilities in a basically homogeneous, rural, agrarian society (say, age 16–17), we have come now to the point where adolescence begins earlier, and where, if we assume the irrelevance to developmental psychology of an arbitrary "legal" age of 18 or 21, we can define its "end" only in terms of highly variable criteria of "maturity." Compare, for example, the lower-class boy or girl who drops out of high school at age 16 or 17 to marry or to go to work full time on an assembly line, and who after four or five years is an experienced, reliable worker or housewife with perhaps three children, a life insurance policy, and a mortgage on a modest house—compare his or her probable "maturity" to those collegiate undergraduates or co-eds, still very much preoccupied with the proprieties of dating, still supported by parents, watched over by house mothers, and probably still thinking of themselves very much as "kids."

Where adolescence may be said to last three or four years, it makes good sense to speak of it as a "transitional stage" (as most textbooks on adolescent and developmental psychology do): the proverbial "stage one goes through"—a difficult but benign period,

to be got through as soon as possible. In a stable, undeveloped society it is possible to escape adolescence after only a few years, by orienting oneself to one's largely ascribed place in an adult world whose social structure, in any case, provides one with few options. But where adolescence begins as early as age 11 or 12—as pubescence occurs earlier—where the prolongation of the status of *student* (in a society in which education is compulsory and in which ascription is said to count for little) may fix one in a quasi-adolescent role (i.e. something less than a fully autonomous and competent adult) often until one's late twenties or early thirties (indeed, sometimes still later—particularly in the professions which require long years of training and apprenticeship), this prolonged period of "preparation" may last twenty years or more, and thus becomes not a relatively fleeting or ephemeral transitional stage but rather a major and substantial segment of life.

It is not surprising that a stage of life which may last this long should develop its own distinctive style, its own traditions, and its own sources of motivation and satisfaction—hence all the discussion in recent years about a so-called youth culture. But the term youth culture is misleading if it suggests that the content of that culture is relevant primarily to people in their teens or early twenties. Although some of the troubles of adolescence arise from the prolonged withholding of adult privileges, others—particularly in late adolescence—arise from a youth so successful in its own terms, so rewarding within the milieu of youth culture itself, that adulthood loses its lure, and the prospect of another ten or fifteen years as a quasi-adolescent (for example, as a perennial student or "nonstudent") can become a very attractive possibility. The spontaneous and "idealistic" qualities of the young that our culture celebrates (and sentimentalizes) the most are precisely the qualities that the conditions of adult life make most difficult to sustain, emphasizing, as they do, an instrumental approach to the world. It is this bad bargain in growing up that makes utopians like Paul Goodman see growing up as "absurd." But even nonutopians like Bruno Bettelheim and Kenneth Keniston have noted increasing reluctance to "grow up" even among those who choose maturity.

Nor is it surprising that a period of life which may last as long as twenty years should evoke what sociologists call "anticipatory socialization": hence the phenomenon known as "preadolescence," in which prepubescent youngsters begin adopting *orientations* to ado-

lescence, a fact which pushes still lower the effective age at which proto-adolescent behavior begins. In any case, it should be clear that, historically speaking, adolescence is a recently invented social category which prolongs the exclusion of the young from full participation in the major institutions of society until they are deemed "ready" to assume adult roles. No wonder, then, that there may be an "identity" problem: the answer to the question "who are you?" is very apt to seem like "nobody very much."

For a society to subject a substantial part of its population to the severe pressures of "adolescence," and then to devote so much of its energies to coping with the problems thus created, seems like a particularly wasteful way for it to handle its youth. But we really don't know what else to do with them, for the "problem" of adolescence is inherent in something we seem unwilling to change: the very structure of advanced industrial societies.

The imposition of "adolescence" on young persons is not a simple accident of history nor the ethical expression of revulsion with the facts of child labor, nor even an attempt by gerontocracies to postpone the succession of generations. It is by now quite common knowledge that, as societies industrialize, their need for the relatively unskilled labor of the young declines, and this tends to render a large part of youth economically superfluous. Such societies have the problem of accommodating economically useless persons while encouraging them to develop the skills that the economy needs. The institutionalization of "adolescence" as a special age-grade—that is, a legal definition and a consensus that young persons are not fully competent citizens—justifies the controls that society exerts over them. It helps keep youth juvenile until society has readied an adult place for them.

The schools, particularly high schools (although colleges too now) are the most important means of controlling adolescents (the military, through the draft, is another), and although the campaigns to reduce the number of "dropouts" are without doubt correct in warning those who are contemplating dropping out that their future occupational chances will be severely reduced, staying in high school is less important for the jobs it will qualify one for than for the reduced pressure it provides on a labor market unable to absorb the unskilled. I doubt that a high school diploma equips one to perform very many jobs that a person with a tenth or eleventh grade education could not perform.

There are two major arguments often made in defense of prolonged

adolescence. The most common is the alleged "complexity" of our society which is said to require a long period of preparation for adequate functioning in it. Now there is no question about the fact that modern occupations increasingly require extended training, and to the extent that an autonomous adulthood requires economic independence, it may be argued that the granting of full adult privilege should be withheld until the achievement of such independence. But the criterion of economic independence is far from adequate by itself as a measure of maturity (is an eighteen year old dropout who is working and supporting a family likely to be a more mature and responsible citizen than a college freshman?—it can be argued either way). And the evidence is less than convincing (far, even, from being adequately gathered) that a contemporary American adolescent, for example, has more to learn about adult functioning *in general* than a young member of a primitive society, who may have to master the intricacies of a very complex kinship system (ours is relatively simple) or a system of highly elaborate religious ritual (our rituals are increasingly simplified). No doubt our society is complex, but there is no evidence to suggest its young people understand it any less well than other young people have understood less complex ones. Nevertheless, much social practice is devoted to reminding the young that they are less than fully competent citizens (while at the same time a great deal of cultural rhetoric is spent urging them to behave "responsibly"); and that more "youngsters" (the patronizing analogue of "oldsters") do not protest their relative powerlessness is testimony to the effectiveness of socialization which has persuaded them that others (elders) know better what is good for them, one of these things being, conveniently, a firm and stable identity—something without which, it is commonly asserted, one is not ever likely to be truly mature.

The more important argument made in defense of a prolonged adolescence, however, is precisely its alleged role in helping young persons to find or achieve a stable identity. One of the allegedly most civilizing features of prolonged adolescence is what Erikson calls the "psycho-social moratorium": a period of years free from adult pressures and commitments in which a young person is encouraged to engage in "the search for identity," that stormy process in which the young person plays and experiments with social roles in an attempt to find out who and what he is and where he belongs in a changing society which does not ascribe his place from birth. In this

view adolescence terminates with the development of a firm and stable ego-identity capable of adult choices and commitments; and this development, promoted by a long adolescence, is frequently praised as one of the triumphs of modern civilization because of the optimum individuality it is said to engender.

There are several difficulties with this view. First of all, there is little evidence that the institutions designed to care for the young during the psycho-social moratorium are contributing much to identity play or experiments with social roles. It seems, rather, as Friedenberg has emphasized, that the schools (as well as other adult-sponsored youth organizations) are devoted less to the cultivation of individuality than to the fabrication of junior grown-ups, which is not the same thing.

The comprehensive high school is the basic institution in industrial societies for detaching young persons from families and locales, the primary sources of identity—a process which helps fit the young for social mobility. Industrialism largely destroys the traditional capacities of families to train their children (particularly fathers to train their sons) for economic roles. But schools do more than take over the educational function from families; by bringing large numbers of young people together for a common purpose, the schools help shift the orientations and loyalties of the young away from their families to their peer groups, and this makes excellent sense for the future. Getting on in the adult world increasingly means the probability of physical removal from the persons and places of one's youth, and strong family and kinship identities as well as psychological ties to "soil" and locale make it more difficult for one to move. The structure of opportunity, then, *systematically* weakens the sources from which the most comprehensive identities might be expected to spring. Blood may indeed be thicker than water, but for the sustenance of the kind of society we are making, it had better not be.

Moreover, the continuing fear of a shortage of college openings creates great pressure among middle-class adolescents for early commitment, especially occupational commitment, which tends to foreclose rather than extend the horizons of personal identity. It is as if the theory encouraged one to find out *who* one is in order to be able to make intelligent adult choices, occupational and otherwise, whereas practice constrained one to make these choices first, and only then begin accommodating one's identity to the *fait accompli.*

Second, even if practice were consistent with theory, there would still be serious question about the social relevance of a firm, stable identity. Although it is not difficult to see how *convenient* it is in social, economic, and familial terms for the "search for identity" to end when occupational and kinship choices are made, there is no self-evident psychological reason for the stormy search to end at any point before the grave, since presumably personal growth and change continue as one goes on accumulating significant experience. Erikson, in one of his long essays on the subject, attempts to have it both ways, arguing that a "final" identity is *fixed* at the end of adolescence, and a few pages later suggesting that identity formation is a lifelong process. I do not see how he can have it both ways.

Moreover, I know of no good reason to believe that a firm and stable identity is under all circumstances preferable to its opposite—presumably an unstable and flexible (or even flabby) one. These days, a firm identity often seems to express itself as pig-headedness, and a stable one as smug or stubborn rigidity. In a rapidly changing society which continually confronts persons with new situations to which one must adapt, a flexible, unstable identity seems like a very useful thing to command—however offensive such plasticity of personality may seem to those thinkers intellectually bred on psychiatric euphemisms for "strength" of character. Kingsley Davis observed years ago that dominant conceptions of "mental health" or "healthy personality" looked suspiciously like the Protestant Ethic. Similarly, it may well be that contemporary sociological and psychological fashions about "finding one's identity" may be suspiciously close to traditional Victorian notions about character strength.

Actually, there are good reasons to believe that in the by now proverbial "search for identity," inducing the process of search is sociologically more important than anything one may happen to find along the way. While young persons are discovering that it is important to "find themselves," what they are actually learning is that they are *immature* until they do. And this knowledge performs two very important functions for the emerging social structure. First, it helps accommodate them to their juvenile status and therefore constrains them to keep out of markets and arenas where only the "mature" belong. In this sense, the theory of the identity crisis is part of the juvenilization process. Second, and here I come to the heart of my point, if identity is inherently something elusive or un-

graspable, *if the self is an onion rather than a nut*, then the most important function performed by institutionalizing the search for something unfindable is to induce the sort of anxiety that *promotes the mobility of the psyche*. A person who does not know who he is *might just be anybody*, and hence is fit for the unanticipateable opportunities and eventualities which rapidly changing industrial societies provide.

Moreover, the belief that in finding an identity one creates or becomes oneself, puts a psychological gloss on (and hence reinforces) two of the core values of our culture. It affirms the legacy of liberal individualism which confers upon the person an essential autonomous reality transcending the social categories in terms of which he has his public being. In this sense an "identity" is a secular equivalent of a soul or a spirit. Second, the belief in identity search, as an important part of the motivational apparatus inducing persons to reach for achieved statuses, sustains the idea that one *makes* one's own future. In this sense the search for identity is implicated in the American search for success.

But public approval or tolerance of the "search for identity" is less a general cultural value than a fairly strictly age-graded one. This tolerance declines as the young person gets older; a lifelong or perpetual search for identity threatens the stability of family and career choices that may have been made, and as the young person gets older, strong negative sanctions against the disorder implied by continued "search" increase. Indulgent or otherwise sympathetic attitudes toward the tensions and instabilities accompanying the search for identity become increasingly severe or punitive when these tensions and instabilities continue beyond the point at which they can comfortably be attributed to the structure of age-grading.

Is it too radical to entertain the idea that we may be moving into a period when men and women will be called upon to sustain greater and greater disjunctions among and between the different dimensions of their lives, and that to urge the development of an integrated identity is to exacerbate rather than alleviate the problem? Isn't the "individual" whom many of us most admire precisely the person who sustains the most unusual combination of social statuses and hence lends to each of his role performances some unexpected features derived from his other lives—in short, the man who never finds *an* identity because he is too busy accumulating being: a "free man" at

home in a society in which *all* traditional institutions are tottering? I don't know the answer to these questions, and I'm not even sure they are the sort of questions which social science can answer. But I think they are the sort of questions it is useful for us to ask ourselves when a young person appears in our offices telling us that his problem is that he has no identity.

Student Unrest and the Crisis in the Universities

1969

When I was an undergraduate, twenty years ago, I was Chairman of one of the radical student groups at my college, and an active official in the regional intercollegiate association of that group. I marched in my share of picket lines, published an article attacking my college President for anti-Semitism, was sung to by the sirens of the local Communist Party, and even, in a burst of creativity, wrote what in this age of instant classics I suppose qualifies as a classic militant's love song. I called it "You and I and the Mimeograph Machine" and dedicated it to all the youthful romances born amidst the technology of moral protest. Later, when I got older and became a sociologist, I resisted becoming a "political sociologist," by which in this context I mean what a lot of the militants mean: a former activist who traded his credentials as a conscious moral and political agent in exchange for the rewards of expertise *about* political behavior.

I mention these things not in any middle-aged confessional mood nor even as part of my qualifications to speak but as a statement about a past which I do not disavow, and as preface to my remarks

From *The New York Times Magazine*, 2 November 1969. © 1969 by The New York Times Company; reprinted by permission.

about student militance which, though they are analytic, yield nothing to the young in the way of moral credentials. Not unlike that prostitute of legend whose morality was no better than anyone else's, I like to think that mine will stand comparative scrutiny. It brings me certain rewards, and these rewards have certain costs, and I am never sure for very long about the wholesomeness of the bargain I have struck (either because of my tendency to get depressed from time to time or because situational changes disequilibrate my delicate balances). My satisfactions as a moral agent in academic disguise come from using sociological analysis to pose moral problems subtler than the ones which originally occasioned the analysis. That, I think, is part of what a "humanistic" education is all about. But in attempting to deepen problems one must try very hard to say neither more nor less than one actually thinks and feels. That, I know, is a luxury which student activists and "hard line" administrators may say we can ill afford in the present crisis in the universities. They may well be right. I comfort myself with the thought that in a crisis, men (I include intellectuals in this company) seldom act with consummate consistency. When the chips are down and the barricades are up, we agonizers may find ourselves out there on the line, under fire, while the shrillest militant or the most self-righteous defender of order may find it convenient to be in another city delivering a speech he could not afford to cancel.

One final prefatory remark. In trying to throw some sociological light on the nature and character of student unrest, I'm going to try to avoid both the self-congratulatory perspective of the students and the defensive self-righteous perspective of their elders both in and out of the academic establishements. So I won't, on the one hand, comfort the militants by saying that students protest because this is a racist, plastic society or because the curriculum is irrelevant or because the university has sold its soul to the military-industrial complex or because the university is a machine in which students are treated as raw material—when, indeed, their uptight teachers take time from their research to treat them as anything at all. On the other hand, I won't comfort their critics by saying that students rebel for kicks or because their upbringing was too permissive or because they are filled with a seething self-hatred or because they are symbolically murdering their fathers in a recurrent ritual melodrama of generational conflict. And certainly not because there's a communist

plot to destroy the moral fiber (fresh phrase, that) of our youth with sex, drugs, and treason (that's Max Rafferty's phrase).

What I will try to do is to show how certain conditions generic to the direction of our present societal development have helped to bring about the present situation among youth and in the universities. An analysis of these conditions reveals their usually ambiguous character. Understanding this will not make the solutions to our problems any easier (for knowledge is not power) but it can at least arm us against panaceas—the militant ones from the Left and the "firm" ones from the Right. It may even add some humaneness to the actions we undertake; there is never enough of that.

Prolonged Adolescence

The problem of student unrest is rooted in the prolongation of adolescence in industrial countries. It should be understood that "adolescence" is only minimally a biological category; there are only a very few years between the onset of puberty and the achievement of the growth and strength it takes to do a man's or woman's work. But as we know, culture has a habit of violating nature, and adolescence as a social category has been stretched far beyond these few years. Proto-adolescent behavior now begins even before puberty (which itself is occurring earlier) with the action—and the orientation —we call "pre-adolescent," while at the other end, technological, economic, and social developments conspire to prolong the dependence of the young, to exclude them from many of the privileges and responsibilities of adult life, and therefore to *juvenilize*[1] them.

The casual evidence in support of this deep institutionalization of adolescence is diffuse and quite remarkable. It includes such spectacles as six-foot, two-hundred pound "boys" who in another time and place might be founders of dynasties and world-conquerors (like Alexander of Macedon), cavorting on the fraternity house lawn hurling orange peels and bags of water at each other (their girl friends

---

[1]"Juvenilize": a verb describing a process through which "childish" behavior is induced or prolonged in persons who, in terms of their organic development, are capable of participating in adult affairs. When I used this verb recently in the description of a new course I was preparing to offer, an English professor on the courses committee objected on the grounds that there was no such word. If the process exists there ought to be a verb to describe it.

looking after the ammunition supplies), while tolerant local police, who chuckingly *approve*, direct traffic around the battlefield. It includes the preservation of child-like cadence and intonation in voices otherwise physically mature. It includes the use of the term "kid" in common discourse to refer to people under thirty (the power of socialization and usage is such that they often refer to themselves that way). It includes the common—and growing—practice (even in official university documents) of opposing the word "student" to the word "adult"—as if students were by definition not adults, even as the median age of university students rises with the increase of the graduate student population. It includes all sorts of preferential and "protective" treatment for students, for example, special admission prices to theaters, special treatment in the courts, and special transportation fares, to say nothing of the *in loco parentis* functions which many schools still exercise regardless of the age of the students involved.

Adolescence, then, is not the relatively fleeting "transitional stage" of textbook and popular lore but a substantial segment of life which may last fifteen or twenty years, and if the meaning of adolescence is extended only slightly, it can last longer than that. I have in mind the age-graded norms and restrictions in those professions which require long years of advanced training, and in which the system of sponsorship makes the advancement of one's career dependent upon being somebody's "boy" perhaps well on toward one's middle age—a fact not uncharacteristic of university faculties. Indeed, the postponement of advent to "full" adulthood is almost caricatured in the attempts of several recent publications to argue that new age-statuses *between* adolescence and adulthood are in the process of being institutionalized.[2]

Much of the discussion of "youth culture" in recent years reflects the prolongation of adolescence, since it is not surprising that a period of life which may last from age twelve to age thirty-five might

[2]See, for example, Allen J. Moore, *The Young Adult Generation*, (Nashville, Tenn.: Abingdon, 1969); and Kenneth Keniston, *Young Radicals* (New York: Harcourt, Brace, and World, 1968). See also two new anthologies, both called *The Young Adult*, one edited by Winter and Nuss (Glenview, Ill.: Scott, Foresman, 1969) and the other edited by Mortimer Gross and published by the Forest Hospital Foundation. In addition, *Sociological Symposium*, a new behavioral science journal, in planning a series of issues on the sociology of the life cycle, is including three separate issues for "adolescence," "pre-adulthood," and "early adulthood."

develop its own cultural style, its own traditions, and its own sources of motivation and satisfaction—and dissatisfaction. It can apparently even afford its own kind of internal differentiation, as is suggested by the range of its manifestations: from the ritualized, half-approved antics of the fraternity boys to the outright revolutionary games played by the Yippies. However various its consequences (factors other than age affect those consequences), the prolongation of adolescence creates an enormous stratum of persons caught in the tension between their experience of peak physical strength and sexual energy on the one hand, and their public definition as culturally "immature" on the other.

This tension is exacerbated further by a contradictory tendency: for while modern industrial conditions promote juvenilization and the prolongation of dependence, they also create an "older" more experienced youthful cohort. They have more and earlier experience with sex and drugs; they are far better educated than their parents were; urban life sophisticates them more quickly; and television brings into their homes worlds of experience that would otherwise necessarily remain alien to them. Young people, then, are faced not only with the ambiguity of the adolescent role itself (no longer a child, not yet a grown-up) and its prolongation, but with forces and conditions that, at least in some ways, make for *earlier* maturity. The youthful population is a potentially explosive stratum because this society is ill-equipped to accommodate it within the status system.

The Search for Identity

Erik Erikson's well-known theory of the "psycho-social moratorium" of adolescence adds to the tension of the ambiguities I have already suggested. That theory takes the facts of adolescent prolongation and transforms them into a triumph of civilization. By emphasizing the increased time provided for young persons to postpone commitments, to try on social roles, and to play the game called "the search for identity," Erikson suggests that the moratorium on lasting adult responsibilities contributes to the development and elaboration of personal individuality. But there is an important fact which contradicts Erikson's assertions about the moratorium on adult commitments. Although Erikson's theory has been enormously influential

(an influence, I should add, not unrelated to the ideological reinforcement it provides to the social processes prolonging adolescence), its influence has been exercised in spite of the increasing and clearly documented pressures to which young people are subjected for earlier and earlier occupational planning and choice. "Benjamin," asks that famous Graduate's parents repeatedly, "what are you going to *do*?" And the question is echoed by millions of prosperous American parents, who despite their affluence, cannot assure the future economic position of their heirs. One does not, after all, drift into medical school after a long adolescence devoted to "finding oneself."

Logically, of course, prolonged identity play and early occupational choice cannot be encouraged at the same time; the fact is they are. And like other ambiguous values (and most moral values are ambiguous, or can be made so) this pair permit *different* groups of youngsters to rationalize or justify the kinds of adaptations that differing circumstances in fact constrain them to make. The public attention generated by protesting youth in recent years (hippies, The New Left, black militants) obscures the fact that the majority of young people are still apparently able to tolerate the tensions of prolonged adolescence, to adjust to the adolescent role (primarily, student), to take some satisfaction from the gains it provides in irresponsibility (i.e. "freedom"), and to sail smoothly through high school into college where they choose the majors, get the grades, and eventually the certifications for the occupations which they want, which want them, and which higher education is equipped to provide them. I mean degrees in education, business, engineering, librarianship, optometry, dentistry, and so on.

For others, however, the search for identity (quote unquote) functions as a substitute for an occupational orientation; it gives them something "serious" to do while coping with their problems of sex, education, family, and career. In college most of these people tend to major in the humanities or social sciences (particularly sociology) where they may take ten years or more between the time they enter as Freshmen, drop out, return, graduate, and go on to pursue graduate degrees or give up on them entirely. I will return to this matter, but for the moment I want only to cite these developments regarding prolonged adolescence and the role of "the search for identity" in it, and make two general points:

(1) that the contradictions (between the prolongation of adolescence and the greater sophistication of the young, between the exhortations to seek one's identity and to make an early occupational choice) create understandable tensions in the young and feed their appetite to discover "hypocrisy" in their elders; (2) that this condition is largely beyond the control of the universities; it is generated by the exigencies of a "postindustrial" society which uses institutions of higher education as warehouses for the temporary storage of a population it knows not what else to do with.

The situation has become critical over the past ten years because the enormous *numbers* of the young (even small percentages of which yield formidable numbers of troops for worthy causes) and their *concentration* (in schools and cities) have promoted easy communication and a sense of group solidarity among them. Numbers, concentration, and communication regarding common grievances have made increasingly viable, in almost precisely the way in which Karl Marx described the development of class consciousness among workers, the creation and maintenance of "deviant subcultures" of youth.

The "Moral Idealism" of Youth

This youthful population is "available" for recruitment to moral causes because their marginal, ambiguous position in the social structure renders them sensitive to moral inconsistencies (note their talent for perceiving "hypocrisy"), because the major framework of their experience ("education") emphasizes "ideal" aspects of the culture, and because their exclusion from adult responsibilities means that they are generally unrestrained by the institutional ties and commitments which normally function as a brake upon purely moral feeling; they also have the time for it.

The two great public issues of the decade (the Viet Nam war and the rights of despised minorities) have been especially suited to enlist the militant predispositions of the young precisely because these issues are clearly moral issues. To take a strong "position" on these issues requires no great expertise or familiarity with arcane facts. And the moral fervor, involved in taking such a position nicely reflects our traditional age-graded culture to the extent that it

identifies virtue with "idealism," unspoiledness, and innocence—precisely the qualities adults like to associate with the young. Commencement rhetoric and similar institutional practices have long praised youth for these qualities and actively encouraged them to pursue their "dreams" and to realize their "ideals."[3]

It is almost as if the young, in the unconscious division of labor which occurs in all societies, were delegated the role of "moral organ" of society—what with all the grown-ups being too busy running the bureaucracies of the world (with their inevitable compromises, deals, gives and takes) to concern themselves with "ideals." This even makes a sort of good structural sense because the unanchored character of the young (that is, their relative unfetteredness to family, community, and career) fits them to perform their "ideal" functions—in the same sense and for the same reason that Plato denied normal family life to his philosopher-kings and the Roman Catholic Church denies it to their Priests. The "idealism" of youth is structurally underpinned by the prolongation of adolescence which, by discouraging for a longer period of time the involvement of the young in the important adult business of the tribe, weakens their ties and loyalties to major organizations and institutions of modern society which, as I said, normally function as constraints on purely moral impulses.

It is this combination of alienation–moral sensitivity that accounts both for the extreme juvenophile postures of moral critics like Edgar Friedenberg, Paul Goodman, and John Seeley (which sometimes reaches the belief that the young are simply better people than the old or middle-aged, and hence even a belief in juvenocracy), and the fear of and hostility toward militant youth by writers epitomized by Lewis Feuer in his new book on student movements. In the latter view, the idealism of the young becomes corrupt, violent, terroristic, and destructive precisely because, alienated, detached from institutions, youth is not "responsible," that is, not accountable for the consequences of their moral zealotry upon the groups and organizations affected by it.

If "irresponsibility" seems to be a condition for the exercise of youth's "moral functions," it is consistent with an old tradition of

---

[3]As a favorable stereotype which flatters youth, this probably helps seduce them to acquiesce in the process of juvenilization, in the same way that favorable stereotypes of other subordinated groups help compensate them for their subordination.

intellectual dilemma in which a virtue seems inextricably bound to a vice. Veblen saw the intellectual pre-eminence of Jews as a function of their exclusion from the mainstream of the societies in which they lived; Henrik Ibsen thought that women had a fuller and deeper "humanity" than men because women were excluded from the de-humanizing male world of economic competition. The English sociologist Frank Musgrove suggests that the repression of youth is a condition of their tendency to perform innovative roles. The tradition is older than old; it is ancient. Sophocles tells of Philoctetes to whom the gods gave a magic bow whose arrows never missed their mark. But Philoctetes suffered a snakebite which would not heal; festering, it gave off a stink so powerful as to make him unfit for the company of men. His comrades needed the bow but were unwilling to accept the stink of the wound that went with it. Call it dialectics, call it ambiguity, the parallel is clear: the moral fervor associated with the young is intimately related to their "irresponsibility."

So one is tempted to say that society may just have to accept youth's irresponsibility if it values their moral contributions. But evidence suggests that adult society is in general sympathetic neither to their moral arrows nor toward granting the young any greater responsibility in public affairs. Musgrove's research in England clearly documents that adults are unwilling to grant real responsibilities any earlier to the young, and there is good reason to believe the same is true in the United States, as is suggested by the strong opposition to the movement to lower the voting age to eighteen. And as for the "idealism" of youth, when it goes beyond the innocent virtues of praising honesty, being loyal, true, and brave, and helping old ladies across the street, to serious moral involvements promoting their own group interests ("student power") or those of the domestic or "third world" dispossessed, the shine of their "idealism" is likely to be tarnished rather quickly by ideology.

Moreover, the moral activism of youth *is* sometimes vulnerable to attack on several counts. The "morality" of a political action for example, is weakened when it has a self-congratulatory character (and the tendency to produce a holier than thou vanity in the actor). It also loses something when it does not involve substantial risk of personal interests or freedom (as it unambiguously *does* with the young only in the case of draft resisters). In the end, like the society's prolongation of adolescence and its encouragement of "the search for identity," continuing praise of the young for their "idealism" (except when it

becomes serious) and continuing appeals to them to behave "responsibility"—in the face of repeated refusal to grant them real responsibilities (except in war)—are understandable as parts of the cultural armory supporting the process of juvenilization.

The Cry for Relevance: The University as Home Territory

Colleges, universities, and their environs are the places apparently designated by society as the primary locations where prolonged adolescence, "the search for identity," and youthful idealism work themselves out. It is clear that the schools, particularly institutions of higher learning, are increasingly being asked by society to perform a kind of holding operation for it. The high schools do their part by encouraging unskilled sixteen and seventeen year olds to stay in school and out of the labor markets which are unable to absorb them. The military institutions, through the draft, help store (and train) many of the working-class young, and the colleges and universities prepare many of the heirs of the middle classes for careers in business, the professions, and the semiprofessions. But higher education also gets the identity seekers: those sensitive children of the affluent, less interested in preparing themselves for occupations which the universities are competent to prepare them for than in transcending or trading in the stigmata of their bourgeois backgrounds (work ethics, money-grubbing, status-seeking) for a more "meaningful" life, either through the development of elite style or through identification with the oppressed or through experiment with and exploration of the erotic and other frontiers of psychological experience and community development.

It is these students, the ones *not* in the relatively technical majors which supply salable skills after an undergraduate education, who are heavily represented among the student activists and among whom the cry for "relevance" is heard most insistently. We do not hear many cries for relevance in schools of business, engineering, optometry, or dentistry because their relevance is manifest in their ability to provide clear occupational certification. Does it seem odd that the cry for relevance should be coming from those students who are *least* interested in the curricula whose relevance is palpable, at least with respect to occupations? Not if one observes that many of these students are, in a sense, classically "intellectuals," that is, oriented toward statuses or positions for which the universities

(as well as other major institutions) have seldom been able or competent to provide certification. The statuses such students (and occasional students) want are not those for which one gets trained and certified, but those to which one appoints oneself or which one drifts into: artist, critic, writer, intellectual, journalist, revolutionist, philosopher. These statuses, by tradition deeply involved in the creation of *Zeitgeist*, have been undermined for two generations or more by technical and bureaucratic elites whose training has become increasingly specialized and scientific. In this context the cry for relevance is a protest against technical, value-neutral education whose product (saleable skills or the posture of uncommitment) contributes nothing to the search by these students for "identity" and "meaningful experience."

Adding final insult to the injury of the threatened replacement of traditional humanistic intellectuals by technical elites is the ironic transformation of some of their traditional curricula (social sciences particularly) into instruments useful to the "power structure" or "the establishment" in pursuing its own ends. It makes no sense to call a curriculum "irrelevant" and then to turn right around and accuse its chief practitioners of "selling out"; the powerful do not squander their money so easily. The ironic point, then, is not that these curricula are "irrelevant" but that they are far *too* relevant to the support of interests to which the Left is opposed.

The villains here are the methodological orthodoxies of the social sciences: their commitment to objectivity, detachment, and the "separation" between facts and values. In the view of radical students, these orthodoxies rationalize the official diffidence of social scientists regarding the social consequences of their research, a diffidence which (conveniently—and profitably—for social scientists, goes the argument) promotes the interests of the established and the powerful. This is true but it is far from the whole truth. There is plenty of research, supported by establishments, whose results provide the establishment with no comfort. Social scientists, no less than others, like to bite the hands that feed them. But like other "nonpartisan" or value-neutral practices and procedures, the methodological orthodoxies of the social sciences tend in general to support established interests simply because the powerful, in command of greater resources and facilities, are better able to make use of "facts" than the weak, and because avoidance of ideological controversy tends to perpetuate the inequities of the *status quo*.

Still the demands for a more activist and "committed" social science and for social scientists to function as advocates for oppressed and subordinated groups may not be the best way of correcting the inequities. In calling for a more politicized social science, radical students are demanding doctrinal recognition of the fact that the orthodox view does indeed have "political" consequences. But they do this usually without full consideration of what a thorough *doctrinal* politicization of social science in the university would mean. One of the things it is likely to mean is the total loss of whatever little insulation remains against the ideological controversies rending the larger society; and the probable result would be that the university, instead of being more liberal than the society as a whole, would more accurately reflect the still burgeoning reactionary mood of the country.

For students who tend to be "around" a university for a long time—the ten year period mentioned earlier is not uncommon—the university tends to become a kind of "home territory," the place where they really live. They experience the university less as an elite training institution than as a political community in which "members" have a kind of quasi-"citizenship" which, if one believes in democratic process, means a right to a legitimate political voice in its government.[4] This conception of the university is quite discrepant with the conception held by most faculty members and administrators. To most faculty members the university is an elite training institution to which students who are both willing and able come to absorb intellectual disciplines—"ologies"—taught by skilled and certified professionals whose competences are defined by and limited to those certifications. Behind much of the controversy between radical students and liberal *or* conservative faculties lies this very sharp discrepancy, still largely implicit, in the conception of what a university is.

But the way one sees the university—as a political community or as an elite training institution—is not purely a matter of ideological preference. The fact seems to be that where training and certification and performance in politically neutral skills are clearest, the more conservative view is virtually unchallenged. This is true not

[4]Much remains to be clarified about the nature of "membership" in academic communities. So much cant has gone down in the name of "community" that I often feel about this word much like that Nazi who is reputed to have said, "When I hear the word 'culture' I reach for my revolver."

only for dentistry and optometry, but for athletics as well. Presumably not many militant Blacks are for a quota system with respect to varsity teams, and presumably football players in the huddle do not demand a voice in the decisions that shape their lives. But where one's education confers upon one (as much liberal education does) a smattering of "high culture" or "civilized manners" or the detached sensibility and ethics of a science whose benefits, like other wealth, are not equitably distributed—in short, where the main result of liberal education is *Weltanschauung* it indeed has "political" consequences. These consequences were not controversial so long as the culture of the university was fairly homogeneous and so long as the "aliens" it admitted were eager to absorb that culture. They have become controversial in recent years because the democratization of higher education has revealed the "class" character of academic culture and because of the appearance on the campus of students who neither share nor aspire to that culture (or who have it and reject it) —and in sufficiently large numbers to mount a serious challenge to the hegemony of traditional academic culture.

The New Student and the Expendability of the University

Despite their many differences, the new militant "ethnic" students and their supporters among "white radicals," "street people," hippies, and other young people on the Left have in common their anti-academicism, which is the campus version of the anti-establishment outlook. This invites explanation because in spite of the fact that academic establishments do tend to be inextricably bound to establishments in government, business, and the foundations, it is also true that the academy has been the most liberal sector of establishment thought and the most sympathetic to at least some of the aspirations of dissident students. Partly, of course, their hostility to the academy is rooted in the fact that the university is where they're at, the institutional location in which they have to work through their prolonged adolescence and the problems associated with it. But beyond this, there is real conflict between the traditional criteria of academic performance and what dissident students demand from academic life.

Research suggests that most of the white radical students have grown up in a milieu where "intellectual" matters were discussed, where books were probably available in the home, where middle-

class manners and style were their birthright, and where, therefore, they learned how to "talk"—that is, where they developed the sort of verbal facility that enables them to do well enough in high school and to seem like promising "college material" if only because they look and sound much like college students have always looked and sounded. And with the ascendence of the view that everybody has a right to a higher education (along with the fact that there's no place else to send well-born adolescents) most of them have wound up in colleges and universities.

Some of them, despite their verbal facility, are not really bright in the ways that higher education rewards; many others, despite their ability to get good college grades, strongly resist conforming to many of the requirements for professional certification, which they demean as mere "socialization." Confronted by academic demands for rigor in their thinking, for sufficient discipline to master a systematic body of knowledge, for evidence that they can sustain a line of logical thinking beyond one or two propositions and bring evidence systematically to bear upon a problem, many of them are found seriously wanting, some because they are not bright enough, others because they think it a point of honor to resist the intellectual demands made on them.

When their numbers are large enough to enable them to turn to each other for mutual support, it is not surprising that they should collectively turn against the system of criteria which derogates them and, in a manner not unanalogous to the "reaction formation" of slum delinquents who develop a subculture in opposition to middle-class school norms which judge them inadequate,[5] develop an anti-academic viewpoint which defines abstraction, logical order, detachment, objectivity, and systematic thinking as the cognitive armory of a repressive society, productive of alienation from self, rigidity of personality, and truncated capacity for "feeling."

Preoccupied as most of these students are with "identity problems" and moral protest, it is again not surprising that they should be less interested in the mastery of academic disciplines, even if they have the ability, than in pursuing what they are likely to call "gut-issues" or nitty gritty, both of which phrases are intended to suggest their interest in the immediate and the concrete and, by extension, their disdain for the remoteness of academic "ologies" from their problems. The kinds of problems they apparently are

[5]See Albert Cohen, *Delinquent Boys* (Glencoe, Ill.: Free Press, 1955).

interested in studying can be inferred from the examination of almost any "Free University" brochure, and what these add up to is a sort of Extension Division for the Underground: practical, topical "rap-sessions" on Viet Nam, civil rights, encounter groups, pottery, psychedelics, macro-biotics, Eastern religion, rock music, revolution, Marxism, imperialism, "women's liberation," and so on.

In the conflict with the established interests of science and scholarship in the university, radical students do win significant victories. New courses do get approved; experimental curricula do get tried out; students do get appointed to important committees; greater weight is attached to teaching in the appointment and promotion of faculty members. But large numbers of these radical students, exhausted by conflict and depressed by negative criticism, drop out of school. In dropping out, however, they do not immediately disappear into the labor market. They tend to remain in the university community, employed occasionally or part time in dead-end jobs, living in furnished rooms or communal houses near the university, and most important for my purposes here, still participating in the marginal student culture which they know so well.

Their participation in this culture is made possible to some extent by the fact that their youth protects them from the degrading consequences of being poor and having no regular or "approved" status in the community. Part of the age-grading system which postpones adulthood is the temporary protection of the young against the stigmata which, for older people, are normally attached to poverty and marginal or irregular status. But over time, this group of "nonstudents" can be regarded as downward mobile, and thereby hangs an interesting prospect.

The United States has no major tradition of large scale downward mobility. The only major image of intergenerational decline is associated with decadent aristocratic families in ruined Southern mansions. But the general prospect of a significant minority of the children of the vast middle and professional classes of the American population not being as well or better off economically than their parents is unprecedented. Given the general tendency for downwardly mobile groups to resent the system which derogates them, and given the fact that the channels of upward mobility today are largely through higher education, the hostility to the university of these radical, middle class "nonstudents" is probably maintained even after they leave it. The irony is that in dropping out, the hippie

and New Left children of the middle classes provide opportunity for the upward mobility of the new black and other ambitious "disadvantaged" students.

The militant black students complain about "relevance" too, but they seem to mean something somewhat different from what the white radicals mean. The Blacks and other ethnic militants are presently using higher education in a manner different from that in which their predecessors from the lower class used it. For earlier ethnics, the university served as a channel of mobility *for individuals* from the talented poor, enabling them to rise out of their backgrounds into the middle or professional classes. Today, the Blacks and other ethnics are attempting to use the university as a means of *collective* mobility for the entire group. There are two aspects to this movement. For them, "relevance" means first, the emphasis on ethnic studies programs which are designed to provide the members of the respective ethnic groups with a sense of pride in their history and culture, to legitimate that history and culture through their institutionalization in university curricula as an honorable part of the American tradition, and therefore to reduce the constraints to disavow participation in that culture by the more successful ethnics. It means, second, demands that the university play a more active role in ameliorating suffering in the ghettos, not merely through programs of research which exploit the cooperation of ghetto residents without helping them measurably, but by taking the university off the campus, bringing it to them, in their terms, on their turf, for their own purposes.

In the struggle to achieve these ends of the militants blacks and white, the traditional university is very vulnerable because the militants have great leverage. Just as the Blacks can conceivably turn the urban core into a guerilla battleground, militant students can bring the universities to the proverbial grinding halt. Hard line administrators may refuse formally to close down the campus, but higher education can nevertheless be made substantially impossible by the well known techniques developed over the past several years. Continual rallies, classroom disruptions, picket lines, building seizures, student intimidation, and general paranoia, to say nothing of the almost continual meetings by faculty and administration committees to cope with the crises and the continual corridor and coffee room gossip by knots of faculty members can bring the teaching and other academic functions of the university to a virtual standstill.

This prospect raises seriously for the first time the question of whether the traditional university, as we know it, is an expendable institution. Since, for reasons I have tried to make clear, student unrest on the campuses is really unrepressible, given their numbers and the inability of the social structure to accommodate them elsewhere, is it possible that a decision has been made somewhere that it is better to risk the destruction of the university by confining the unrest to the campus than to allow it to spill over into more critical institutions? Pickets, sit-ins, building seizures, and nonnegotiable demands are one thing on the campuses. Imagine them at CBS on Madison Avenue: no TV until SDS gets equal time; at the Stock Exchange: the ticker tape does not roll until corporation X gets rid of its South African holdings; at the headquarters of the Bank of America: no depositors get through the doors until interest-free loans are made to renovate the ghettos. There would be machine guns in the streets in no time at all!

In 1969, despite the tear gas and the national guard, it is still hard to imagine tanks and machine guns used against student radicals so long as their militance is confined to the campus. Because if they do close the universities down, exactly who would miss them? The most practical functions the university performs and those of its activities that are most directly relevant to the national economy (engineering, science, law, medicine, etc.) could be transferred to the private sector. The beginnings of such a transfer are apparent already in the educational functions carried on by private foundations, institutes, and industrial corporations.

But if the English departments and history and political science and sociology and art and rhetroic and anthropology and so on closed tight shut tomorrow, who would miss them? Despite the implication of some social science departments in the military-industrial complex, the bulk of the work that goes on in humanities and social science departments are civilized luxuries with very few sources of support. The student radicals have little sympathy for them and there is probably even less sympathy for them among the students' severest critics. These days, even conservative legislators, in the same breath that they denounce student militance, will quickly add, "of course, this doesn't mean that there isn't plenty wrong with the university; there is." And if the student revolution can be bought off by substituting Bob Dylan for Dylan Thomas, McLuhan for Freud, Marcuse for Plato, Rock for Bach, Black Culture for Greek Culture, rap ses-

sions for formal examinations, how many will care? Who needs high culture anyway? For the radicals it's an instrument of class oppression, and their oppressors, at least in America, have never been too keen on it anyway, except as a tax dodge.

Short of machine guns in the streets and outright revolution, what one can expect to see over the next decade in academic life is greater adaptation by the university to the new kinds of students it must serve and to the new publics whose anticipated support or hostility it must take into account in its planning. By the new students I mean ghetto youth dedicated to a vanguard role in the movement to liberate their people, middle-class white radicals dedicated to moral criticism of the inequitable distributions of wealth and power, and the identity seekers dedicated to "finding themselves" (at least to the romance of looking) through participation in culturally avant-garde styles of life. By the new publics I mean those millions of citizens whose taxes support the great state universities but who never thought of the university as "theirs" until its politicization encouraged ambitious politicians to call this fact to their attention. Having once been reminded (by Governor Reagan and others), the voters are not likely to forget it soon.

If it comes about, this adaptation is likely to occur in a manner not dissimilar to that in which the major political parties have adapted to third party movements in the larger political community: by isolating the *most* radical elements through the adoption of some of their programs and demands, while at the same time adopting severe and punitive policies toward the more intransigent and violence-prone who are still unsatisfied. For ghetto youth, then, there will be more ethnic studies programs, compensatory admissions and grading policies and practices, and more energetic recruiting of ethnic students and faculty. But there will be less indecision or tolerance in the handling of sit-ins, seizures, and other disruptions. For the radicals (ethnic as well as middle-class white), there will be a greater emphasis on programs granting academic credit for extension-type activities such as tutoring of ghetto children, neighborhood seminars on consumer savvy, community organization, and other "activist" programs which take the university off the campus into the communities whose residents have not received "their fair share" of the benefits which, as taxpayers, they have a right to expect from the university their money supports. For the identity seekers there will be more encounter groups, more classes emphasizing "openness

and honesty" in dialogue, more experiments with less structured curricula and residential communities, more "retreats," more student-initiated courses on subjects which engage their sense of "relevance" to their interests: from sex to drugs to rock to film to "identity" to education—there will be a virtual orgy of "self-exploration," potentially running through the whole catalogue of "youth culture." For all, there will be further loosening of the *in loco parentis* restrictions which hardly anybody in the university believes in anymore, and a little more student power (at least influence) on faculty and administrative committees. All this, combined with a more effective public relations campaign explaining the mission of the university and its problems in coping with the consequences of prolonged adolescence, may just bring about a semblance of peace on the campus. But without peace in Viet Nam, it will be uneasy at best.

There will be opposition. Academic conservatives will see in these new programs the prospect of the dilution or outright abandonment of traditional standards of scholarship. The legitimation of ethnicity, the amelioration of suffering by the poor, and the search for identity by the young may all be noble endeavors, they will say, but the major functions of the university are the creation and transmission of systematic bodies of abstract knowledge. Political conservatives will see in these programs harbingers of social changes which they oppose. Militant students imply more leaders and troops for restive ghettos; "the search for identity" and the self-exploratory activities the phrase suggests are redolent of the "liberalism," "permissiveness," and self-indulgence offensive to the traditional Protestant ethics which "made this country great."

Yet academic conservatives might well be reminded that the university is facing radically transformed constituencies (among students and other citizens), that academic disciplines which are well institutionalized and "traditional" today were themselves academically born in the blood of earlier periods of such transformations, and that they were initially opposed by still more "traditional" fields. Political conservatives might well be reminded that student unrest was not invented by outside agitators, that its source is in social conditions conservatives affirm, and that it is not repressible short of military measures. The alternatives to the adaptable university involve blood on the quad and an expendable university.

Ecstatic Youth

1966-1968

Hippie Morality / 1967*

When the organizer of this meeting asked me a few months ago to speak on the new morality, my first impulse was to say *what* new morality, and then, why me? I think (and thought then) that I know the answers to these questions, but didn't offer them, because the answers raise more questions than they resolve—the kinds of persistently interesting questions that I call boring when I am in a mood to evade the frustration of not being able to answer them. Without it ever having been stated, it was clear that I was being asked to talk about hippies, or about their amalgam with the New Left (and now referred to in some quarters as the "pot left"), in short about that national scene which is so visible here in the San Francisco Bay Area, which the mass media has given a virtual orgy of coverage, and about which the entire country (at least that part of it which talks) seems unable to stop talking. Indeed, far more interesting than the hippies themselves is America's inability to leave them alone.

*From a speech to the Plenary Session of the Society for the Study of Social Problems, San Francisco, 27 August 1967.

The question was whether there was a new morality in this milieu, beneath all the beads, bells, bubbles, feathers, and flowing robes, that could be rendered in words as a series of fresh moral dicta. I will get to answering this in a moment. Before I do, however, a word about why me. Because I am an "intellectual," which in this context means a sociologist without specialization, who hence has no expertise, no expert reputation to risk by talking about something that everyone wants talked about and on which everyone has opinions that, as we all know, are as good as anyone else's. In an indiscreet moment, Talcott Parsons once described himself with a devilish grin as having *"got away with"* being a pure theorist in the empirical science called sociology. I am one of that small-but-growing-group of sociologists who has so far been able to get away with being an intellectual—untainted by expertise.

Well, for a few months I've been going around asking hippies what the new morality is all about, and for more than a few months I've been reading and listening to their sympathizers and spokesmen present and former: Paul Goodman, Edgar Friedenberg, Herbert Marcuse, Norman Brown, John Seeley, Alan Watts, Tim Leary, Ken Kesey, among others. I read the East Village *Other* and the Berkeley *Barb* and the San Francisco *Oracle* (when I can bear to), and I've been doing more than my share of café sitting, digging the moral feeling of the young as it comes across through their talk. On the basis of this—forgive the expression—data, it would be very easy to argue (as I will) that there isn't much, if any, New Morality around, and certainly none that warrants upper case letters (although how unprecedented or unheard of or, indeed, out of sight, a morality must be to be regarded as "new" is a question too difficult for me to attempt here). But I am reluctant to suggest that there isn't any new morality, because this conclusion inevitably functions as a put-down of various activities some of which I actually want to encourage. Thus I am confronted with the very old problem of whether to speak the truth when it may have undesired consequences. To love the truth is no doubt a great virtue; but to love to speak the truth is a small vanity, and I should like to be very clear that it is my vanity which constrains me to risk dampening the ardor of some of those who belong to a movement which in many respects I admire, by attempting to speak the truth about it. It is small comfort to a group whose spirit may rest on an erroneous conviction that it is doing

something new and revolutionary to be told that they are (only) the most recent expression of what is by now an old tradition, even if it is, as I believe, an important and an honorable tradition as well.

I am talking, of course, about the contemporary version of bohemian youth, and it is noteworthy that discussions of a new morality usually wind up talking about kids (as if morality were relevant only to them). One is reminded that this tendency to talk about the young when the subject at hand is moral innovation reflects a commitment to a very old theory: the generational view of change, in which the elites of an age-group function as the major agents of culture change by usurping the right to speak in the name of an entire cohort or generation. A recent addition to this theory is the view that youth are structurally induced to perform innovative "idealistic" or "cultural" functions (and to assume appropriate corresponding roles) by virtue of their relative exclusion from responsibility for the major institutions of adult society and hence their relative insulation from the informal sanctions that induce conformity in the more institutionally vulnerable. In the sense that Robert Park once unfortunately referred to Negroes as "The Lady of the Races," youth are often characterized as what might be called the lady of the age-grades, with attributed qualities such as warmth, emotionality, sensitivity, etc., the sort of stereotyping which fits them for their apparently ascribed moral functions. If ladies seem to have fewer of these qualities than ever before, it may well be that men will eventually become the lady of the sexes (hopefully, the last of the hot-blooded minorities).

I suggested a moment ago that the moral dimensions of the hippie community are part of a long and honorable tradition, and I'd like to put some meat on the bare bones of this assertion. More than thirty years ago (a "generation," as Karl Mannheim reckoned social time, two generations as Ortega y Gasset reckoned it, and three, four, or more, as contemporary journalists and other grabbers of the main literary chance reckon it)—in any case, exactly thirty-three years ago (1934) the literary critic, Malcolm Cowley, published *Exile's Return*, a book about the experience of American literary expatriates in Europe in the 1920s. In it he treats to some extent the history of bohemianism, starting back in the middle of the nineteenth century with that important document of bohemian history, Henri Murger's *Scenes of Bohemian Life*. By 1920, Cowley says, Bohemia had a relatively formal doctrine, "a system of ideas that could be roughly summarized as follows" (and as I go through these eight basic ideas,

I ask you to keep the hippies in mind—and also the fact that these ideas were formulated thirty-three years ago about phenomena that were then more than a hundred years old.[1]

1. *"The idea of Salvation by the child.*—Each of us at birth has special potentialities which are slowly crushed and destroyed by a standardized society and mechanical modes of teaching. If a new educational system can be introduced, one by which children are encouraged to develop their own personalities, to (listen!) blossom freely like flowers, then the world will be saved by this new, free generation." [The analogues here are hippies innocence or flower power (more on this later) and the educational revolution.]

2. *"The idea of self-expression.*—Each man's, each woman's purpose in life is to express himself, to realize his full individuality through creative work and beautiful living in beautiful surroundings." This, I believe, is identical with the hippie's moral injunction to "do your thing."

3. *"The idea of paganism.*—The body is a temple in which there is nothing unclean, a shrine to be adorned for the ritual of love." The contemporary paganism, by no means limited to the hippies but especially prevalent among them, is manifest in the overpowering eroticism that their scene exudes: the prevalence of female flesh (toe, ankle, belly, breast, and thigh), male symbols of strength (beards, boots, denim, buckles, motorcycles), the gentler and more restrained versions of these, or the by now hardly controversial assumption that fucking will help set you free.

4. *"The idea of living for the moment.*—It is stupid to pile up treasures that we can enjoy only in old age. . . . Better to seize the moment as it comes. . . . Better to live extravagantly . . . to 'burn (your) candle at both ends'." Today, this might be formulated as something like being super WOW where the action is in the NOW generation who, like, know what's happening and where it's at. (I am reminded that it was an English cleric who said many years ago that the man who marries the spirit of his own age was likely to be a widower in the next. Prophets of rapid social change please take notice.)

[1]From *Exile's Return: A Literary Odyssey of the 1920s* by Malcolm Cowley. Copyright 1934, copyright renewed 1962 by Malcolm Cowley. Reprinted by permission of The Viking Press, Inc.

5. "The idea of liberty.—Every law . . . that prevents self expression or the full enjoyment of the moment should be shattered and abolished. Puritanism is the great enemy. . . ." Today, this is manifest in the movement to legalize marijuana, to render ecstasy respectable (dancing in the park, orgiastic sex, the impulse to turn everybody on, etc.), to demonstrate the absurdity of laws against acts which harm no one, and the hypocrisy of those who insist on the enforcement of these laws.

6. "The idea of female equality.—Women should be the economic and moral equals of men . . . same pay . . . same working conditions, same opportunity for drinking, smoking, taking or dismissing lovers." For the hippies, insistence on equality in smoking and the taking and dismissing of lovers is already quaint, and drinking is increasingly irrelevant. But the theme of sexual equality is still important with respect to still strong sexually related cultural differentials, and evident in the insistence that men may be gentle and women aggressive, and in the merging of sexually related symbols of adornment (long hair, beads, bells, colorful clothes, and so on).

7. Hippies often tell me that it is really quite difficult, if not impossible, to understand their scene without an appreciation of the importance of the psychedelic drugs in it. Although I am inclined to believe this, the importance of "mind-expansion" in the bohemian doctrine was plain to Cowley thirty-three years ago. The references are dated—even quaint, but the main point of his seventh basic idea is unmistakable: *"The idea of psychological maladjustment.*—We are unhappy . . . because we are repressed." And for Cowley, the then contemporary version of the doctrine prescribed that repression could and should be overcome either by Freudian analysis or (listen to this) by *a daily dose of thyroid* or by the mystic qualities of Gurdjieff's psycho-physical disciplining. Today, repression may be uptightness or "game reality," and it is not Freud but Reich, not thyroid but LSD, not Gurdjieff but Yoga, I Ching, The Book of the Dead, or some other meditational means of transcending the realities that hang one up.

8. Cowley's final point in the bohemian doctrine is the old Romantic enamor of the exotic. *"The idea of changing place.*—They do things better in . . . ." (you name it). The wisdom of old cultures has

been affirmed at some times, that of wild and primitive places at other times—anything that will break the Puritan shackles. Paris, Mexico, Tahiti, Tangier, Big Sur. The contemporary hippie fascination with American Indians has a triple attraction: they were oppressed, nobly savage, and by a symbolic act of identification, they become a part of one's American collective unconscious, reachable under the influence of drugs.

Hippie morality, then, at least that part of it perceivable from the outside, does not seem to be new but the most recent expression of a long tradition. But having said this, I don't want to just leave it there, because if I am right that saying the morality isn't new functions as a put-down of what it actually is, then my conclusion is misleading, and I do not want to mislead you. Let me try to clarify what I am getting at.

Some months ago I gave a talk on black culture to what I then mistakenly thought was the usual sort of polite, university extension audience of culture-hungry school teachers and social workers— many of them Negro. I argued—tentatively, without much emotion, in the dispassionate style I have argued so far in this paper—that although the idea of black culture seemed useful to me as a Myth to bind Negroes together in a way that would enhance their ability to press their political demands, there seemed to be little in what the Nationalists and other militants were touting as "Black Culture" that couldn't be attributed to a combination of Southern regional patterns, evangelical Christianity, and lower-class patterns of the metropolitan ghetto. I had hardly finished when I found myself facing an angry and shouting group of people who felt they had been insulted, and who, under other circumstances, might simply have killed me as an enemy of the people (I am not being melodramatic). Later, it was pointed out to me that black culture was in the process of being made, and if I didn't see it, it was because I didn't know where it was at (both of which may be true); and besides, my implying that there wasn't any was not only likely to weaken the Myth but to impede the actual growth and development of the reality—which made me an enemy.

The logical form of this problem is an old one for sociologists who deal with issues of public resonance: the problem of self-fulfilling and self-denying assertions. So although I do not see among the hippies any system of values that warrants the pretentious solemnity

of the phrase "New Morality," I believe that moralities old *and* new rise and fall in part through self-fulfilling and self-denying processes which may be activated by descriptive statements innocent of pre-scriptive intent. Knowing this, however, destroys the possibility of innocence for those who make statements which affect outcomes in which they are interested. There are, that is, always potentially ascendant deviant or subterranean moralities around, the numbers of whose adherents are subject to expansion or contraction partly on the basis of how persuasively the morality is talked up or down, glamorized or mystified, vitalized or stultified, and its prevalence exaggerated or minimized. Such processes affect the rigor with which sanctions are or are not applied, and therefore obstruct or facilitate not merely moral deviance but the prospects that deviance will become legitimate and proclaim its own propriety. Joseph Con-rad, that famous Polish sociologist, used as an epigraph for his very sociological *Lord Jim*, the following words: "It is certain that my conviction increases the moment another soul will believe it."

Hippie morality is not new, but I think that more souls are believing it. The proportions of the age-grade may not be any larger, but the absolute numbers are enormous for two very good, and rather new reasons. First, there is the unprecedented, colossal size of the cohort between, say, fifteen and twenty-five years of age, even a small per-centage of which produces very large numbers indeed. Second, this cohort of morally deviant youth have been further swelled by the group known as "Teenyboppers," preadolescents and early ado-lescents who have not to my knowledge previously played any significant role in bohemian movements. Their presence on the contemporary scene is, I think, a function of the institutilization of adolescence as a major substantial period of life, allocating indi-viduals to a something less than fully adult status, which may last as long as twenty years, and which therefore evokes its own orien-tational phenomena and behavior which we have learned to under-stand as "anticipatory socialization."

In addition to their large numbers, their peculiar visibility is playing an important contemporary part in the gradual legitimation of their traditional subterranean morality. Exactly *un*like the invisible poor in Michael Harrington's *The Other America*, the hippies are unequally distributed in ways which magnify their visibility. They are concen-trated, segregated in universities or recently out of them and into the bohemian ghettos of the more glamorous big cities. They are

colorful, disturbing, and always newsworthy. Moreover, they have a substantial press of their own and radio stations which play their music almost exclusively. And not only are many of them the children of relatively affluent and influential people, but they have their sympathizers (secret and not so secret) in the universities, and let's not forget the ballet, and in the mass media which, as I have said, seem incapable of leaving them alone.

How do I know the morality is gradually being legitimated? I don't for sure, but when John Lennon said the Beatles were more popular than Jesus—something that probably wasn't even quite true—he got away with it, *and helped make it truer by getting away with it*. But there's better evidence, take for example sex, which in this country seems to be the quintessence of morality. More important and more reliable than survey data reporting premarital sexual experiences are the revealing attitudes of more or less official moral spokesmen. Hollywood films, for example, as good an indicator of acceptable morality as one is likely to find (appealing, as their producers say they must, to mass sentiments) not only affirm unmarried sex but go even further to suggest that your life may be ruined by the decision *not* to climb into bed with the person you love. It is still news when Christian ministers refuse to condemn unchastity, but it gets the inside pages now, and is not nearly so startling an event as it was a few years ago. And now, finally, the topic is ready for discussion in the public schools: Is premarital intercourse wrong? William Graham Sumner gave us the answer: the moment the morés are questioned, it is a sign that they have lost their authority. And when they are questioned publicly by official representatives of the major institutions, they have not only lost their authority but are ready to be replaced—not, let me repeat, by a "New Morality," but by an old one which has been underground, and which now, like Yeats' rough beast, its hour come round at last, slouches toward Bethlehem to be born.

So what else is new? Well, several things which, although they don't exactly express what I would call a new morality, do express traditional bohemian virtues in so fresh, unusual, and potentially consequential a manner, that they are worth noting.

1. I said I would say a word about hippie innocence. Clearly, the symbols of childhood and innocence are very much in: flowers, ice

cream, kites, beads, bells, bubbles and feathers, and sitting on the ground like Indians, or with legs outstretched in front of one, like Charlie Brown and his friends (perhaps reflecting the guilelessness of the prose styles of Paul Goodman and Alan Watts?). Just recently, hippie innocence was a major theme in a CBS documentary oddly titled "The Hippie Temptation." CBS, Harry Reasoner that is, disapproved, pointing out how the innocence was used in a hostile way (girl taunting an annoyed policeman by insistently offering him flowers), and concluding with the (smug?) observation that people who can grow beards and make love ought to go beyond innocence to wisdom. What CBS apparently chose to ignore (and I say chose, because it seems so obvious) was the fact that innocence *as* wisdom and the child *as* moral leader are two ideas which go back a couple of thousand years to very respectable sources. Harry Reasoner, a man with a usually reliable sense of irony, also chose to ignore the irony of network TV prescribing wisdom—and to the "TV generation!" Of *course* hippie innocence is provocative; it angers the police, it angers CBS, and it is potentially consequential, because Authority finds it difficult to fight. Wisdom might be a good antidote, but there's very little wisdom around (and more people pleading incompetence to preach it). There's only sophistication, and not too much of that.

2. Another interesting development in the hippie milieu is the panhandling. It's interesting because of its relation to the innocence theme and because of the peculiar moral relevance of the interaction. The approach is usually the standard "Do you have any spare change?" But it is often consciously winsome and "charming." A teen-age girl, for example, asks me to lend her 15¢ for an ice cream cone, then asks for 2¢ additional so she can have the ice cream in a sugar cone. The mood of the interaction is different from skid row panhandling in which the bum plays humble and subservient, thus allowing his mark to feel generous or powerful—or even contemptuous—which is what the giver gets in return for giving. Hippie panhandling is innocent, offhand, as if to say: you've got it and can spare it, I haven't; all men are brothers, and if you don't give, you're a kind of fink; or, if you think it's principle that prevents you from giving, it reveals only your uptightness about money, your enslavement to an obsolete ethic about the virtue of *earning* what you get. Indeed, one of the things one may learn from being approached is the shocking discovery that one *does* truly believe in that virtue. But what-

ever the specific character of one's response, the people I have spoken to invariably find it obscurely disturbing, an occasion for reflection, and this is important.

3. The hippies have also played an important role in the gradual institutionalization of the use of formerly obscene and other taboo language in public, even on ceremonial occasions. This trend is part of the general eroticization of public life, from print, to advertising, to film, to styles of dress and undress, and it has within it the potential of changing the quality of public life through its effect on spoken rhetoric, which may help reclaim the language from the depths of degradation to which public speech has sunk it. Lenny Bruce was a prophet of this movement. The so-called filthy speech movement at Berkeley in the summer of 1965 is well known, and so are the fairly severe sanctions that were invoked against the offenders. What is not so well known is that shortly after this controversy, the university sponsored a poetry conference on the campus. For almost a whole week, there were daily and nightly readings by, among others, several of the more successful "Beat" poets of the fifties, as well as by many very young and relatively unknown hippie poets. I remember sitting in the hallowed halls of Wheeler auditorium (now gutted by a fire of obscure origin) and the only slightly less hallowed Dwinelle Hall, amidst little old ladies with knitting, suburban housewives from Orinda, and cashmere sweatered undergraduates holding tight to their boy friends' hands. And I remember listening to Allen Ginsberg rhapsodize about waking up with his cock in the mouth of his friend Peter Orlovsky; I remember listening to other poets wax eloquent about cunnilingus and about what they repeatedly insisted upon calling fucking. Now because I am a sociologist as well as a person interested in poetry, I not only remember sitting and listening to the poets, I remember also observing that the ladies hardly looked up from their knitting, the undergraduates listened raptly (with that almost oppressive quiet reminiscent of museums), and I heard neither a titter nor a gasp of shock. I saw no outraged exits, not an indignant word in the press that week about pornography or obscenity, nor was I aware of any other complaints against the use of university facilities for such goings on—although the organizer of the conference told me, when I spoke to him about it later, that there had been one or two letters of complaint. One or two! And, I must confess, it is the improbability of negative sanctions that encourages me here to contribute to the tend-

ency I am describing, that is, to *show* you my point rather than argue it: that formerly taboo language is increasingly used in public, and that, yes, Virginia, it is erotic. Nor is the poetry conference the only example at hand. As Bay Area residents well know, Lenore Kandel's *The Love Book* was read aloud at a mass meeting of faculty and students at San Francisco State shortly after it was banned by the San Francisco police. And I have been told by the cast of "The Beard" —a one-act play that had a long run in San Francisco before its New York opening, which uses all the four-letter words and winds up with an act of cunnilingus on stage—that their performances on campuses before college groups have been invariably successful—the audiences laugh in the funny places, not in the dirty ones—but that the Saturday night audiences in their San Francisco theater still leave a good deal to be desired.

4. The music (rock, folk-rock, etc.) of course is new, but I will not discuss it at any length, except to point to some features of it that I think may have important social consequences. First of all, the lyrics of many of the songs are for the first time in the history of popular music in this country lyrics that a thoughtful person of some sensibility and taste can sing without embarrassment. Think of it! Very intelligent people singing popular songs seriously! Cole Porter was an exception to the rule of banality. Bob Dylan is not an exception because there is no longer a rule. Dylan is not a great poet; he's not even a very good one, but he *is* a poet in a country whose lyricists have usually been versifiers rather than poets. Second, I am struck by the fact that few, if any, of the traditional popular baritones sing rock well, or at all. It seems apparent that rock songs are not made for deep or mature voices; there is a prevalence of high, reedy, thin, sometimes even falsetto male voices—indeed it is often difficult to tell the difference between a male and a female voice; enunciation, when it can be understood at all, is often childlike, sometimes even infantile; postures tend to be limp, and facial expression unformed and vulnerable. All this tends to identify the music with an age-group and a life-style, a distinctive kind of music for a distinctive kind of people, which outsiders may admire, if they do, only as a tourist admires an exotic scene, but closer intimacy with which exposes one to the dangers of infection by other aspects of the life-style. Finally, there is the fact that rock groups typically do their own material almost exclusively, something so far as I know unprecedented in Amer-

ican popular music. And even when a song is very successful, other groups do not generally do it. This may well express the importance of the idea of authenticity in the subculture, that doing your thing should be doing *your* thing, which would discourage a rock group from doing something that wasn't "theirs."

It is of course easy to deflate the authenticity balloon by pointing out that certain "things" can be authentically evil, and that doing *your* thing can be indirectly damaging to lots of people including yourself. Qualifications, then, are necessary, but they are not usually made by moralists; the great moral dicta are typically stated in absolute terms, and never with all the qualifications necessary to live with them. The Commandment prohibiting homicide does not, after all, say except in self-defense, or except at the order of the commander-in-chief; and we all know that we may be pardoned our inability to honor our mothers and fathers if they push heroin in the high school cafeteria.

But it occurs to me that sociologists are among the least likely people imaginable to speak with sympathy or *Verstehen* about expressive morality because, of all data, data on morality reveal the greatest disparity between the point of view of the actor and that of the observer; the actor sees consummation, whereas we observers typically treat expressive morality à la Durkheim: as social facts whose prime significance lies in the institutional functions they facilitate or obstruct. As sociologists, we avoid moral discourse and resist indulging our moral feelings, because our scientific education has taught us that all moralities are ultimately arbitrary, and because, as men of science, we have learned to abhor arbitrariness. Moralists frequently embarrass or bore sociologists, because their moral passion keeps demanding a like response from us, whereas our impulse is to look only for latent functions. But like Philoctetes, the moralist has a magic bow as well as a festering wound, for one of the important manifest functions of the moralist's passion is to define or affirm or redefine for all members of the community the standards with reference to which expressive satisfactions are achieved. And to the extent that scientists get expressive satisfactions through their work, these standards are never irrelevant.

Like other creative work, the best scientific work is usually informed with a moral energy which ultimately owes nothing to science, and the best sociologists have found ways of living with the tension posed by this dilemma: Weber, passionately detached, a brilliant and elo-

quent spokesman for cognitive criteria skeptical of brilliance and eloquence, dealt with it by honorably impaling himself on its horns; Simmel by transfiguring the study of interaction into a connoisseur's art;
Parsons by dedicating himself to Systematic Theory as if he were
called to it by the Almighty Himself.

The closest that sociologists usually get to real moral judgment is
when they invoke comparative data as a source of norms to appraise
morally relevant situations (Lipset's work is a good example). This
angers and frustrates moralists, because their mission is utopian. In
moral discourse, reliance on norms of evaluation derived from comparative data leaves one impotent to affect the standards in terms of
which the evaluations are made; it renders one morally acted upon
rather than morally active, which is a way of saying that sociologists
make poor moral leaders. For moralists, the invocation of comparative
norms is irrelevant. If they appear fanatical, intransigent, unreasonable, it is because they must believe that moral feeling is not negoti-
able, that half a consummation is no consummation at all. It makes
no difference that Americans are freer than Peruvians or Iranians and
more humane than Guatemalans or Guineans; America may still be
found wanting in terms of some current moral vision of human possibility. Where expressive values rather than facts or judicious estimates
are at stake, the utopian standard is more relevant than the comparative norm. Let me conclude with an old Jewish joke that may clarify
this somewhat. Jake says: so nu, Sam, how's your wife? And Sam
says: compared to what? It's funny because of the inappropriateness
of the comparative norm. How, then, is the hippie morality? Compared
to what? No worse than anybody else's, better than many, still not
good enough.

Self-Hatred and the Politics of Kicks / 1969*

You ask for my top-of-the-head thoughts on "the enragé or the beat
or simply the deviant," and one of the first things that occurs to me
is that it is precisely that sort of question—and the purpose for which
it is asked—that enrages the enragés and induces the confirmation
of the beat. I do believe (and in this respect I may be beat—though

*Reprinted from *Dissent*, (July–August 1966).

I doubt it) that conferences of the kind in which you (and I) are engaged are significant less for their contribution to a solution of the problems which occasion them than for what they reveal about the way in which problems are "handled," as we turn into the last third of this century. Probably the very best thing they do is come up with what J. K. Galbraith called positions of "permissible originality."

"The enragé or the beat or simply the deviant" are people whose naiveté is in a way charming, almost quaint, because their orientations are still primarily moral and expressive, by which I mean that they still get terribly upset by discrepancies between what is practiced and what is preached, and extract deep satisfaction from passionately expressing that upsetness. Which may or may not help explain why so many of us are profoundly ambivalent about their "idealism," regarding it as morally praiseworthy, of course—pure, innocent, and all that—and yet deeply distrustful of those virtues when they intrude themselves into arenas of domestic and international conflict where we have learned to believe that other virtues, the ones we call "sophisticated," properly belong.

I remember Marty Lipset one winter (1965) presiding at a hastily called meeting of interested University of California faculty to consider what to do about Clark Kerr's suddenly announced resignation in the midst of the so-called "filthy speech controversy." I remember Lipset muttering over and over with a bitter and sarcastic anger rare for him, "the moral men have won"—suggesting that Kerr had been squeezed between the moral indignants of the Right and Left until he had no more room to maneuver. But behind the impatience and the occasional anger that political moderates or centrists like Lipset feel for the politically enraged and indignant, I often suspect there lies a good deal of latent resentment that the enragés seem always to capture the *moral* ground, leaving the moderates with little but their more or less sophisticated preoccupation with tactics aimed, apparently, at nothing more grand, ennobling, or exciting than the sustenance of the present precarious institutional balance, which is precisely what the enraged idealists scorn, preferring their own vulnerable and corruptible utopias.

Now "idealism" and "sophistication" are terms that describe polar attitudes toward the possible. The sophisticated ("Realists" of course, are people who expect the worst) are people concerned only with the presently possible, devoting their energies to finding and using the

most efficient means of achieving it. The enragés, as "idealists," are tilters at windmills, who, if they had the choice and were conscious of its consequences would prefer a grand moral gesture to a politically calculated act. Where one has hold of a political issue that is at the same time a burning moral issue (as one has with peace and civil rights), then involvement in it can easily become its own reward; you don't have to win in order for it to have been worthwhile. Win, lose, or draw, to fight for the moral right is ennobling, and this is what rebellious students want to do. I call this the politics of kicks, but I don't intend the term as a put-down because there is a part of me that thinks one has a right to expect one's political acts to be morally satisfying regardless of the ends they may or may not achieve. So to say that the politics of the campus militants is for kicks is not a damaging criticism in a sense analogous to that in which it is not damaging to try to impugn the motives of the Vietnam or civil rights activists by saying that they do what they do "just for publicity" (since publicity influences people, and public opinion is what presumably influences policy makers). Politics as kicks is expressive, redemptive; even if one loses (does one hope to lose?) the experience enlarges one. The nobility of defeat is certainly easier to handle than the responsibilities of victory.

On the other hand, using politics for redemptive or expressive purposes is very dangerous in a world armed to the nuclear teeth. The student Left which today shouts so righteously against "this immoral war" in Viet Nam is composed of much the same sort of people who less than ten years ago were deploring John Foster Dulles' conduct of foreign policy for, among other things, the inappropriateness of its moral evangelism in delicate political situations. My recent memories include not only Lipset searching for an accommodation but also a young leader of the student militants insolently baiting an editor of *Dissent*, a veteran of the radical movement, not on any substantive issue of politics, but—believe it or not—about whether his "expectations" were still "heady." The hostile arrogance in the young man's voice, which showed through his patronizing attempt at affecting a teasing good humor, suggested that if the veteran radical was old and tired (he was neither), that is, did *not* have "heady expectations," then it was about time he ceased posing as a radical since only the politically erotic—wild eyed and possessed—had a right to the label. Trying to imagine him conducting negotiations with the leaders of a foreign government, the peace

of the world hanging in the balance, is almost enough to turn one into a conservative. Still, most of the available models of political men seem hardly more attractive, and to be exquisitely immobilized, hung up with Coleridge's "feelings all too delicate for use," is no better. Under the circumstances, political rage may seem like far from the worst alternative.

I think the enragés are enraged at "they," at a system of social order which they perceive as robbing them of kicks, as denying them satisfaction ("I can't get no satisfaction") which they see as the price of an admission ticket to the prosperous, orderly Great Society, where men are reasonable, willing to compromise, ready to give a little in order to get a little; a place where men "maintain themselves by the common routine/ Learn to avoid excessive expectation/ Become tolerant of themselves and others/ Giving and taking in the usual actions/ What there is to give and take . . ." and so on to the end of Mr. Eliot's bleak sermon.[1]

One day not very long ago while sitting in front of a typewriter trying to write something on the reluctance of youth to grow up, I thought: "this is a society which hates itself." I said to myself (with, I noted, an immediate touch of defensive irony) *there's* an arresting (arrestable?) thought, and started to type it out to see how it looked on paper, when my inner censor said no no, that won't do; I'm not the sort of *ressentiment*-filled intellectual who says things like that, and besides, what it means is not even clear. But the feeling persisted, and I kept asking myself what I could have meant (a stubborness I like to think is salutary since, for an intellectual who is not an artist, one of the few functions left to feeling is to evoke analytic thought about itself and about the extent to which it—the feeling— represents an authentic response to something perhaps only dimly perceived but really there, or whether it's simply another dreary projection of private need which would be much better suppressed).

A society which hates itself is cne that is unwilling or unable to honor or reward the social roles and the types of human character which the organization of its major institutions commits it to produce. Honor and reward are probably not the right words, for money and prestige are in pretty good supply (in any case our cultural rhetoric is rich in ways to derogate money, and as for prestige, it is enough

---

[1] From T. S. Eliot, *The Cocktail Party*. Quoted with the permission of the publishers, Harcourt Brace Jovanovich, Inc., and Faber and Faber Ltd.

to observe that the world's Latin source means delusion). I mean that our cultural–emotional rhetoric is poor in symbols which glorify or glamorize or even simply praise the roles and the types of character the society has actually devoted itself to fabricating. When little boys are asked what they want to be when they grow up, they should be able to say (with swelling chest and brimming eyes and trembling voice) "I want to be a registrar in a college" or "I want to be a dental technician" or "I want to be a console operator." A society which hasn't yet learned how to make heroic images out of the types of people it really needs and is committed to, creates an uneasy population vulnerable to ideological appeals which cater to its need for heroic models. And a society which is apparently unable convincingly to glorify those men who manifest its most representative virtues may be said to be a society which doesn't like itself very much, and this will be true so long as "organization men" and "status seekers" are not flattered when they are called by these names. Willy Loman's wife, exhorting us to "pay *attention* to this man" is Arthur Miller insisting that his salesman is a tragic hero because he's typical. He *is* typical, but he's also a bore. And to be typical *and* a bore is a fact very painful to face.

If, as you say, the novel (indeed, as you suggest, all of culture) is "anti-institutional" it is because the institutions are perceived as encouraging the behavior which our values (culture) do not celebrate, and sometimes actually disdain. A "decline in the attitude toward authority" means that there are no more authors or that the emperor has no clothes or, to put it more formally, that assent in the legitimacy of a power source is being withdrawn, which, of course, is a conventional step in "revolutions" (many of which are not revolutions at all but an attempt to restore something perceived as lost or usurped). To all but the most intransigent authoritarian, after all, defiance is a vice or a virtue depending on what one thinks about its object. Presumably Patrick Henry and Nathan Hale (those Bronzes from our Grammar school texts) experienced a decline in their attitude toward authority—which is not a fresh thought by any means.

There are several ways of dealing with conflicts between practice and preachment, or social structure and values. One can choose to modify practice, to bring it into better accord with what is preached or valued—as we are trying to do with regard to race relations. Or, one can take the "sophisticated" position, and observe that all

societies institutionalize duplicity, and, having observed it, begin getting used to the fact by searching for the functions of the duplicity. Or, finally, one can try to alter beliefs and values in order to bring them more into line with "the realities of the situation" (or, as Marxists would say, get rid of "false consciousness," and thus, as Marxists would not say, reduce cognitive dissonance). In this context, irony of ironies, most of the hip are not moral avant-gardists at all, but old-fashioned moralists who prefer finding some relatively insulated niches in the social structure, relatively safe from the sort of sanctions the major institutions can invoke against their own personnel. But the practice of their old fashioned moralities leads them, as Erving Goffman has suggested, to where the action is, to live with the sorts of danger and exploit that our moral vocabulary is well equipped to celebrate, but our social structure ill equipped to accommodate. "Action" in this sense is found in extreme circumstances where something very valuable is risked (like physical safety or self-conceptions). I think that part of our ambivalence toward these enragés is founded in the ritual function they perform for us; we live a bit of our vicarious lives through them.

The Hippie Trip/1969*

In George P. Elliott's novel, *Parktilden Village,* there's a vicious portrayal of a young sociologist who makes love to the teenage daughter of one of his colleagues in order to get access to a motorcycle gang she knows and which he wants to study as a participant-observer. Threatened in his participant role by a tough, former boyfriend of the girl, the sociologist shows yellow and backs off into his role of detached observer, surprising the girl, who remarks with withering contempt how, playing it safe, he's got it made both ways: her guy when he's not threatened, the disinterested researcher when he is. The author of *The Hippie Trip* reminds me of Elliott's sociologist. Not that there's any hanky-panky with his respondents; quite the contrary. Lewis Yablonsky might have written a better book (as well as learned a little more about himself) if he *had* made love to the hippie chick who casually offered herself to him in the back of a

*A review of Lewis Yablonsky's *The Hippie Trip* (New York: Pegasus, 1968). Reprinted from *Trans-Action* (February 1969).

station wagon under the stars on a cliff over the Pacific Ocean. Rather, it's that Yablonsky, like Elliott's sociologist, seems equally incapable of the insight that might come from really daemonic detachment (Erving Goffman's strength) or from giving himself over wholeheartedly to his subject matter, thus transcending his own ideological defenses in a way that would enable him to take full advantage of the opportunities offered by his participant-observation in hippie communes.

Accompanied by his trusty tape recorder (the research instrument Yablonsky calls "unobtrusive" but which was at least twice the cause of serious tension on the research scene) and his hippie "guide," Yablonsky sets out on his research trip which takes him to communes such as Strawberry Fields and other hippie sites in the Los Angeles area, to Big Sur, Haight-Ashbury, New York's East Village, Holiday Lodge near Santa Cruz, and Morningstar Ranch in Sonoma County. What do we learn? That the hippies are predominantly young; that there are "core" participants and marginal participants, "high priests," "novices," and "plastic hippies"; that they see themselves as having "dropped out" of an oppressive society which is racist, plastic, and uptight; that the flower children (and the children's children) are prey to disease, violence, and chaos in their urban and rural communes. We learn that marijuana use is near universal, that LSD is prevalent, and that they are regarded by many as religious sacraments. We discover that nudity is casually regarded, that sex is "free" for the tuned-in, and that the hippies believe in everybody doing his thing—in spite of the problems this creates in organizing viable communities. The tape records also a great deal of inflated rhetoric by the hippies regarding the corruption of American institutions and expressing their mystical, religious, and other oceanic feelings.

Did we need Yablonksy's research in order to "know" this? Do we know it any more firmly or conclusively than we knew it before through the efforts of *Time, Life, Look, Newsweek, CBS, NBC* and the small library of quick-production paperbacks which have exploited the hippie craze? I think not. The value of research like Yablonsky's lies not in the conclusiveness of its findings; its frivolous methodology makes this impossible.[1] The potential value of field

---

[1] "In more cases than not" his interviews were carried out in live situations. "Whenever possible" the discussions took place in natural settings. "In my research participation in the hip world, I utilized all of the relevant social

work like this lies in its insight, in the freshness of its on-scene perceptions, in a theory about deviance or youth or community that such perceptions might generate, and in the proposal of specific hypotheses which further, more rigorous, research might set out to test (good hypotheses do not fall from the sky).

Unfortunately, there is very little of this in Yablonsky's book. He does make the repeated—and interesting (for the first few times) observation that the hippie role may be a way of legitimating psychosis. And we get an application to the hippies of his old idea (which predates his first book, *The Violent Gang*) about "near groups." But on the whole Yablonsky seems to have been unable to learn anything new about the hippies or to express very much that is analytically fresh because he was too busy defending himself against threats to his own sense of moral safety. It is his apparent unwillingness to deal squarely with this fact (except on the one occasion with the girl in the station wagon), combined with his avuncular posture of hippie-sympathizer, which gives the book its smug, self-satisfied tone, and which makes me so angry with it. Even when he is praising the "integrity" of his guide (Gridley Wright) Yablonsky seems to be congratulating himself for his own moral generosity in making that grand gesture.

One of these days (in this time when a vulgarized phenomenology has given a new lift to participant-observer research) a sociologist is going to come along who exemplifies in his own research experience the insight of Joseph Conrad's Kurtz ("the horror! the horror!"), Melville's Benito Cereno, and Elliott's Negro anthropologist (in another story called, "Among the Dangs," which all field workers should read) who went carrying light into the Heart of Darkness and either never returned or reemerged irrevocably scarred by their knowledge of the Dark. Lewis Yablonsky is not that sociologist. There's an irony here, because in his preface Yablonsky makes pious noises (about how "emotionally involving" his "research trip" was, and about what a "very personal document" his book is) which suggest that he was profoundly affected by the experience. I don't believe it. Readers don't generally have to be *told* when an author's experience was emotionally involving or when a book is a highly intimate record of that experience; a book speaks for itself on these

---

theories I know of in directing my research camera. In writing my findings I attempted to blend my personal observations with pertinent theoretical perspectives." This is frivolous methodology.

accounts. Never trust the teller, trust the tale, said D. H. Lawrence, and what *The Hippie Trip* tells us loud and clear is that Yablonsky patronizes his subjects, deceives himself, and insults his readers by his apparent assumption that the patronization and the deception will not be visible.

These are harsh words, I know, but not, I think, unjust. If Yablonsky "knows" the hippie scene, what do I mean when I say that he has learned nothing from it, and that in thinking otherwise he has deceived himself? Well, he sees people casually screwing, so he knows that that goes on; he sees them smoke dope and drop acid, so that surely goes on; he sees little children wandering about obviously high, and smelling of urine and feces, and he sees the squalor and disorganization of the communes, so he knows that those exist. *But he seems unable to believe that they believe in what they're doing; he doesn't really "hear" them.* For example: he frowns on their being "hedonistic and selfish" in matters of love when "self-sacrifice and responsibility" (which Yablonsky affirms) are precisely what in the hippie view corrupts honest intimacy. He chides them for giving in to "slovenliness, laziness, and disorder" in their communes when they clearly consider these the price they may have to pay for the opportunity for everybody to do his thing. He criticizes their responses to "plastic" America as "extremist" when extremism in the defense of freedom is for them clearly no vice. He wrings his hands over the "anarchy" of their lives as if he didn't "know" that lots of hippies are serious anarchists.

He is, moreover, consummately conventional in interpreting their drug abuse (he evades the question of when drug use becomes drug abuse) as an "escape" from, not a solution to their problems. He never for a moment questions (as a serious thinker, affected by his research experience, might) the received virtue of "facing" one's problems, particularly when (as his own discussion of anomie suggests) the prospects of a solution are not encouraging; nor does he consider the possibility that "escape" (particularly when it's successful) may have a good deal to recommend it. (If the possibility did occur to him, he'd probably get that smug look and pronounce piously that no escape can be successful—thus solving by definition what is potentially a good empirical question.) Nor does Yablonsky consider the even more extreme possibility that drug trips express a classic *American* concern with the application of science (in this case chemistry) to the more "rational" solution of human problems.

What the hippies obviously want (and what their anomie prevents them from getting legitimately) are certain desirable states of *feeling* (their condemnation of American culture boils down simply to the assertion that it doesn't make people happy). Our reigning value systems say that desirable states of feeling should come *indirectly*, as the natural concomitant of good or right action. Science makes all this complex indirection unnecessary; if chemistry can make you feel good *directly*, the hippies seem to be saying, why go through all the hassles over *doing* good and *being* good in order to *feel* good?

Yablonsky, who thinks he has real sympathy for the hippies, has no sympathy for what they essentially are. Where they are anarchic, he wants them orderly; where they are given to Dyonisian excess, he wants them moderate and self-contained. But make no mistake; he digs the hippie philosophy. He's against plastic and "the machine;" he too is for love and spontaneity and doing your thing and spiritual enlargement and all that. It's just that their philosophy in its present form is not quite viable for the sustenance of community, what with all the unruliness, violence, drug abuse, aimlessness, and child neglect. What he'd really like to do is take the philosophy, scrub it good and clean, turn its adherents into liberals and Unitarians, and send them into group therapy where they'll learn the need for discipline and strong leaders—like the "forty-three year old rather 'hip' professor" who studied them.

I am not being too harsh. "Rather hip" professors don't patronize their respondents. After finding an East Village hippie who is willing to serve as guide and informant, and who tells him " 'What you're doing as a sociologist is what I love to do. Like man, I really like to find out what's happening, not only for me but in general,' " Yablonsky remarks "I was more than pleased to conclude that I now had acquired a very articulate and knowledgable research assistant." Rather hip professors don't repeatedly congratulate themselves on their "firm beliefs" in the rights of researchers to go where the data are (even if being there *is* illegal) or on their own "smoothness" and "grace" in extricating themselves from threatening situations, or on their "wisdom" in yielding petty cash tribute to a Hell's Angel bent on extortion. And finally, rather hip professors don't report their own first drug experiences with the portentousness and melodrama suitable to a Victorian virgin on her wedding night.

Two of the high points in the book report Yablonsky's personal introduction to marijuana and LSD, experience with which he care-

fully decided was vital to his research. So one day in the company of a group of hippies he takes "five or six" drags on a joint, just enough, apparently, to convince him that he didn't like it, but enough to make him see that it produces a mild high, giggles, and illusions of great wittiness. But his LSD experience apparently blew his mind, or so he seems to think. He and his wife each ingested 500 micrograms in their own home sometime after midnight while in the company of two old friends and his wife's grown daughter. Once he got over his initial panic at the hallucinations, it was apparently a good, fifteen hour trip. He keeps repeating the word "Excalibur," and it becomes the "theme" of his trip. He discovers that he is a red, white, and blue patriot, with deep love of country, friends, and Synanon (the drug-rehabilitation organization he has been associated with and written a book about). He talks volubly about movies of the 1930s he remembers seeing as a child; in high spirits he affects an English accent. He is suffused with feelings of well-being, good fellowship, and love for his wife and daughter, who seem very beautiful to him. He and his wife say candid things to each other that they would not have said under ordinary circumstances. They make love, bathe, drive over to the beach, visit friends, come home, and by early evening they have both come down.

Yablonsky believes that his LSD trip gave him profound insight into himself in ways that he cannot fully communicate. As with the marijuana, he feels no desire to try the acid again, but unlike his experience with marijuana he is unwilling to believe that the LSD insights were "illusory." If marijuana makes one *feel* witty when "in fact" one is not (or not very), why is Yablonsky convinced that his LSD-induced feelings were authentic? I think it is because the feelings were self-supportive and self-congratulatory; he and his wife discovered they loved each other deeply. More importantly for the subject of his book, the experience "affected [his] viewpoint as a sociologist. I am more than observer; I have to assume the responsibility of action to change the society I love." I think, in the final analysis, that it is this redemptive posture of his that lies at the heart of his failure to see and hear the hippies with the clarity that his access to them made possible. There's a final irony too; for it is *they* who have changed the society (with their cultural innovations in music, graphic and decorative art, in clothing, and in language) and their success may be rooted in a final ambiguity: that many of them are beyond redemption.

American Cultures

Introduction

The Myth of Suburbia is the intellectual center of what was, first, my Ph.D. dissertation and, later, the book *Working-Class Suburb* (University of California Press, 1960; revised 1968). It represents, in a way, the making of something out of nothing. Like many graduate students in the 1950s, I had passed my qualifying examinations for the doctorate, and faced the prospect of the dissertation without much sense of the kind of research I wanted to undertake. And after one false start, I even found myself without a job. Then I heard about a Professor of Business Administration at Berkeley who had some money to study the consequences of the closing of a Ford assembly plant in Richmond, California, and the opening of a new one near San Jose. He was looking for a sociologist to study the impact on the families of Ford workers who had moved with the plant. I got the job, and my investigations became the basis of my dissertation.

The making of something out of nothing occurred in a way that reverses the usual process of dissertation writing. Most students, at least in those days, would begin their dissertations with high hopes and high motivation, some because they chose topics in which they were really interested, others because it was the last hurdle to the Ph.D. But many would gradually get fed up to the point where they

could hardly bear to look at the result of their labors by the time it came out of the typewriter. I finished with high hopes and high motivation after starting out with little of either: I needed a job and I needed a dissertation topic, and the Ford opportunity seemed to provide both. It certainly provided a job. The question of whether the job could lend itself to a dissertation had to wait until I had begun to investigate the scene because unlike many professors who hire graduate students for research, the professor I went to work for did not have any very specific ideas about what he wanted studied. He knew the problem was "sociological," and that's what he hired a sociologist for. And my interest grew as I attempted to find a focus for the research.

William Whyte's book, *The Organization Man*, with its several chapters on the new mass-produced suburbs, was having much influence then (1956), and "suburbia" was an idea (with its connotations of middle-class "conformity" and status anxiety) and a word that was just coming into widespread common usage. The seed idea for the dissertation was planted as I drove through the new suburbs (near the new Ford plant) where many of the workers had bought homes. Unskilled and semiskilled factory workers in suburbia? It could provide me with an opportunity to *watch* suburbia work its magic to transform them into middle-class conformists. The ways in which I was mistaken, and why public images about suburbs persist in spite of the facts became the subject of my dissertation.

While the dissertation was becoming a book, the promotion people at the University of California Press thought it would be good for sales if a piece of the book appeared in a good general magazine shortly before publication date. "The Myth of Suburbia" was prepared for this purpose. I sent it first to *Commentary*, where it was accepted subject to some revision. A couple of revisions were done, and the editors and I were discussing still further revision when the Editorship at *Commentary* changed hands, and the article never appeared. It was subsequently turned down by *Harper's*, and never did see print before publication of the book.

I was rather depressed by these experiences, not only because I fancied myself a sociologist whose work would interest a general intellectual audience without losing the interest of my colleagues, but also because I was a young assistant professor not entirely innocent of what it took to advance an academic career. The dittoed manuscript was then circulating among friends in other universities,

and Joseph Adelson, the psychologist, heard about it and asked to see it for a special issue of *The Journal of Social Issues* he was editing. It finally appeared in that journal in 1961.

Working-Class Suburb was well received for the most part, and its modest success acquired for me a modest reputation as an "urban sociologist" (something I had never thought of myself as). It also acquired for me several invitations over the next few years to lecture and participate in conferences and forums regarding urban problems. The most important of these invitations was to a conference on "Planning for the Quality of Urban Life," held at Washington University at St. Louis in the Spring of 1965: **Suburbs, Subcultures, and Styles of Life** is the paper I prepared for that conference. It was my first experience on the big league academic conference circuit, and although the papers were on the whole excellent, the most memorable thing about the conference for me (with the possible exception of a small argument about ethnicity I had with Gunnar Myrdal) was the new motel near the campus in which we conferees were housed. It was "done" in rough-hewn, half-timbered, imitation Elizabethan style, and I remember much used brick, leaded windows with flower boxes, and an atmosphere of hammered brass and rare beef in its public rooms. As I arrived I noticed the bright flowers in the window boxes. It was still a quite cold April, and it did not surprise me to discover that the flowers were plastic; it *did* surprise me to discover that they were "growing" out of real soil. The motel was so new that there was a workman in my room still fitting the TV picture tube into an "antiqued" cabinet. As I watched, the man misread the ironic smile on my face and tried to reassure me about the cabinet by saying, "It just *looks* old, sir; it's really new." I remember having the distinct feeling I was not going to learn very much more about the quality of urban life over the next few days than I learned in my first few moments at the motel.

As it happened, I learned another thing or two. For example, that well-funded conferences (particularly if they had, as this one did, a "practical" function—its emphasis was on "planning") tend to be less interested in morally edged criticism than in practical and feasible proposals made within a context of assumptions shared by an "establishment." The emphasis toward the end of my conference paper on the insolubility of many "social problems," on the symbolic functions performed by their public recognition, and the general bias in favor of cultural pluralism was regarded by some of the conferees

as "romantic," and when the time came to prepare the conference papers for publication it was suggested to me that I might eliminate the section on Occupation and Social Class, severely blue-pencil much of the concluding section, and add some considerations on alternatives for planning the urban future. With some misgivings, I complied—largely because I was uncertain of what grounds I might have for noncompliance and because the suggestions did not seem unreasonable, given the purpose of the conference and the limits on space. But upon reflection, I think that the essay I wrote for the conference is on the whole a more interesting piece of work than the versions which finally appeared in print, and it is very nearly the original paper which appears in this book. For those who are interested in such literary transformations I invite them to compare the essay printed here with the versions published earlier.[1]

The Sociology of Leisure has a much simpler history. When I went to the University of Illinois in 1959 as Assistant Professor of Sociology, I inherited a course on the sociology of leisure which my department had given for some time largely as a convenience for students majoring in Recreation who needed some bona fide liberal arts credits. I had never thought much about the meaning of leisure before, but discovered that a good way to learn a few things fast about a subject is to be faced with the obligation to teach a course in it. I was helped considerably by my predecessor in the course (he had moved elsewhere) who provided me with hard to get curricular material and other data as well as with manuscript of the book on leisure that he was writing. I reviewed that book for *The American Journal of Sociology* in 1961, and the review came to the attention of Margaret Gordon, who had been instrumental in gaining for me the support of Berkeley's Institute of Industrial Relations earlier when I was doing my work on suburbia. The Institute was then planning a special issue on leisure for its new journal, *Industrial Relations*, and she asked me to contribute an article. (I remember doing much of the work for that article on an old typewriter on an even older table in an Illinois kitchen with the dirty dinner dishes pushed aside to make room, and I have wondered from time to time why I can't seem to write any better now that the typewriters are newer, the surfaces

[1]See "Suburbia and the American Dream" in *The Public Interest* (Winter 1966) and/or "Suburbs, Subcultures, and the Urban Future," in Sam Warner, ed., *Planning for the Quality of Urban Life*, (Cambridge, Mass.: MIT Press, 1966).

teak, and the room book-lined, quiet, and private.) The only difference between the original manuscript and the finally printed version was the elimination of some of the technical sociology language for the sake of *Industrial Relations'* nonacademic readers.

I spent the summer of 1966 in Hanover, New Hampshire, working on a project for the American Sociological Association at Dartmouth College. One of the small joys of an Eastern summer for a California academician is *The New York Times* at breakfast, and I remember the cool mornings in a rocking chair on the veranda of the old Hanover Inn (before it fell to the wrecker's ball) in that idllyic New England setting, reading of Richard Speck and his nine nurses in Chicago, of the sniper in the University of Texas tower, and of the riots in American cities. It was that summer, too, that the crisis in the civil rights movement (the term itself sounds obsolete four years later) began to be visible, that Stokeley Carmichael became a household name, and "black power" became a slogan announcing the accession of a new kind of militant mentality to influence in the councils of Negro organizations. I had been invited to participate in a conference of the American Institute of Planners in Portland, Oregon, in August of 1966, and, under the influence of the events of the summer, I wrote a brief paper on the developing splits in the civil rights movement, emphasizing (because it was for a conference of planners) the serious problems posed for integrated housing by the new insistence by militant Blacks on the authenticity and legitimacy of their "culture."

Earlier research had suggested that when interracial contacts occurred under conditions where shared interests and common tasks were available, and where the members of the different ethnic groups were in other respects of relatively equal socio-economic status, negative stereotypes weaken and prejudice is considerably reduced. But such findings would be encouraging only to those liberal middle-class Whites and Negroes who would see them as evidence that under the right conditions race or ethnicity need not matter. These findings could be interpreted quite differently by the apparently increasing number of young Negroes who want to maintain "Black Culture" and demand respect for it, while at the same time taking advantage of open occupancy and similar opportunities to improve the physical conditions of their housing. Under such conditions, inter-racial contacts could exacerbate hostile feelings and reinforce negative stereotypes.

Black Culture, my review of Charles Keil's *Urban Blues,* together with the essay *Racist, Plastic, Uptight* express my belief that the rising rhetoric about black culture and black identity is part (probably the most important part) of the wider revolution by the "underground" cultures of America against the dominant cultural conception of what "American" means, a conception in which the price of Toleration by the majority (or, more precisely, the politically effective majority) of the minority cultures was the latter's implicit acceptance of the inferiority inherent in the idea of being "tolerated." Actually, my interest in the newer currents of thinking among black militants was less an expression of my interest in contemporary political conflict than of my old and continuing interest in cultural pluralism and in the conditions of the viability of subcultures in America—interests which were expressed in my initial work on suburbs, in my writing on youth, and in the paper prepared for the St. Louis conference in 1965.

If one finds the pluralist idea at all attractive, one immediately runs into the problem of deciding how to respond when your friends call you a segregationist. I say this only half-jokingly because sociological theory and research suggest that the social conditions which sustain subcultures add up to something not unlike segregation. There is little question, for example, that such success the Jews and the Chinese have had in maintaining their subcultures in America has been made possible by the segregation of their social systems, by the relatively clear territorial boundaries which circumscribed them to their distinctive institutional structures (economic, religious, political, educational, familial, aesthetic, etc.), separate, yet sufficiently differentiated and elaborated to provide a framework within which an individual can live a relatively full life, *if he chooses it.* If your friends call you a segregationist, I think a good response is to point out this relation between subcultural preservation and social segregation. I think it worth pointing out, too, that the "separate but equal" doctrine is vulnerable not primarily because of the inequality of the facilities provided but because the separation was *unjust*; it was, that is, arbitrarily imposed, not chosen by the people concerned. Where, under conditions of free choice and opportunity for interethnic mobility, groups actually do choose to segregate themselves it is not clear to me what moral mandate urges one to disapprove.

Charles Keil's book, *Urban Blues,* caught my attention because

the blurbs announcing its publication emphasized its discussion of blues as a feature of its wider concern with Negro culture. I had gone back earlier to re-read the controversy among anthropologists and sociologists about the survival of elements of African culture among American Negroes, and I found Keil's book a fresh contribution to the discussion. My review of it (published in *Trans-action* in June 1967) was written in the Autumn of 1966 while I was revising my draft of the paper for the Portland conference, and the review reflects my thinking in that early period (remarkably distant already) of the present mood of militant confrontation.

I had my first personal involvement with this mood early in the Spring of 1967 when I used some of the material from these two papers in a talk I gave to a University of California Extension group in Santa Barbara. The group was composed in about equal parts of Blacks, Whites, and Mexican-Americans who had been working in community action groups all through southern California, and they responded with distinct hostility to my remarks. I was supposed to talk on "white identity" (a black intellectual and a Mexican-American intellectual were there to talk on the other two kinds), and used the occasion to say that I (a New York Jew) had never thought of myself as "white" (certainly not as "Anglo"—an angry Chicano rose to say I looked Anglo to him), that I regarded the whole "identity" idea as having more mythic significance than anything else, and that while I could understand and appreciate oppressed groups using such myths to abet the political effectiveness of their people by increasing their solidarity, I thought, too, that intellectuals ought to feel some obligation to avoid being deceived by their own political rhetoric. It seemed to me then (and seems to me still) that a primarily political preoccupation with one's own "culture" or "identity" is not unlike absorbing oneself with other virtues of one's own (like "humility" or "modesty"); it alters the character of the object by fitting it for ideological purposes, usually to the detriment of its authenticity.

Well, this was not what my audience had come to hear, and I was met with fiery rebuttals, angry shouts, and mutterings about goddam know-it-all professors. Clearly I had made an error—although two Negro women later told me quietly they agreed with me—admitting, however, that they would not say so publicly. The error was in assuming I had an academic audience when, in fact, it was an activist audience which, when it asembles to hear a talk, expects from its

speakers a sort of ritual performance which *invokes* the appropriate sacred and profane objects rather than analyzes them. Indeed, in 1970, it seems sometimes as if almost any public forum on a controversial issue risks ending in chaos because the issues are so volatile, opinion so polarized, and audiences so unrestrained that debate becomes theater, in which literally almost anything can happen.

Racist Plastic Uptight was written in the spring of 1968 for *The New York Times Magazine* which wanted an article on contemporary criticism of "middle-class values." That criticism is coming these days mostly from militant Blacks, from hippies, and from student activists, and the criticism has a common core. Since I had been thinking and writing about the newer militance among Blacks, had written a piece on the hippies in the summer of 1967, and had been following student radicalism closely since my own under-graduate days when I had written an article denouncing my college President as an anti-Semite, the material for the article was fresh in my mind. The *Times* never used the article; it was turned down by the editorial board, over the objections of the editor I worked with on it. I think they made a mistake, which is why I include it here.

The Myth of Suburbia

1961

In recent years a veritable myth of suburbia has developed in the United States. I am not referring to the physical facts of large-scale population movement to the suburbs: these are beyond dispute. But the social and cultural "revolution" that suburban life supposedly represents is far from being an established fact. Nevertheless, newspapers and magazines repeatedly characterize suburbia as "a new way of life," and one recent textbook refers to the rise of suburbia as "one of the major social changes of the twentieth century."

To urban sociologists, "suburbs" is an ecological term, distinguishing these settlements from cities, rural villages, and other kinds of communities. "Suburbia," on the other hand, is a cultural term, intended to connote a way of life, or, rather, the intent of those who use it is to connote a way of life. The ubiquity of the term in current discourse—suggests that its meaning is well on the way to standardization—that what it is supposed to connote is widely enough accepted to permit free use of the term with a reasonable amount of certainty that it will convey the image or images intended. Over the last dozen years, these images have coalesced into a full-blown myth, complete with its articles of faith, its sacred symbols, its rituals,

Reprinted from the *Journal of Social Issues* 17, no. 1 (1961): 38–49.

its promise for the future, and its resolution of ultimate questions. The details of the myth are rife in many popular magazines as well as in more highbrow periodicals and books; and although the details should be familiar to almost everyone interested in contemporary cultural trends, it may be well to summarize them briefly.

The Elements of the Myth

Approaching the myth of suburbia from the outside, one is immediately struck by rows of new "ranch-type" houses, either identical in design or with minor variations built into a basic plan, winding streets, neat lawns, two-car garages, infant trees, and bicycles and tricycles lining the sidewalks. Nearby is the modern ranch-type school and the even more modern shopping center dominated by the department store branch or the giant super market, itself flanked by a pastel-dotted expanse of parking lot. Beneath the television antennas and behind the modestly but charmingly landscaped entrance to the tract home resides the suburbanite and his family. I should say *"temporarily* resides" because perhaps the most prominent element of the myth is that residence in a tract suburb is temporary; suburbia is a "transient center" because its breadwinners are upwardly mobile, and live there only until a promotion or a company transfer permits or requires something more opulent in the way of a home. The suburbanites are upwardly mobile because they are predominantly young (most commentators seem to agree that they are almost all between twenty-five and thirty-five, well educated, and have a promising place in some organizational hierarchy—promising because of a continuing expansion of the economy and with no serious slowdown in sight. They are engineers, middle-management men, young lawyers, salesmen, insurance agents, teachers, civil service bureaucrats—groups sometimes designated as Organization Men, and sometimes as "the new middle class." Most such occupations require some college education, so it comes as no surprise to hear and read that the suburbanites are well educated. Their wives, too, seem well educated; their reported conversation, their patois, and especially their apparently avid interest in theories of child development all suggest exposure to higher education.

According to the myth, a new kind of hyperactive social life has developed in suburbia. Not only is informal visiting or "neighboring"

said to be rife, but a lively organizational life also goes on. Clubs, associations, and organizations allegedly exist for almost every conceivable hobby, interest, or preoccupation. An equally active participation in local civic affairs is encouraged by the absence of an older generation, who, in other communities, would normally be the leaders.

This rich social and civic life is fostered by the homogeneity of the suburbanites: they are in the same age range, they have similar jobs and incomes, their children are around the same age, their problems of housing and furnishing are similar. In short, a large number of similar interests and preoccupations promotes their solidarity. This very solidarity and homogeneity, on top of the physical uniformities of the suburb itself, is often perceived as the source of the problem of "conformity" in suburbia; aloofness or detachment is frowned upon. The "involvement of everyone in everyone else's life" subjects one to the constant scrutiny of the community, and everything from an unclipped lawn to an unclipped head of hair may be cause for invidious comment. On the other hand, the uniformity and homogeneity make suburbia classless, or one-class (variously designated as middle or upper-middle class). For those interlopers who arrive in the suburbs bearing the unmistakable marks of a more deprived upbringing, suburbia is said to serve as a kind of "second melting pot" in which those who are on the way up learn to take on the appropriate folkways of the milieu to which they aspire.

The widely commented upon "return to religion" is said to be most visible in suburbia. Clergymen are swamped, not only with their religious duties but with problems of marriage family counseling and other family problems as well. The revivified religious life in suburbia is not merely a matter of the increasing size of Sunday congregations, for the church is not only a house of worship but a local civic institution also. As such it benefits from the generally active civic life of the suburbanites.

On week-days, suburbia is a manless society that is almost wholly given over to the business of child rearing. Well-educated young mothers, free from the interference of tradition (represented by doting grandparents), can rear their children according to the best modern methods. "In the absence of older people, the top authorities on child guidance (in suburbia) are two books: Spock's *Infant Care*, and Gesell's *The First Five Years of Life*. You hear frequent references to them."

Part of the myth of suburbia has been deduced from the fact of commuting. For a father, commuting means an extra hour or two away from the family—with debilitating effects upon the relationship between father and children. Sometimes this means that Dad leaves for work before the children are up and comes home after they are put to bed. Naturally, these extra hours put a greater burden upon the mother, and have implications for the relationship between husband and wife.

The commuter returns in the morning to the place where he was bred, for the residents of suburbia are apparently former city people who "escaped" to the suburbs. By moving to suburbia, however, the erstwhile Democrat from the "urban ward"[1] becomes the suburban Republican. The voting shift has been commented on or worried about at length; there seems to be something about suburbia that makes Republicans out of people who were Democrats while they lived in the city. But the political life of suburbia is characterized not only by the voting shift, but by the vigor with which it is carried on. Political *activity* takes its place beside other civic and organizational activity, intense and spirited.

The Sources of the Myth

This brief characterization is intended neither as ethnography nor as caricature, but it does not, I think, misrepresent the image of suburbia that has come to dominate the minds of most Americans, including intellectuals. Immediately, however, a perplexing question arises: why should a group of tract houses, mass produced and quickly thrown up on the outskirts of a large city, apparently generate so unique and distinctive a way of life? What is the logic that links tract living with suburbia as a way of life?

If suburban homes were all within a limited price range, one might expect them to be occupied by families of similar income, and this might account for some of the homogeneity of the neighborhood ethos. But suburban developments are themselves quite heterogeneous. The term "suburbia" has not only been used to refer to tract housing developments as low as $8,000 per unit and as high as

---

[1]William Whyte has a way of making the phrase "urban ward" resound with connotations of poverty, deprivation, soot, and brick—as if "urban ward" were a synonym for "slum."

$65,000 per unit, but also to rental developments whose occupants do not think of themselves as homeowners. The same term has been used to cover old rural towns (such as those in the Westchester-Fairfield County complex around New York City) which, because of the expansion of the city and improvements in transportation, have only gradually become suburban in character. It has been applied also to gradually developing residential neighborhoods on the edges of the city itself. The ecological nature of the suburbs cannot justify so undifferentiated an image as that of "suburbia."

If we limit the image of suburbia to the mass produced tract developments, we might regard the fact of commuting as the link between suburban residence and "suburbanism as a way of life." Clearly, the demands of daily commuting create certain common conditions which might go far to explain some of the ostensible uniformities of suburban living. But certainly commuting is not a unique feature of suburban living: many suburbanites are not commuters, many urban residents are. It may be true that the occupations of most suburbanites presently require a daily trip to and from the central business district of the city, but it is likely to be decreasingly true with the passage of time: The pioneers to the suburban residential frontier have been followed not only by masses of retail trade outlets, but by industry also. Modern mass production technology has made obsolete many two- and three-story plants in urban areas. Today's modern factories are vast one-story operations that require wide expanses of land, which are either unavailable or too expensive in the city itself. With the passage of time, "industrial parks" will increasingly dot suburban areas, and the proportions of suburbanites commuting to the city each day will decrease.

If the occupations of most suburbanites were similar in their demands, then this might help account for the development of a generic way of life. And, indeed, if suburbia were populated largely by Organization Men and their families, or, lacking this, if Organization Men, as Whyte puts it, gave the prevailing *tone* to life in suburbia, then one could more readily understand the prevalence of his model in the writing on suburbia. But there is no real reason to believe this. Perhaps the typical Organization Man is a suburbanite. But it is one thing to assert this and quite another thing to say that the typical tract suburb is populated or dominated by an Organization way of life.

Clearly, then, one suburb (or *kind* of suburb) is likely to differ from

another not only in terms of the cost of its homes, the income of its residents, their occupations and commuting patterns, but also in terms of its educational levels, the character of the region, the size of the suburb, the social and geographical origin of its residents, and countless more indices—all of which, presumably, may be expected to lead to differences in "way of life."

But we not only have good reason to expect suburbs to *differ* markedly from one another; we have reason to expect striking *similarities* between life in urban residential neighborhoods and tract suburbs of a similar social cast. In large cities many men "commute" to work, that is, take subways, buses, or other forms of public transportation to their jobs which may be over on the other side of town. There are thousands of blocks in American cities with rows of identical or similar houses within a limited rental or price range, and presumably occupied by families in a similar income bracket. The same fears for massification and conformity were once felt regarding these urban neighborhoods as are now felt for the mass produced suburbs. Certainly, urban neighborhoods have always had a class character and a "way of life" associated with them. Certainly, too, the whole image of the problem of "conformity" in suburbia closely parallels the older image of the tyranny of gossip in the American small town.

In continually referring to "the myth of suburbia" I do not mean to imply that the reports on the culture of suburban life have been falsified; and it would be a mistake to interpret the tone of my remarks as a debunking one. *I mean only to say that the reports of suburbia we have had so far have been extremely selective.* They are based for the most part, upon life in Levittown, N.Y., Park Forest, Ill., Lakewood, near Los Angeles, and, most recently (the best study so far) a fashionable suburb of Toronto, Canada. The studies that have given rise to the myth of suburbia have been studies of *white collar suburbs* of large cities. If the phrase "middle-class suburb" or "white collar suburb" strikes the eye as redundant, it is testimony to the efficacy of the myth. Large tracts of suburban housing, in many respects indistinguishable from those in Levittown and Park Forest have gone up and are continuing to go up all over the country, not only near large cities, but near middle sized and small ones as well. In many of these tracts, the homes fall within the $12,000 to $16,000 price range, a range well within the purchasing abilities of large numbers of semi-skilled and skilled factory workers in unionized

heavy industry. Many of these working-class people are migrating to these new suburbs—which are not immediately and visibly characterizable as "working class," but which, to all intents and purposes, look from the outside like the fulfillment of the "promise of America" symbolized in the myth. Even more of them will be migrating to new suburbs as increasing numbers of factories move out of the city to the hinterlands. Many of these people are either rural-bred, or urban-working class bred, with relatively little education, and innocent of white collar status or aspiration. And where this is true, as it is in many low-price tracts, one may expect sharp differences between their social and cultural life and that of their more sophisticated counterparts in white collar suburbs.

This should be no surprise; indeed, the fact that it should have to be asserted at all is still further testimony to the vitality of the myth I have been describing. My own research among auto workers in a new, predominantly "working-class" suburb in California demonstrates how far removed their style of life is from that suggested by the myth of suburbia. The group I interviewed still vote 81% Democratic; there has been no "return to religion" among them—more than half of the people I spoke to said they went to church rarely or not at all. On the whole, they have no great hopes of getting ahead in their jobs, and an enormous majority regard their new suburban homes not as a temporary resting place, but as paradise permanently gained. Of the group I interviewed, 70% belonged to not a single club, organization, or association (with the exception of the union), and their mutual visiting or "neighboring" was quite rare except if relatives lived nearby.[2] Let me summarize, then, by saying that the group of auto workers I interviewed has, for the most part, maintained its working class attitudes and style of life in the context of the bright new suburb.

The Functions of the Myth

Similar conditions probably prevail in many of the less expensive suburbs; in any case, semi-skilled "working-class" suburbs probably constitute a substantial segment of the reality of suburban life. Why,

[2]The details of my findings were published in *Working-class Suburb* (Berkeley and Los Angeles: University of California Press, 1960; 2nd ed, with a new introduction, 1968).

then, is the myth still so potent in our popular culture? Suburbia today is a public issue—something to talk about, everywhere from the pages of learned journals to best sellers, from academic halls to smoke-filled political rooms, from the pulpits of local churches to Hollywood production lots.[3]

One source of the peculiar susceptibility of "suburbia" to the manufacture of myth is the fact that a large supply of visible symbols are ready at hand. Picture windows, patios and barbecues, power lawn mowers, the problems of commuting, and the armies of children manning their mechanized vehicles down the sidewalks, are only secondarily facts; primarily they are symbols whose function is to evoke an image of a way of life for the nonsuburban public. These symbols of suburbia can be fitted neatly into the total pattern of the "spirit" of this "age." Suburbia is the locus of gadgetry, shopping centers, and "station wagon culture"; its grass grows greener, its chrome shines brighter, its lines are clean and new and modern. Suburbia is America in its drip-dry Sunday clothes, standing before the bar of history fulfilled, waiting for its judgment. But like Mr. Dooley's court, which kept its eyes on the election returns, the "judgments of history" are also affected by contemporary ideological currents, and the myth of suburbia is enabled to flourish precisely because it fits into the general outlook of at least four otherwise divergent schools of opinion whose function it is to shape the "judgment of history."

To realtor-chamber of commerce defenders of the American Way of Life suburbia represents the fulfillment of the American middle-class dream; it is identified with the continuing possibility of upward mobility, with expanding opportunities in middle-class occupations, with rising standards of living and real incomes, and with the gadg-

---

[3]In the movie version of the novel *No Down Payment*, ostensibly a fictional account of life in the new suburbia, Hollywood makes a pointed comment on social stratification. The sequence of violence, rape, and accidental death is set in motion by the only important character in the story who is not a white-collar man: the rural Tennessee-bred service station manager. Frustrated at being denied the job of police chief (because of his lack of education), he drinks himself into a stupor, rapes his upper-middle-class, college-educated neighbor, and then is accidentally killed (symbolically enough) under the wheels of his new Ford. The film closes with his blonde, nymphomaniacal widow leaving the suburb for good on a Sunday morning, while the white-collar people are seen leaving the Protestant church (denomination ambiguous) with looks of quiet illumination on their faces.

eted good life as it is represented in the full-color ads in the mass circulation magazines.

To a somewhat less sanguine group—for example, architects, city planners, estheticians, and designers—suburbia represents a dreary blight on the American landscape, the epitome of American standardization and vulgarization, with its row upon monotonous row of mass produced cheerfulness masquerading as homes, whole agglomerations or "scatterations" of them masquerading as communities. To these eyes, the new tract suburbs of today are the urban slums of tomorrow.

Third, the myth of suburbia seems important to sociologists and other students of contemporary social and cultural trends. David Riesman says that John R. Seeley et al., the authors of *Crestwood Heights*, "collide like Whyte, with a problem their predecessors only brushed against, for they are writing about *us*, about the professional upper middle class and its businessmen allies. . . . They are writing, as they are almost too aware, about themselves, their friends, their 'type'." There are, obviously, personal pleasures in professionally studying people who are much like oneself; more important, the myth of suburbia conceptualizes for sociologists a microcosm in which some of the apparently major social and cultural trends of our time (other-direction, social mobility, neoconservatism, status anxiety, etc.) flow together, and may be conveniently studied.

Finally, for a group consisting largely of left-wing and formerly left-wing critics of American society, the myth of suburbia provides an up-to-date polemical vocabulary. "Suburb" and "suburban" have replaced the now embarrassingly obsolete "bourgeois" as a packaged rebuke to the whole tenor of American life. What used to be condemned as "bourgeois style," "bourgeois values," and "bourgeois hypocrisy," are now simply designated as "suburban."[4]

But while the myth of suburbia is useful to each of these four groups, it cannot be written off simply as "ruling class propaganda," or as an attempt to see only the sunny side of things, or for that matter, as an attempt to see only the darker side of things—or even as a furtive attempt to peer into a mirror. Too many responsible intellectuals, while uncritically accepting the *myth* of suburbia, are nevertheless extremely critical of what they "see" in it.

---

[4]In 1970, "plastic" seems to be the most common term of general rebuke.

But precisely *what* is it that they see that they are critical of? Is it conformity? status anxiety? chrome? tail fins? gadgetry? gray flannel suits? No doubt, these are symbols powerful enough to evoke images of an enemy. But the nature of this "enemy" remains peculiarly elusive. Surely, there is nothing specifically "suburban" about conformity, status anxiety, and the rest; nor is there anything necessarily diabolical about mass-produced domestic comfort and conservatively cut clothes. It is extraordinary that, with the single exception of William H. Whyte's attempt to trace the "web of friendship" on the basis of the physical structure of the Park Forest "courts," no one, to my knowledge, has come to grips with the problem of defining what is specifically *suburban* about suburbia. Instead, most writers are reduced to the use of hackneyed stereotypes not of suburbia, but of the upper middle class. When most commentators say "suburbia," they really mean "middle class."

The sources of this way of life, however, lie far deeper than mere residence in a suburb. These sources have been much discussed in recent years, most notably perhaps, by Mills, Riesman, Fromm, and Galbraith. They go beyond suburbs to questions of wealth, social status, and corporate organization. Even Whyte's famous discussion of suburbia (upon which so much of the myth is founded) was undertaken in the context of his larger discussion of the Organization Man, a social type created by the structure of corporate opportunity in the United States—something a good deal more profound than the folkways of suburbanites. Seen in this light, suburbia may be nothing but a scapegoat; by blaming "it" for the consequences of our commitment to chrome idols, we achieve ritual purity without really threatening anything or anyone—except perhaps the poor suburbanites, who can't understand why they're always being satirized.

But heaping abuse on suburbia instead of on the classic targets of American social criticism ("success," individual and corporate greed, corruption in high and low places, illegitimate power, etc.) has its advantages for the not-quite-completely-critical intellectual. His critical stance places him comfortably in the great tradition of American social criticism, and at the same time his targets render him respectable and harmless—because, after all, the critique of suburbia is essentially a "cultural" critique; unlike a political or economic one, it threatens no entrenched interests, and contains no direct implications for agitation or concerted action. Indeed, it may be, as Edward Shils has suggested, that a "cultural" critique is all that is possible

today from a left-wing point of view[5]; the American economy and political process stand up fairly well under international comparisons, but American "culture" is fair game for anyone.

Despite the epithets that identify suburbia as the citadel of standardization and vulgarization and conformity, suburbia is also testimony to the fact that Americans are living better than ever before. What needs emphasis is that this is true not only for the traditionally comfortable white collar classes. but for the blue collar, frayed collar, and turned collar classes also. Even families in urban slums are likely to be paying upward of $85 a month in rent these days, and for this or only slightly more, they can "buy" a new tract home in the suburbs. There is an irony, therefore, in the venom that left-wing critics inject into their discussions of suburbia because the criticism of suburbia tends to become a criticism of industrialization, "rationality," and "progress," and thus brings these critics quite close to the classic conservatives, whose critique of industrialization was also made in terms of its cultural consequences. It is almost as if left-wing critics feared the seduction of the working class by pie—not in the sky, not even on the table, but right in the freezer.

What Middle Class?

The "achievement" of suburbia by the working class is a *collective* achievement made possible by prosperity and the labor movement. As such, it does not constitute evidence of individual social mobility. In a prosperous society there occurs not only individual mobility between strata in a relatively stable hierarchy; the entire hierarchy is pushed up by prolonged widespread prosperity and rearranged by changes in the distribution of occupations and income. Systems of social stratification maintain viable, hierarchical distinctions between different categories of people, and when symbols which formerly distinguished rank no longer can, because they have become available to all, we should expect a change in the symbolic aspects of social stratification—if, that is, symbols are to retain the power to make distinctions.

It is perhaps for this reason that in recent years there has been such a relative de-emphasis on economic criteria of stratification in favor of the distinctly cultural ones—that is, those having to do with

[5]See "Daydreams and Nightmares: Reflections on the Criticism of Mass Culture," *Sewanee Review* 65 (Autumn 1957).

style of life. For in a society in which even a semi-skilled factory worker can earn $5000 a year, own two cars, a ranch house, and a TV set, it should perhaps be no surprise that groups with higher prestige (but perhaps without considerably greater income) should defend themselves against the potential threat posed by widespread material abundance to their "prestige" by designating such economic possessions "vulgar" and by asserting the indispensability of a certain style of life—that is, something that cannot be immediately purchased with no down payment. Like universities, which respond to the clamor for higher education by tightening their entrance requirements, prestige groups respond to the clamor by money for prestige by tightening *their* entrance requirements. This has been common enough among aristocratic groups for a long time—money and possessions have rarely been sufficient to admit one to the select circles of old wealth—and the increasingly sharp symbolic distinction between the upper middle class and the lower middle class (not only distinctions of income) suggest that something similar may be occurring on lower levels of society.

Whereas at one time in recent history, the phrase "middle class" evoked images of Sinclair Lewis, Main Street, *The Saturday Evening Post* families of smiling faces around brown-turkeyed dinner tables, and a concern with "respectability," today the phrase is just as likely to evoke images of cocktail parties, country clubs, other-directedness, *The Atlantic Monthly*, and a hypersensitivity to considerations of status. Sociologists recognize this ambiguity by designating the style suggested by the former series of images as "lower" middle class, and the style suggested by the latter series of images as "upper" middle class, and tend to think the issue has been clarified. But the real problem implicit in the terminological need to break the middle class into an upper and a lower stratum is too complex to be solved by a simple linguistic device. The problem is not only one of drawing a line between two contemporary "middle class" styles of life; the immense difference between the life styles of the lower middle class and upper middle class also involves an historical dimension.

Nineteenth century America was a middle-class society in the sense that its typical (if not its statistically modal) individuals were shoestring entrepreneurs; the covers of *The Saturday Evening Post* were testimony to their former hegemony and to the continuing power of the myth they created. Today, we designate the style of those who

follow the lead of the "old" middle class as "lower" middle class in order to make room for the style of the burgeoning "new" middle class, which we designate as "upper" middle class because this latter style is a tailored, truncated version of an older upper-class model emphasizing "taste" and "grace," and made possible—even necessary—by the bright vistas looming before the increasing numbers of college educated people with a promising place in our burgeoning bureaucratic hierarchies. We have no clear images of American "working-class style" precisely because the lowest positions on our socio-economic ladder were traditionally occupied by the most recent groups of European immigrants, each of which, as they arrived, pushed earlier groups of immigrants up. Our images of working-class life, consequently, are dominated by ethnic motifs. But with the end of mass immigration from Europe, it is possible that an indigenous urban working-class culture may develop in the United States in the near future. In its visible manifestations, however, this style is likely to approximate the style of the "old" middle class, for with the gradual disappearance of shopkeepers as a significant stratum in American economic life, the organized, well-paid, industrial workers have apparently taken over the style of the "old" middle class, *without*, however, inheriting the mantle of social mobility.

It is only in this sense that America can be called a middle-class society and, to be sure, a substantial minority of the people I interviewed identified themselves as "middle class." But our society approves of this usage as synonomous with "homeowner," or "respectable standard of living"; and the myth of suburbia itself may reinforce the propensity to identify oneself with "America" because America is increasingly characterized in the mass media as a "middle-class society" and the new suburbs are submitted as strong evidence of this. "Anybody with a steady job and income is middle class," one of my respondents told me, and certainly this is true if we conceive of lower middle-class people as upper middle-class people with slightly lower incomes. For although it is true that these suburbanites I studied do have only slightly lower incomes than a young insurance salesman or a junior engineer, it illumines nothing to call them middle class because their style (whether it be designated as lower middle class or working class) is a *terminal* one; they live in the present, mostly in the solid, respectable style their income permits, but mobility is something that is possible only for their children. With a house in the suburbs, two cars, a TV set, a wife

and two children, and many "major" and "minor" kitchen appliances, one respondent, explaining why he didn't want to be a foreman, said "I'm a working man; I don't like to be sitting down or walking up and down all the time." Another, explaining why he quit being a foreman after six months, said, "I got nothing against guys in white shirts, but I just ain't cut out for work like that." These are the statements of working-class (or, if one insists, lower middle-class) men, who, because of prosperity and the labor movement have been able to achieve a material standard of living never before possible on any large scale for manual workers. But the element of social mobility is missing; aspiration and anticipation as well as "status anxiety" and "conformity" are things for educated people with a fluid position in an organizational hierarchy, and it is the lack of this which makes suburban domesticity in a $12,000 house a *final* fulfillment.

Nothing I have said about suburbs gives us the right to doubt the truth of what many observers have said about places like Park Forest and Levittown. I do, however, question the right of others to generalize about "suburbia" on the basis of a few studies of selected suburbs whose representative character has yet to be demonstrated. It is remarkable how, despite the efflorescence of the mass produced suburbs in post-World War II America, references to "suburbia" more often than not cite the examples of Park Forest and Levittown—as if these two communities could represent a nationwide phenomenon that has occurred at all but the very lowest income levels and among most occupational classifications. If "suburbia" is anything at all unique, we'll never know it until we have a lot more information about a lot more suburbs than we now, unfortunately, have.

Suburbs, Subcultures, and Styles of Life

Problems of Cultural Pluralism   1965
in Urban America

Several times over the past four and a half years (since, that is, my book on Suburbs was published), I have been asked to give public lectures with titles like "Has Suburbia Created a New American?" or "Is there a Suburban Style of Life?" Until recently, however, I always declined these invitations because I could not imagine taking an hour or more to answer the questions. In a Steigian dream of glory, I would rise before a distinguished audience assembled to hear me, and say simply, "No, suburbia has not created a new American," or "No, there is no single suburban style of life," and then sit down to wait for questions from an audience stunned by the daring of my brevity.

Terseness, however, is not the sociologist's virtue, and rather than a flat no it would be more accurate to say that I know of no evidence that should lead anyone seriously to believe that suburbia *has* created a new American or a new style. But I want to make a stronger statement than that, for I cannot even conceive of any *logic*

Prepared for the Washington University Conference on Planning for the Quality of Urban Life, March 1965. Shorter versions of this essay have been published in *The Public Interest* (Winter 1966) and in Sam Warner, ed., *Planning for a Nation of Cities* (Cambridge: M.I.T. Press, copyright 1966). Reprinted with the permission of the M.I.T. Press.

that should have led one seriously to entertain even the *possibility* that suburbia (whatever *that* is) is a profound enough fact of life to be credited (or discredited—depending on one's point of view) with the creation of a "new American"—whatever *that* is. Having said this, I shall not now sit down to wait for questions; instead, I shall tell you at some length what has led me to this conclusion; why the conclusion, though necessary, leaves me unsatisfied and disturbed; and finally, the thoughts about subcultures and styles of life evoked by this unease.

Social Character and Social Change

When intellectuals speak of new styles of life, or, more specifically, new social types (e. g., a "new American"), I assume that what they mean is something in the way of a radically transformed character structure or "modal personality"—something perhaps kin to the "other-directed" character which David Riesman originally attributed to changes in the economic and demographic structure of our society. Or to the kinds of distinctive (or allegedly distinctive) mentalities referred to by phrases like "Soviet man," or "industrial man," or "urban man." Or to C. Wright Mills' characterization of labor leaders as "new men of power," or to C. P. Snow's reference to recent additions to the British elite as "new men," or perhaps even to post-Nietzscheian "existential man" who, affirming the death of God, has looked into the abyss of Nothing to come away with an ability to find comfort only in irony and expertise about the absurd.

In general, "new" types of men appear on the historical scene either as a response to far-reaching changes in social structure which eventually affect a society's child-rearing practices (as has been persuasively argued by David McClelland in his book *The Achieving Society*): or as a result of sudden historical discontinuities created by wars, revolutions, colossal natural disasters, and the like, which require a radical adaptation to new conditions of existence; or through vast and unprecedented opportunities which "old" types of men are for a variety of reasons unable to exploit. In these senses, it would perhaps be reasonable to speak of new types of men appearing on the historical scene in the commercial medieval cities, which were insulated from the rural social structure of feudalism, or of new types of men engendered by the Protestant reformation's redefinition of the relation of the individual to God, or of the new types of men

whose recruitment to prominent historical statuses was made possible by the virtually limitless economic opportunities created by industrialism, and made necessary by the traditional aristocracy's disdain of "trade," which inhibited them from exploiting these opportunities. A new man is also implicit in the French version of the rags to riches story, best exemplified in life by the figures of Rousseau and Napoleon, and in literature by Stendhal's Julien Sorel—all self-made, socially mobile men (as we say today), picaresque and tragic heroes of modern society.

In this broad historical frame, the very question of whether suburbia has created a new American sounds enormously trivial. But even if we narrow our perspectives to recent American history and to relatively familiar American types, we cannot endow the question with very much more dignity. For if we try to brush aside for the moment, the myths, the legends, the distortions, the comforting fictions to which we as a nation are no more immune than any other (and considerably less so than many, since our mass media are so powerful and our insulation against them so fragile), and ask ourselves with as fresh a mind as we can muster what it is in the American experience that best accounts for such apparent changes in our culture and personality (and I put it this weakly because it is a matter of some contemporary dispute whether major changes have in fact occurred[1]), we find ourselves involved in the analysis of major social institutions—surely no great surprise to a sociologist. Major changes in the structure of economic opportunity, the widespread diffusion of higher education, the state of permanent political and military crisis since the end of the Second World War all affect social character through, for example, their impact upon the decline of ascetic Puritanism; the physical and then psychological metropolitanization of the population; and the gradual infiltration and then the sudden *coup* of the collective imaginative life by advertising and the mass media, which have wrought a revolution on all levels of culture by at one and the same time providing the masses with the major source of their entertainment and the upper classes with the major source of the macabre, satiric revolution of the absurd which has recently dominated most of the higher arts from drama to painting to the

[1]Talcott Parsons and S. M. Lipset are among those influential sociologists who have committed themselves publicly to the idea that there have been no changes in basic American values since colonial times. See *Culture and Society: the Work of David Riesman Reviewed*, ed. Seymour Martin Lipset and Leo Lowenthal (New York: Free Press, 1961).

novel to music to American stand-up comedy. And the accumulated effects of these changes converge and lodge, finally, in the family, where the incipient shape of the next generation can be observed— previewed is perhaps the apt metaphor. But whatever the disagreements that exist regarding the qualities or magnitudes of influence exercised by these institutions, I want to emphasize that there is virtually *no respectable intellectual ground* I can think of for even entertaining as a moderately plausible hypothesis that simple residence in a mass produced tract of new houses can wreak profound changes in character and style of life.

The Myth of Suburbia

I should, of course, admit that this, which seems so obvious to me today, did not seem at all obvious to me late in the 1950s when I undertook to interview a hundred families of suburbanites who happened to be blue collar employees of the Ford Motor Company. (But, then, the obvious tends to become so only by being apprehended and clearly stated). Having read *Time, Life, Fortune, Harper's* and other popular magazines which showed interest in the new suburbs before social science did, it seemed obvious (since no one had taken the trouble to observe that it was not obvious at all) that there was indeed something about suburbia which transformed men and women into the figures which these magazines described.

Surely I need not repeat the characterization; in spite of research, it is still the "official" version of the suburbanite: a well educated middle-management man, anxious, a joiner, neighborly, conforming; and his wife, absorbed with Spock, Gesell, and ballet lessons for the children. In this age of rapid superannuation, the image is hoary by now. But in the middle of the 1950s it all seemed to make obvious sense, and it seemed to me that my extraordinary good luck in finding a working-class population more than two years settled in a new suburban setting (without any other major changes in their life conditions) provided an almost natural experimental setting in which to document the processes through which suburbia exercised its profound and diffuse influence in transforming a group of factory workers and their families into those model middle-class Americans obsessed with the problems of crab-grass.

Well, it is now a matter of public record that my basic assumption was wrong. As the interview evidence piled up, it became clearer and clearer that the lives of the suburbanites I was studying had not been profoundly affected in any statistically identifiable or sociologically

interesting way. They were still overwhelmingly Democrats; they attended church as infrequently as they ever did; like most working-class people, their informal contacts were limited largely to kin; they neither gave nor went to parties. On the whole they had no great hopes of getting ahead in their jobs, and instead of having a transient psychology, most of them viewed their new suburban homes as paradise permanently gained.

But I was cautious in the general inferences I drew from that study. It was, after all, based only on a small sample, of one suburb, of one metropolitan area, in one region, and it suffered from all of the methodological limitations inherent in small case studies. None of my findings gave me any reason to doubt the truth of what William F. Whyte, for example, had said of his Organization Men, but it also seemed to me that there was little reason *not* to believe that my findings in San Jose would be repeatedly confirmed in many of the less expensive suburbs around the country whose houses were priced well within the means of unionized workers in heavy industry, and lower white collar employees as well. I did, in short, question the right of others to generalize freely about suburbia on the basis of very few studies of selected suburbs which happened to be homogeneously middle or upper middle class in character—especially when it seemed apparent that suburban housing was increasingly available to all but the lowest income levels and status groups.

The considerable bulk of research that has been done on suburbs in the years since I did my own work has given me no reason to alter the conclusions I drew then; quite the contrary, it has strenghtened those conclusions. Today, in addition to my own study of a working-class suburb, William Whyte's study of transient middle-class suburbs, and Seeley's study of Crestwood Heights (a stable, older upper middle-class suburb), we have Herbert Gans' study of predominantly lower middle-class Levittown, Pennsylvania, S. D. Clark's survey of a variety of suburbs around Toronto, Scott Greer's study of a Negro suburb of St. Louis, Charles Tilly's suburban work around Wilmington, Delaware, and the studies of William Dobriner and John Liell of Levittown, New York[2]—Liell being the first I know

[2]John R. Seeley et al., *Crestwood Heights: A Study of the Culture of Suburban Life* (New York: Basic Books, 1957); Herbert J. Gans, *The Levittowners: Ways of Life and Politics in a New Suburban Community* (New York: Pantheon, 1967); Samuel D. Clark, *Suburban Society* (Toronto: University of Toronto Press, 1966); John T. Liell, "Levittown: A Study in Community Development and Planning," unpublished PhD dissertation (Yale University, 1952) and "Social Relationships in a Changing Suburb," a paper presented at the 1963 Annual Meeting of the American Sociological Association.

of to study a suburb over time (shortly after its founding in 1951 and again in 1960). A Master's thesis at Berkeley a few years ago replicated my own study, and largely confirmed its findings. With the cooperation of the National Opinion Research Center at the University of Chicago, and the Survey Research Center at the University of Michigan, research is now going beyond case studies to get generalizations about suburbia based upon national samples of population broken down in terms of place of residence.

I want to emphasize that none of this research can be expected to give much comfort to those who find it convenient to believe that the suburbs exercise some mysterious power over their residents to transform them into replicas of Whyte's practitioners of "The Outgoing Life." There seems to be increasing consensus among students of suburbia that suburban development is simply the latest phase of a process of urban growth that has been going on for a long time, that the cultural character of suburbs varies widely in terms of the social make-up of its residents and the personal and group dispositions that led them to move to suburbs in the first place; that the variety of physical and demographic differences between cities and suburbs (and there *are* some) bears little significance for the way of life of their inhabitants; and that some of these differences, although statistically accurate, are sociologically spurious, since the appropriate comparisons are not between suburbs and cities as wholes, but between suburbs and urban residential neighborhoods. The high degree of order that was asserted as characteristic of suburbia was a reflection of highly ordered suburbs that were selected for study, and in general the reported changes in the lives of suburbanites were not caused by the move to suburbia, but were the reasons for moving there in the first place. In suburbs, as in city apartments, the degree of sociability is determined not primarily by ecological location but by the homogeneity of the population (although as Whyte indicated, the particular flow patterns of sociability may be affected by the specific locations of domicile). Social class, the age-composition of residents, and the age of the neighborhood are much more profound predictors of style of life than is residential location with respect to city limits. Transient attitudes (if they were there to begin with) apparently decline with the increasing age of the suburb, as the neighborhood settles into the style of life determined largely by its dominant social and demographic characteristics, a settling sim-

plified by the economic homogeneity of specific suburban housing tracts. Analysis of national samples has provided confirmation of neither a trend to Republicanism in politics nor a return to religion. Suburbs, in short, seem, as Leonard Reissmen and Tom Ktsanes characterized them, "New Homes for Old Values."

There are, then, if I may repeat it once more, no grounds for believing that suburbia has created a distinctive style of life or a new social character for Americans. Yet the myth of suburbia persists, as is evident from the fact that it is still eminently discussable over the whole range of our cultural media, from comic books to learned journals. Myths are seldom dispelled by research; they have going for them something considerably more powerful than mere evidence. And although nothing I say here can change this fact, it may give us some comfort to understand the sources of the myth, the functions it performs for the groups by whom it is sustained, and the nature of its appeal to America's image of itself.

In my book, and again in an article, I undertook a functional explanation of the myth of suburbia which I thought—and still think—was pretty good, although then, as now, there is still a good deal about it that puzzles and disturbs me. I pointed first to the fact that suburbs were rich with ready made visible symbols—patios and barbecues, lawnmowers and tricycles, shopping centers, station wagons, and so on—and that such symbols were readily organizable into an image of a way of life that could be marketed to the non-suburban public. I also pointed out that this marketing was facilitated by the odd fact that the myth of suburbia conveniently suited the ideological purposes of several influential groups who market social and political opinion, odd because these groups could usually be found disagreeing with each other not only about matters of opinion but about matters of fact as well. Realtor–chamber of commerce interests and the range of opinion represented by the Luce magazines could use the myth of suburbia to affirm the American Way of Life; city planners, architects, urban design people, and so on could use the myth of suburbia to warn that suburbs would become the urban slums of tomorrow. Liberal and left-wing culture-critics could—and did—use the myth of suburbia to launch an attack on complacency, conformity, and mass culture, and found in the myth of suburbia an up-to-date polemical vocabulary with which to rebuke the whole slick tenor of American life. In short, the *descriptive* accuracy of the

myth of suburbia went largely unchallenged because it suited the *prescriptive* desires of such a wide variety of opinion, from the yea sayers of the Right to the agonizers of the Center to the nay sayers of the Left.

But although I still think this makes very good sense, I think too that there is something more, something, if I may be permitted to say so, deeper, profounder, and which I was only dimly aware of then. "Suburbia," I wrote "is America in its drip-dry Sunday clothes, standing before the bar of history, fulfilled, waiting for its judgment." I suspect now that when I wrote this I was less interested in understanding the full significance of what I felt to be true than I was in simply turning a fancy phrase. But I see now that the myth of suburbia, i.e. the notion that Suburbia *is* America, is our society's most recent attempt to come to terms with the melting pot problem, a problem that goes straight to the heart of the American ambivalence about cultural pluralism.

Cultural Pluralism and the Melting Pot

America has never really come to terms with the legend of the melting pot. That legend, if I may quote the windy prose of its original source, saw America as the place where "Celt and Latin, Slav and Teuton, Greek and Syrian, Black and Yellow, Jew and Gentile, the palm and the pine, the pole and the equator, the crescent and the cross" would together build "the Republic of Man and the Kingdom of God."[3] Despite the hope that a unified American culture might emerge from the seething cauldron, it didn't happen; instead, ghettos and other ethnically homogeneous communities helped the immigrants preserve large segments of their cultures, and the tendency to endogamy helped them preserve it beyond the first generation. But in spite of the evident facts of our cultural pluralism, attempts are continually made to create an image of *the* typical or genuine or representative American or his community, attempts which have succeeded only in creating stereotypes—usually a caricature of one or another variety of Our Town, white, Anglo-Saxon, protestant, and middle class. Saturday Evening Post covers, white picket fences, clapboard houses, maple hutches and such have historically played

[3]Israel Zangwill, *The Melting Pot* (New York: Macmillan, 1909).

an important role in such attempts. The myth of suburbia is the latest attempt to render America in this homogeneous manner, to see in the highly visible and proliferating suburbs a new melting pot which would receive the diverse elements from a society fragmented by class, region, religion, and ethnicity, and from them create *the* American style of life. Suburbia as America is no falser a picture than Babbitt or Our Town as America, but it fails as a melting pot for the same reason that the original idea failed: suburbs became ghettoes, this time segregated not primarily by ethnicity, (although many new suburbs do have a distinct ethnic cast), but by income and social class.

Indeed, it is hard to see how a unified national culture could even be imagined as a distinct reality, for until quite recently the United States was a society without very powerful *national* institutions. Without an Established church or a powerful Federal government, without national political parties or a standardized educational system, with enormous distances and poor communications, local customs and local economies were able to breed a highly differentiated system of native subcultures—in addition to those created by the immigrants. The fact, of course, is that even today there are literally dozens of distinctive American styles: Vermont farmers and Boston Brahmins, Southern Bourbons and Tennessee hillbillies, Gary steelworkers and Jewish garment workers, Beatniks and Organization Men, Plainvillers, Middletowners, and cosmopolitan intellectuals, to say nothing of teen-agers, the jet set, and many, many more—all American, all different, and none probably very eager to be integrated into a conceptualization of "American" at a level of complexity suitable for a patriotic movie.

It is not surprising, then, that when one tries to abstract from American life a system of values which can be called representatively American, the task is immensely difficult. The most ambitious attempt by a sociologist, that of Robin Williams in his book *American Society*, fails because important groups in American life do not share the fifteen or sixteen values which he offers as basically American. There is no question that values such as "achievement," "success," "work," "efficiency," "equality," "secular rationality" and the rest have played an important part in creating the quality of American life, but important parts of the lower and working class (important because of their numbers) do not share them, and important parts of the

upper class (important because of their influence) do not share them. This is not the place to document in detail the sources of indifference or outright resistance to the American values discussed by Williams, but upon examination these values turn out to be the ones that characterize the great middle mass of the American population—a group whose values certainly deserve to be called American, but not at the cost of exiling the values of those at the very top and the very bottom.

The Viability of Subcultures

The most durable and effective subcultures in the United States have been the ones which combined class, ethnic, and religious factors to create a symbolically enclosed community. This fact has been most visible with regard to recent immigrants: an ethnic status, a lower-class job, a personal church, a local politics, a residential neighborhood composed of one's own "kind" provides most of the necessary conditions for the maintenance of a way of life. A subculture, that is to say, is made viable by its ability to enclose the lives of its members, and this is made possible by a kind of quasi-territory over which the group's authorities can successfully claim hegemony through a set of institutions which sustain its implicit values by facilitating the activities which constitute the style of life and discouraging the one's that threaten it. A completely successful subculture encloses the life of the person by providing a framework of institutions which minimize the necessity for him to go outside of that framework to find what he regards as a "full life." Jews in the ghetto, of course, are the classic example of what I have in mind. There are other examples: The Amish represent perhaps even more thoroughly than ghetto Jews the extent to which a subculture can be maintained in a relatively hostile environment so long as the territorial and institutional conditions are met. Similarly, an upper-class, aristocratic subculture can be maintained in a hostile demo-cratic environment to the extent that it goes on in places (territories) others can't afford to enter and to the extent that it is *enclosed* by a system of exclusive institutions—from school, club, college and church, through special courting and kinship institutions which pro-mote endogamy, to careers in strategic sectors of the economy. But these are all matters of degree. The important thing to remember is

that a subculture is made viable *to the extent that* territorial and institutional factors (the conditions are variables) provide sustenance and support to its norms, insulate the members of the group from outside pressures, and hence discourage, forestall, or minimize defection, i.e. mobility.[4]

Groups whose basic values and style of life are to some extent distinctive but which fall severely short of providing their members with an enclosed institutional environment are exposed to strains and pressures which threaten the integrity (and eventually the continuation) of the subculture. Even so traditionally viable a group as the Amish are periodically threatened by demands of local authorities that their children remain in school beyond the eighth grade. Bohemian subculture is continually threatened because of its meager institutional support and the consequent rapid turnover of its population. Were it not for the quasi-territoriality of urban Bohemias (the Greenwich Villages of the world *belong*, in a sense to bohemians; that they *are* Bohemias suggests both their economic role and the source of their toleration by dominant urban authorities) and their attractiveness to the young, the subculture would be still more fragile and continually threatened than it is. Some urban delinquent gangs provide another example of groups whose subculture is precariously maintained in spite of its institutional vulnerability. Like bohemians, certain delinquent gangs survive periodic police harrassment. The survival of their deviant subculture is achieved with the help and support of the deviant institutions of the slum, and the proverbial emphasis of delinquents on the importance of their authority over "turf" may well be their own way of recognizing their own need for territoriality. (I should add that the tenacity of the subculture is in part a function of the less than enthusiastic attempts to recruit delinquents into the dominant culture.)

[4]At this point, one runs into the melting pot problem again if, as I have suggested, the maintenance of a genuine cultural pluralism requires the kind of *segrgeation* implied in my emphasis on territoriality and institutional enclosure. When the walls come tumbling down, there is no question but that culture contact, borrowing, and diffusion occur, but the experience of anthropologists indicates that the borrowed elements are absorbed in such a way to make them homogeneous with what they join. The pot has not exactly melted, but things do run into one another: pizza is created from English muffins, kosher salami is washed down with milk, and the bleeding madras has a button down collar. Distinctive ethnic and other subgroup motifs are visible but they infrequently warrant the fulness and consistency suggested by the term subculture.

The precariousness of the subcultures and the instability of the subgroups which exist without territorial and institutional support are of two sorts. They are vulnerable to institutional penetration from outside, as when local authorities compel the Amish to continue their children in school or a bohemian to shave off his beard or a teen-ager to trim his long hair. But there is also a threat to personality represented by the necessity of the participant in a subculture to go "outside" for some needs, and hence to "pass," that is to regularly seem to be what he is not; he must pass through some parts of the institutional environment in a sociological disguise, and under such conditions is probably most vulnerable to seduction or recruitment.

To speak excusively of the conditions for the viability of subcultures, however, may be misleading because it suffers from a static bias; it leaves out of consideration the dynamic character of the subculture itself. I think this can be brought into the theory I am offering by conceiving subcultures as patterns of norms with distinctive competences and limitations, norms which enable their adherents to cope with certain exigencies, to undertake certain activities, to move in certain directions, to create certain personal and collective styles. But culture patterns which enable in some respects, disable in other respects—an insight made excellent use of by Veblen, Dewey, Kenneth Burke, and many others. "The poor pedestrian abilities of the fish are explainable in terms of his excellence as a swimmer."[5] To conceive subcultures, then, with a kind of double vision, as enabling or adaptive for some contexts and eventualities and disabling or abrasive for others, provides us with a systematic vocabulary for analyzing subcultural dynamics and hence discourages the excessive sentimentality implicit in the transparent fondness or hostility characteristic of many ethnographies with a moral point to make.

Thus, the bias inherent in a sentimental description of the solidarity of the Jewish family and the psychological advantages it provides is corrected somewhat by Bruno Bettelheim's criticism of Anne Frank's family, where a little less solidarity might have let them survive. Under conditions of Nazi persecution, the desire to remain together meant to be slain together, when, separated they might have escaped. Or, as William F. Whyte made clear a long time ago, the cultivation of warm and loyal feelings to the persons and places

[5]Kenneth Burke, *Permanence and Change*, 2d rev. ed. (Los Altos, Calif.: Hermes, 1954).

of one's childhood and adolescence may nourish the spirit, but impedes social mobility—if social mobility means, as it often does, geographical removal. We need not even go back as far as Whyte. In his paper for this conference, Marc Fried suggests that the homogeneous working-class neighborhood is a way of providing a familiar and stable context for new recruits to the industrial work force. As they go through the several crises of adaptation to the industrial environment (from the learning of basic working-class roles to the "occupational morality" of the middle class), formerly peasant psychologies are provided with a measure of security by the stability and familiarity of the homogeneous neighborhood. Lee Rainwater's paper, on the other hand, emphasizes not the evolutionary or transitional character of lower-class life, but the distinctive culture that the lower class develops, and which provides the material for distinctive identities. These "expressive" identities (as he calls them), in turn, are likely to impede mobility, however psychologically compensatory they are for the deprivations which are suffered. For Rainwater, the distinctive culture of the lower class (particularly the Negro lower class) facilitates the the achievement of certain benefits and satisfactions but obstructs the achievement of others. That Rainwater's Negro cats are poor climbers may be partially explained in terms of their excellence as swingers.

Social Class, Occupation, and Style of Life

Now, with the decline (though by no means the disappearance) of ethnicity as a major source of subcultural differentiation (the ghetto may be a Miami Beach as well as the Bronx, a new suburb of St. Louis as well as the Lower East Side of New York), where can we look for new sources? Occupation and social class are the most likely candidates.[6] American culture actually has been a loose congeries of subcultures based upon various combinations of regionalism, religion, ethnicity, and social class, subcultures maintained through the relative *isolation* from each other of the groups that bore

---

[6]Age-grading is also an important candidate. The facts that the young stay in school longer and the old retire earlier create at both ends of the life cycle longer periods of age-graded homogeneity. The "teen-age" culture and the retirement community are composed of those who, pushed out of the mainstream by the exigencies of advanced industrial life, form their own cultural eddies—bucolic, aristocratic, dyonisian—not usually instrumental.

them, but *related to* one another through the political and economic structures and accommodations characteristic of urban life. But large scale immigration from Europe has ceased, our religions are increasingly at peace with each other, regionalism has declined everywhere and even in the South is under sharp attack, and the latest phases of urban development (residential, commercial, and industrial suburbanization, the redevelopment of central business districts, the destruction of ethnic neighborhoods) have been breaking down the barriers which sustained cultural pluralism. The result is curious: as the culture seems less differentiated, the social structure seems more so. Occupation increasingly becomes the single most important differentiating factor in group life; as occupations become more specialized, more skilled, more complex, more arcane, more *differentiated*, one might have expected that the differentiation of economic interest and function would carry with it corresponding differentiations in style of life. Instead, what seems to be occurring is that the cultures of the occupationally most differentiated strata (professional, executive, white collar, members of large organizations) are becoming increasingly homogeneous, whereas the cultural gap widens between the prosperous middle classes and the young, the poor, the primitive, the isolated, and the dying: the unamerican.

I would like to use this double perspective to analyze some of the difference between middle-class and lower-class occupations as they bear upon differences in leisure and style of life. There exists a relatively large body of data which documents the variety of ways in which large segments of the urban working class and the poor constitute culturally separate strata, i.e., do not share the dominant values of the middle classes. In addition to the indifference or open hostility of large segments of the lower strata to the "dominant values" discussed by Williams, there is the well documented "alienation from work" of assembly line workers and the even more severe alienations of the strata lower than that. Although we know a good deal about the demoralization and other deprivations concomitant with alienated work, we know considerably less about the mitigating or compensatory factors which apparently help make it tolerable. Let us note some of them.

First of all, moral norms in the society about the desirability of "meaningful" or otherwise status-conferring work are such that alienated workers are likely to have collective sympathies (certainly those

of the intellectuals) on their side; no negative moral sanction is attached to alienation from monotonous assembly line work, because no right thinking American could reasonably be expected to get satisfactions from such work.[7] One consequence of this is that the alienated worker from the lower strata is not *doubly* punished by being not only alienated but *blamed* for (and hence guilty about) being alienated. Quite the contrary; one respects the desire of the alienated worker to leave his job at the factory gate, to forget it after 5 o'clock. His wish to completely dissociate his work life from his family and leisure life sems not only sensible but functional as well: it restores him for the next day's work. If he feels, and says, with evident distaste that his work is "just a living," or "just a job," the public is not likely to regard his lack of enthusiasm as a *moral* failing. The sharp separation between work and leisure in the lower class is a condition which permits the lower class, in its leisure, to develop the expressive life styles and the dramatic selves that Lee Rainwater analyzes. But the viability of these selves is dependent upon their *irrelevance* to alienated work; the "personality" of manual workers is "their own" *because* it is not an important factor in their work. I emphasize these perhaps "positive" aspects of alienated work not out of any desire to sentimentalize it or to recommend it to those who would escape the rat race,[8] but to illustrate how the fact that some work is manual and alienated is related to the distinctive personalities and styles of life developed by such workers. The relation between occupation and style of life is mediated by the variability of the relevance of personality.

Compare with this, now, that large mid-section of the population which includes the still ambitious sectors of the lower class, through the aspirant semi-professions, to physicians, lawyers, professors, and so on: strata symbolized well enough by the brief case or attaché case. In the present context, the brief case is above all a symbol of work that can be taken home, and is thus a symbol of the erasure of the line between work and nonwork. The brief case is an announcement that its carrier, unlike the manual worker, but like

[7]Since his alienation is not "his fault," the lower-class worker is under little or no pressure to hide his feelings—which may account somewhat for higher rates of admitted alienation among assembly line workers in surveys.
[8]Although it is interesting to observe that bohemians prefer earning their livings through alienated work which allows them their personalities, to the kinds of jobs which require personal commitments.

the President of the United States, is a man who works at home. To the extent that effective or successful performance in executive or professional occupations involves not only actually working at home but also obligations concerning dinners, parties, civic participation, golf, and so on, work becomes continuous with, sometimes indistinguishable from, leisure. To the extent that bureaucratization continues increasingly to define the conditions of a professional or executive life which no longer ends at the office door, leisure (and hence style of life) tends to become increasingly instrumentalized. The interpenetration of home and job, work and nonwork, creates a milieu which requires increasingly personal commitment from its members. The personality or "self" of the professional or executive is *not* just "his own business": as an essential ingredient of his business or profession, his personal style is always relevant to his work. Unlike the alienated manual worker, he is not free to develop expressive identities independent of—and perhaps in compensation for—the well advertised tensions of the executive life.

If an executive or professional should have the bad luck to feel alienated from his work, the strains implied in the situation described above are exacerbated. There is no question that alienation from work occurs in the more prestigious occupations, but again, unlike manual labor, there are strong constraints against expressing dissatisfaction with economic roles which the culture defines as highly desirable: one must not be ungrateful. To be dissatisfied with a lower-class job is eminently American—almost patriotic. But to be unhappy in a high prestige occupation is an insult to the value system, threatens its validity, and compounds the anxieties of the ambitious. Were the physician or lawyer or clergyman to say of his profession "it's a job, it's a living," public morality would be outraged; faith in the merit and dedication of men of high achievement would be undermined. Unlike the assembly line worker, the professional man is expected to be pious about the "meaningfulness" of his work. If he feels alienated from it, it is likely that he will be doubly punished by being *blamed* for his alienation. His alienation from work will express not only a moral failing but an error of sociological observation as well. For to the extent that his effective work performance requires participation in a whole style of life, his work is objectively *not* "just a job"; it is a life, a life that takes its dominant motifs from the constraints engendered by a social system rather than from the person's own expressive needs. Since personal fulfillment at these

occupational levels is expected to come *through* work, less obligation is felt to honor the satisfaction of expressive needs through an
autonomous leisure.[9]

Cultural Myths and Styles of Life

But there is, finally an irreducible sense in which a style of life is a
myth, and this will bring me back to the still disturbing question
of suburbia. The very idea must ultimately anchor itself to the particular patterns which behavorial regularities form, or to perceived
consistencies or affinities in tone and feeling which pervade a
variety of apparently disparate actions. But a "style" of life is always
to some extent a distortion, a stereotype, first because there are as
many styles as one's perspective directs one to find, and second,
because the styles one finds are always *modal*, and hence distort by
neglect the patterns that occur at more extreme places in the range
of variability. Even under "natural" conditions, then, a pattern of
culture, a style of life, is enormously difficult to describe with salutary accuracy. But a curious thing happens when a society becomes
self-conscious about its culture and rich enough to do something
about it. The maturity and the luxury of our civilization constrains
its elites to define an "American" style, and the miracle of our technology arms us to manufacture it. Our society is wealthy enough to
support a substantial class of intellectuals devoted to staying on top
of contemporary events (from the grossnesses of politics to the pre-
ciosities of art) to "spot the trend," "see the pattern," "find the
meaning," "discover the style." And our media are such that these
spottings and seeings are more or less instantaneously communicated
to audiences of millions, poised to receive and pass on the cues of
their intellectual leaders.[10]

[9]It is perhaps unnecessary for me to add that not all executive and professional occupations are like the one I have described, just as not all lower-
class occupations evoke the kind of expressive identities Rainwater describes.
To the extent that an occupation is a tie which binds persons to a community, the line between work and leisure blurs. This is most typical of
certain bureaucratized professions but not exclusive to them. As Seymour
Lipset has shown, for reasons intrinsic to their work, skilled printing workers
maintain a vital community which reaches far beyond the shops in which
they work. See Lipset et al., *Union Democracy* (Glencoe, Ill.: Free Press, 1956).
[10]Like the TV audience, whose demand to be continually entertained is greater
than the nation's resources of drama, comedy, and music, the increasing

Under such conditions, we certainly do not get serious historical interpretation of contemporary events; we do not even get responsible journalism; we get myth. Under the pressures of deadline, the ephemerality of topical chic, the limitations of time and what the sponsor and the audience will tolerate, the *Time* cover story, the CBS Report, the NBC White Paper, the pot-boiling best seller, the column by James Reston provide us with more or less coherent syntheses of more or less incoherent events, with diagnoses of what is not yet clear—with myths, which themselves become part of the forces shaping what is happening, and which hence function ideologically. Myths are more or less noble fictions; fictions in the sense that they are *made,* and more or less noble depending upon the extent to which we are in favor of the consequences they foster, or the kind of solidarity they promote. What is often at stake is, *whose* version of America shall become "American."

The myth of suburbia fosters an image of a happy, homogeneous America, without ethnicity. The American family of the full color Sunday supplement (spouses, children of both sexes—the children of the American suburban family are never all boys or all girls) makes full use of the marvelous productivity of American industry: the ranch house with the two car garage, the used brick fireplace and the sliding glass door to the concrete patio; the refrigerator and the freezer, the washer and the dryer, the garbage disposal and the built-in range and dishwasher, the color TV and the hi-fi stereo. Suburbia, its lawns trim, its driveways without oil stains, its children happy on its curving streets and in its pastel schools; suburbia, California style, is America.

Most American intellectuals have found this myth repugnant, but the bases of their antipathy have never really been made clear. Somehow associated with these physical symbols of suburbia in the minds of the intellectuals are complacency, smugness, conformity, status anxiety, and all the rest of the by now familiar and dreary catalogue of suburban culture.[11] But the causal connection between the physical character and the alleged cultural style of suburbia has

---

numbers of the literate exert constant demands for sense and coherence on the marketers of opinion and interpretation.

[11] The success of books like *No Down Payment, The Crack in the Picture Window*, and *The Split-Level Trap,* which sensationalize the "under side" of suburban life suggests that there are other opinion markets with prurient and debunking interests in suburbia.

never been clearly established. It is almost as if, like severe old Calvinist prophets, American intellectuals felt that physical comfort necessarily meant intellectual sloth. Perhaps it is because we have been too well trained to believe that there is somehow a direct relationship between the physical structure or the esthetic shape of a residential environment and the possible sorts of values and culture it can engender—so that the esthetic monotony of suburbia could house nothing but a generation of dull, monotonous people, and its cheerful poverty of architectural design could breed nothing but a race of happy robots. The only trouble with this view is that there is little evidence and less logic to support it. The suburbanites were, at least according to the myth, *urban* bred. And although it is a little too early yet to tell what kind of culture will be produced by the generation bred in the manufactured environment of suburbia, we will have small complaint if it is as fertile and as vital as the culture produced by the generation bred amidst the manufactured ugliness and monotony of the endless, prison-like New York tenements.

Or, as I have suggested previously, suburbia may be nothing but a scapegoat; by blaming *it* for the consequences of the nation's commitment to comfort and fun (what Jules Henry calls the "Ever Higher Standard of Living" in *Culture Against Man*), American intellectuals appease the ghosts of their Puritan Gods with cheap tribute; they achieve ritual purity without threatening the general prosperity they share. But power is subtly involved here too. As Herbert Gans has pointed out, a hundred years ago the white, Protestant, Anglo-Saxon elites of small town America blamed the city—that den of iniquity—for the sins that one found among deprived, lower-class, ethnic minority populations *wherever* they lived. When the hegemony of the small town was threatened by an urban population explosion of immigrants from southern and eastern Europe, the critics attacked the city. Now that the city is losing its power to the suburbs, urban intellectual elites take out after the suburbanites.

Myth and Social Problems

Having found little merit in the question of whether suburbia has created a new style of life, then, our attention shifts to the circumstances surrounding the creation of the myth of suburbia, and the

functions this myth performs in the contemporary structure of intellectual discourse. But this does not completely dispose of the matter; for once myths gain currency, once they go, as we say, "into the cultural air," they *become* real; they function frequently as self-fulfilling prophecies. Life copies literature; fact is affected by fiction; history is constrained by myth. "If a situation is defined as real," said William I. Thomas, "it is real in its consequences," and I have no doubt that personal decisions regarding whether or not to move to the suburbs have been affected by the myth of suburbia, just as I have no doubt (and there are plenty of data on this) that the behavior of Negroes and others is affected by myths about them. And despite everything reasonable I have said about suburbs, I *know* that the fact that I *dislike* suburbs has been conditioned, *beyond the possibility of redemption by mere research*, by the fact that the myth of suburbia exists.

And although I don't *know* it, I do believe that the history of recruitment to the medical and legal professions will be affected by the occupational myths which go by the names of Ben Casey, Kildare, Lawrence Preston, and Perry Mason, just as I believe that Huck Finn, Nick Adams, Holden Caulfield, and Andy Hardy have shaped our *images* of adolescence, and having shaped them, added to the conditions which affect "real" adolescence—if, indeed, adolescence may be said to have any reality other than the cultural reality we have given it. If this seems idle or frivolous or reveals excessive doubt in the findings of the most controlled kind of mass communications research, I ask only that you think of the millions of dollars that advertising commits to pandering to the customer's fantasies rather than to asserting the factual merits of the product. Since we must assume that hard headed businessmen do not squander money lightly, I have little alternative but to believe that men smoke Marlboros because they want to be like contemporary cowboys (a group, incidentally, that the census bureau defines as "farm laborers"—as sharp an example I know of a disjunction between image and reality) and that teen-age girls when leaning over a dark mahogany counter at Woolworth's looking at lipsticks are thinking more about soft music under a tropical moon than they are about the role of the Revlon company in the now all but forgotten TV scandals—although I continue to find it difficult to believe that hostesses at elegant parties greet their guests with an invitation to have a pepsi.

What I have said about myth bears upon the *problem* of social problems in general and on suburbia in particular. The spurious problem of suburbia—whether it has created a new, homogeneously "American" style of life (as distinguished from the real problems of the recent phases of urban growth)—is one of those problems to be understood more by giving one's attention to those whose needs are served by the belief that there *is* a problem than by giving one's attention to the objective dimensions of the problem itself. For social problems, of course, *have* no objective existence. It is objectively true that some people live crowded into dilapidated, unheated, and vermin-infested residences, but "slums" become a social problem only when a large enough and powerful enough group of people decide they ought not to. Americans have a propensity to *find* social problems; we thrive on them because by defining them as real and hence setting ameliorative forces into action, we feed our welfare impulse. To find problems, to mobilize opinion about them, to shake our social structure by its metaphorical shoulders and force it to *pay attention* to these matters, nourishes our beliefs in progress and perfectibility. For America is a country dedicated to the propositions that there are no evils which are ineradicable, no problems unsolvable, no recalcitrance beyond conciliation, no ending that need be unhappy (we are a most un-Greek democracy). So that finding and dealing with "problems" are necessary conditions for the verification of these propositions; the very existence of social problems to ameliorate reaffirms our principles more than any imaginable utopia could.

I do not mean to suggest that some problems are not solved, or at least eased; *I do mean to suggest that the problems which we define as real reveal the kinds of solidarity we seek.* Like the punishment of crime, which, as Emile Durkheim noted, was to be understood less as a deterrent of crime or as simple revenge against the criminal than as a collective reaffirmation of cultural values, our concern with certain social problems can be understood less in terms of the amelioration of the difficulties of those who *have* the problems than in terms of the affirmation and the solidarity which the *existence* of the problems provides to those groups who undertake responsibility for ameliorating them. I refer to the ubiquitous "sociologists, psychologists, clergymen, and educators" whose authority journalists are always quoting—the civic officials, teachers,

social workers, and "intelligent homemakers" who become more or less vocationally concerned with the social welfare of others. But not *all* others. The "others" almost always turn out to be the weak and dependent segments of the population: children and youth, the unemployed, the handicapped, the ill and the incarcerated. What these groups have in common is their vulnerability to public action; they tend to be relatively unproductive categories of the population, and lack many of the institutional connections which bind individuals to society. Wealth, however, protects one from the welfare impulses of others. Our concern over and desire to plan for "the problem of" the increasing proportions of aged persons in our society does not extend to Lyndon Johnson, Harry Truman, or H. L. Hunt—all of whom qualify for the statistical category "aged," but not for our image of those who need help—although I must confess that, if consulted, I might have several suggestions as to how they might spend their declining years more wholesomely. The people who have the problems that are defined as real are those who are vulnerable to the desires of problem definers to make these people more like themselves—to affirm their own kinds of solidarity.

If I am skeptical about the possibilities that "Planning for the Quality of Urban Life" can help to sustain the traditional cultural vitality and variety of our cities, it is because such planning is likely to affect primarily the weak, the desperate, and the unrespectable in ways that I have no confidence are benign, because much of what is culturally fertile and vital in American cities is the product of the desperate and the unrespectable, and because I have no confidence that the needs of professional welfarists are met in any way by the sustenance of this kind of pluralism. When we "improve the quality of urban life" what we are most likely to be doing is altering the conditions under which weak and vulnerable segments of the population live—in order to make them a little more like our own. The strong and the autonomous grant no one the right to alter the condition of their lives—that is what strength and autonomy are about.

It may well be that some of our problems get solved, although it seems to me that most of them are as visibly with us today as they were when the Muckrakers gave their name to an "Age" by preoccupying themselves with them. Some social problems go out of fashion, with some we simply get bored (as their relevance to the dominant myths or spirit of the age is obscured); and as they leave the headlines and the public conscience they replaced by new ones,

more appropriate to the wealth and luxury of our affluent time. Hence our preoccupation with "problems" like "conformity," "leisure," "popular taste," "status seeking," "teen-agers," and finally, suburbia, and whether it has a new and distinctive style of life. Has it? No, it hasn't, but it certainly has been a luxury to talk about it as if it were something vital.

The Sociology of Leisure:
Some Suggestions

1962

In a world full of newspapers whose headlines daily remind us of the continuing reign of misery and wretchedness in much of the world, and with the persistent cloud of nuclear war hanging over the heads of even the prosperous, the "problem" of leisure is one that we are distinctly privileged to have. Yet the study of leisure is not trivial—far from it. It is, however, worth noting at the outset that leisure assumes that status of a major problem only in a society which has been gripped by a "revolution of rising expectations." Unlike revolutions in underdeveloped countries, our revolution of rising expectations grows out of the demand for psychological as well as material benefits. An affluent society turns its attention to the pursuit of happiness; a well-fed society turns its attention to mental health, a successful society turns its attention to what Daniel Lerner[1] has called "comfort and fun," to personal "fulfillment," that elusive but supposed concomitant of success.

Despite the fact that "the problem of leisure" is already a conventional phrase in the language of the social sciences, the problem

Reprinted from *Industrial Relations* 1, no. 2 (February 1962).
[1]See "Comfort and Fun: Morality in a Nice Society," *American Scholar* 27 (Spring 1958), 153–65.

has hardly been formulated and the *concept* of leisure has only rarely been directly confronted.[2] To be sure, some problems of leisure may be understood without much attention to the difficulties of conceptualization. Negroes who do not have access to public parks, beaches, theaters, and so on, may be said to have a leisure problem. Culturally deprived persons whose backgrounds handicap them from participation in important voluntary associations, and who are hence deprived of access to sources of power and influence, may also be said by some to have a leisure problem. But these are not situations which are typically referred to as problems of leisure. The phrase, "problem of leisure," usually evokes images of the aged rocking in shabby rooms, poor, lonely, unattended, with little to do but wait for death; of adolescents on slum street corners answering with apparently senseless violence the anxious question of "what'll we do tonight?"; of large blocs of a nation's population sitting each evening in darkened living rooms lit only by that blue light from which emanates the irrelevant shadows which people the imaginative life of a society. These images, and the facts which underline them, are at the core of the concern expressed over the disposition of free time.

Nevertheless, it seems to me that little is contributed to the understanding of these particular problems by conceiving them as problems of leisure. The aged, certainly, have special problems, some of them imposed by sudden retirement, some by the infirmities of age, still others by the breakup of families. Basically, however, these are problems of the aged and can be understood without invoking the unexamined abstraction, leisure. Similarly, problems of adolescents have been intensified or dramatized in recent years by, among other things, their increasingly late entrance into the labor market, by

[2]The classic confrontation is, of course, Johan Huizinga, *Homo Ludens: The Play Element in Culture* (London: Routledge & Paul, 1949). For a Catholic view, see Joseph Pieper, *Leisure, the Basis of Culture* (New York: Pantheon, 1952). Though the word "leisure" is hardly mentioned in it, Werner Jaeger's *Paideia: The Ideals of Greek Culture* (New York: Oxford University Press, 1943), is probably the best single source for a classical understanding of leisure. Clement Greenberg, "Work and Leisure Under Industrialism," *Commentary* 6 (July 1953), 54–62, is a thoughtful consideration of the impact of industrialization on traditional views of leisure. None of these writings, however, are by sociologists. Almost any of David Riesman's several essays on work and leisure are very helpful in the study of leisure, and Max Kaplan makes a heroic but unsuccessful attempt to conceptualize leisure sociologically in *Leisure in America: A Social Inquiry* (New York: John Wiley, 1960), ch. 2. The most promising work is outlined by Harold Wilensky in "Work, Careers, and Social Integration," *International Social Science Journal*, XII Fall 1960), 543–60.

their increasingly early admittance into adolescent status, and by the sight of Negro, Puerto Rican, and other slum youth who are doomed, amid the general prosperity, to an environment of urban blight.

The problems of mass leisure (perhaps best symbolized by the TV narcotic) are inextricably bound up with a technology which renders work progressively more routinized and "easier" (though perhaps not less exhausting), with the purchasing power of large masses of people in the "culture market," and with the consequent rise of enormous "culture industries." In short, each problem of leisure is almost impossible to formulate or to solve without understanding the position of the groups who *have* the problem and the nature of the social and economic changes underlying their problems. More people are presented with more time at various stages of the life cycle than ever before—time when they are free to seek the inner satisfactions which we seem legitimately to expect from leisure. It adds little to our understanding of the difficulties of specific groups to perceive these difficulties as problems of "leisure," unless this approach provides clues to aspects of the problem that were previously hidden and aids in the development of a theory of leisure.

Two Traditions in the Discussion of Leisure

Problems are not self-evident. Thus we may raise the empirical question of *to* whom and *for* whom leisure is a problem—for not everybody is concerned about the leisure problems of everybody else. The more familiar social problems of leisure have developed out of the concern *by* specific groups *for* the leisure of other specific groups, and an examination of these groups may cast some light on the conceptual problem of leisure.

Whose leisure is usually a public concern? Certain salient groups may be identified: the aged, children, youth, the unemployed, the handicapped, the ill, and inmates in prisons and mental institutions are groups that come immediately to mind. In general, these groups are relatively unproductive categories of the population; they also often lack many of the basic institutional connections which bind individuals to society. Perhaps most important of all their common characteristics is their vulnerability to public action: in one way or another, these groups tend to be composed of less than fully competent persons. They are dependent, and by virtue of their dependence the disposition of their free time becomes a legitimate concern

of those who are responsible for them. Who is responsible, who concerned? The groups seem to be composed primarily of civic officials, certain categories of group workers and social workers, some teachers, clergymen, and people at least to some extent vocationally concerned with the welfare of others. The social problem of leisure in this context seems to be one of providing the dependent groups (to the extent that they are unable to provide for themselves) with opportunities for "wholesome" activities. By keeping them busy and productive and by engaging them in social relations, these activities are expected to give meaning to lives otherwise subject to unusually severe stresses.

The leisure of the masses also gives rise to a good deal of publicly expressed concern. This concern, however, is not typically expressed by the groups I have cited above, but rather by intellectuals or cultural elites, whose concern over mass leisure seems to reflect their fear of the power of the masses in the culture market and the consequent threat to the traditional values of high culture. There are two major ideological approaches to this problem. Conservative intellectuals tend to be pessimistic about the possibilities of elevating popular taste on a mass scale and consequently see the social stratification of culture as inevitable. In their view, cultural elites should tend the garden of high culture and ignore the mass media which, after all, reflect the tastes of the markets they serve.

Liberal and radical intellectuals, on the other hand, tend to accuse the suppliers of mass culture of catering to the lowest levels of popular taste in order to achieve the highest levels of net profit.[3] These intellectuals confer upon the mass media an enormous potential for elevating popular taste, a potential which they argue is not only rarely used but is actually perverted by the commitment of the media to diversion, entertainment, and escape. In other words, they consider the media committed to serve as a distraction from, and compensation for, the presumably drab and monotonous routines of the working lives of the masses. Richard Hoggart, in his description of the decline of English working-class culture, gives precise expression to this view when he says, "The strongest objection to the more

[3]Bernard Rosenberg and David Manning White, eds., *Mass Culture* (Glencoe, Ill.: Free Press, 1957), contains several examples of both views. For an especially good example of the conservative view, see Edward Shils, "Daydreams and Nightmares: Reflections on the Criticism of Mass Culture," *Sewanee Review* 65 (Autumn 1957), 587–608.

trivial popular entertainments is not that they prevent their [consumers] . . . from becoming highbrow, but that they make it harder for people without an intellectual bent to become wise in their own way."[4]

These two types of concern about leisure—that is, the concern of intellectuals and elites over popular taste and mass culture and the concern of more-or-less professional "do-gooders" over the "wholesome" disposition of the free time of relatively vulnerable, dependent groups—are contemporary instances of traditional approaches to leisure which go back a long way and have only rarely complemented one another. One tradition, probably dating from the relatively early stages of industrialization in the West, conceives of leisure as "free time" or time not devoted to paid occupations; leisure activities are viewed primarily as recreative and restorative; historically the problems involved are associated with the poor, the dependent, or the laboring classes. The much older, classical tradition conceives of leisure in the Greek sense, as "schooling" or cultivation of the self, as a preoccupation with the values of high culture. Historically this tradition has been associated with the functions of aristocratic, patrician, or leisure classes, since other classes were not culturally important.

To the Greeks, leisure was concerned with those activities that were worthy of a free man, activities we might today call "culture." Politics, debate, philosophy, art, ritual, and athletic contests were activities worthy of a free man because they expressed the moral core of a style of life. Their nobility was not, ideally, compromised or diluted by mere instrumental or productive purposes. "Work" as instrumental or productive activity was regarded as below the dignity of a free man, fit only for slaves and women. Leisure, in this aristocratic usage, is concerned with the maintenance of a style of life expressing the highest values of a culture. There is no problem of leisure because those who have it are bred to it.

What may be called the Protestant or industrial view of leisure is something quite different. When Calvinism sanctified work and industrialism ennobled it, what followed was the separation of work and leisure, the emphasis on economically productive functions as the most significant aspect of life, and the relegation of leisure to the status of spare time—time especially vulnerable to the ministrations

[4]*The Uses of Literacy* (London: Chatto and Windus, 1957), p. 276.

of the Devil (witness the depravity of the poor) unless it were used productively to restore or refresh the organism for its primary purpose, work, or for unambiguously "wholesome" purposes such as prayer, Bible reading, or the disciplining of children. With the onset of industrialism, the functions of creating and maintaining the aristocratic values—formerly the avocations of gentlemen of leisure or the preoccupations of men of talent kept as ornaments by aristocratic families or subsidized by the state—were increasingly taken over by occupational groups whose services were paid for through the market economy.

This brief review of the two traditions of leisure should suggest, above all, that a concept of leisure must be normative. To neither tradition, however different their evaluations of it, is leisure merely neutral time involving neutral activities. For Aristotle, leisure was the aim of life; for the Calvinist divine, it represented a threat to the Protestant virtues. Both classical aristocrat or Protestant preacher had clear ideas about the activities to which this time was to be devoted. Where the viability of the Greek idea of leisure rested on slave labor, the Protestant deification of work was supported by the sin of idleness (which to the Greeks was a virtue). The meanings of work and leisure are inextricably related both to each other and to the cultural norms which define their moral place in a social order. A sociological definition which ignores this fact does so at the peril of becoming irrelevant.

Toward a Normative Concept of Leisure

Is there a way of marrying these normative traditions and their associated concerns, thereby creating a unified, value-relevant approach to the sociology of leisure? To some extent, economic development and the spread of political democracy have answered this question for us by bringing the masses onto the stage of history. At the same time, the more severe and ascetic features of Puritanism have been discredited. As citizens, the masses have had human rights and secular dignity conferred on them; as free men they have been invited to participate in "activities worthy of a free man," to pursue happiness and personal fulfillment. And as possessors of discretionary income they have acquired the means to make these goals more than mere formal possibilities.

At the same time, the modern world has witnessed the near dis-

appearance of a leisure class in the classical sense of an aristocratic group with time completely free of the need to labor productively. Today, practically all of us work and practically all of us have
some "free time" beyond the minimum needed to restore or refresh
the body for its economic tasks. We are all, at least in principle,
compromised Greek citizens carrying the burden of compromised
Protestant ethics. The industrial system has created hundreds of
thousands of jobs that we feel are degrading,[5] but we are unwilling
to do without the wealth which the system creates. We no longer feel
that idleness is sinful, but we still retain something of the expectation
that work should have moral content and feel rather cheated and
slightly betrayed when we discover that moral content has simply
disappeared from much industrial work.

It is out of such ambiguous situations that sociologies are made.
One would expect a burgeoning sociology of leisure. This is not the
case, however. We know a great deal about what people do with
their free time, but only a small part of this knowledge has been
gathered by students who have undertaken a conscious investigation
of leisure. We know, for example, a considerable amount about who
participates in what kinds of voluntary associations with what frequency, but the scholars who have done the work do not typically
think of themselves as students of leisure. Kinsey studying sex is
surely studying leisure. And something like this can be said about
studies of mass media impact, juvenile delinquency, family life, and
many other fields.[6] Moreover, it seems to me that less has been contributed to a sociological understanding of leisure by studies consciously directed to that end than by good community studies which are
only incidentally or peripherally concerned with it. Although books
like *Street Corner Society, Elmtown's Youth, Democracy in Jones-
ville, Middletown, Deep South, Crestwood Heights*, and many others,
do not typically deal with the conceptual problem of leisure, they
contain not only a wealth of data on free-time activities but data
made meaningful through their linkage to a theory of community or

---

[5]Degrading, that is, in terms of the values created by industrialism and which
define what men have a legitimate right to expect.
[6]This is typical of the way fields of specialization develop in sociology and,
perhaps, in other disciplines too: not because of a rigorously logical division
of labor, but rather because of historical accidents in which specific "claims"
are laid to certain kinds of data. Sociology's traditional interests in the family
and in various aspects of "social disorganization" are due in large measure
to the fact that these "fields" had not been claimed by other disciplines at
the time sociology formally developed.

class or subculture or whatever the dominant focus of the book in question happens to be.

This theoretical relevance is precisely what is missing from most of the contemporary empirical work in the sociology of leisure. The sociology of leisure today is little else than a reporting of survey data on what selected samples of individuals do with the time in which they are not working, and the correlation of these data with conventional demographic variables.[7] There are several important exceptions to this general statement, but they do not alter the melancholy fact that empirical proof that rich people play polo more often than poor people gives us little reason to hope that an incipient sociology of leisure is taking shape. No genuine sociology of leisure is likely to emerge until a body of data is reinforced by a theory of leisure—at the very least by a conceptual understanding of what leisure is.

Leisure has been difficult to conceptualize for two very basic reasons.[8] First, conceptualization in sociology requires the abstraction of a common property or properties from a relatively wide range of events or social behavior. Leisure activities include such a colossally varied assortment of behavior (everything from, say, attendance at the President's Inaugural Ball to—as Louis Kronenberger pointed

[7]Wed to an operational definition of leisure as time not spent in gainful employment, such studies can only rarely get beyond the level of empirical generalization implicit in simple correlation. Studies of leisure and stratification are good cases in point. See, for example, R. Clyde White, "Social Class Differences in the Use of Leisure," *American Journal of Sociology*, 61 (September 1955), 145–50; Alfred C. Clarke, "Leisure and Occupational Prestige," *American Sociological Review*, 21 (June 1956), 301–07; Leonard Reissman, "Class, Leisure, and Social Participation," *American Sociological Review*, 19 (February 1954), 76–84. Saxon Graham correlates the data from his study with both class and rural–urban residence. See ch. 18 of his *American Culture* (New York: Harper & Row, 1957). Marjorie Donald and Robert Havighurst relate variations in the meanings attached to leisure to certain demographic variables. See "The Meanings of Leisure," *Social Forces*, 37 (May 1959), 355–60.

[8]That it *is* difficult to conceptualize is implicit in the failure of one recent symposium to come to any agreement on what the term means. See the introductory remarks in Robert W. Kleemeier, ed., *Aging and Leisure* (New York: Oxford University Press, 1961), p. 4. This book is probably the best of the several collections published in recent years on the problems contained in its title, but its utility extends beyond the problems of the aged. Sebastian De Grazia's contribution, "The Uses of Time," presents an enormous amount of data collected for studies under the Twentieth Century Fund; Nelson Foote's chapter, "Methods for the Study of Meaning in Use of Time," carefully reviews the several techniques of data collection in leisure studies. See, in addition, the contributions of Meyersohn, Wilensky, and Gordon.

out—wandering up and down railroad yards collecting the names of Pullman cars and noting them down in a little book) that it has been virtually impossible to conceptualize it on a behavioral basis. Instead, a circumstance of that behavior (that it goes on in time not given over to paid occupations) has typically been made the sole criterion of leisure. Such a definition tells us nothing about the normative content of leisure, nor does it even invite questions about it; it characterizes only the time in which leisure activities occur. Strictly understood, the conventional opposition of work and leisure is a false opposition because these terms characterize different orders of phenomena: leisure is a kind of time, whereas work is a kind of action. Students of leisure, however, do not study time, they study behavior. To contrast work and leisure—and we must contrast them, since they have sociological meaning only vis-a-vis each other —we must conceive of leisure also as a kind of action which, however, is distinguished from work.

The apparently simple characterization of leisure as free time (two of the most complicated words in the language) or unobligated time seems to lead to precisely this kind of distinction: the "free" of free time suggests that leisure activity is voluntary whereas work is constrained. This distinction brings us to the second difficulty with the conceptualization of leisure, because the very idea of free time belongs to a presociological age. If sociology has taught us anything it has taught us that no time is free of normative constraints; what is work for some, is leisure for others, it is said, and of course this is right. Is work work if I love it? Is leisure leisure if I feel it as burdensome or boring? These are the kinds of questions which make students of leisure tear their hair and in despair reach for the operational definition. Any normative distinction between work and leisure as action should be a distinction between the two kinds of norms which constrain them or a distinction regarding the extent to which norms have been internalized.

If, sociologically speaking, no time is unconstrained, how can we save leisure as free time from the status of a sociological myth? One way is to invoke Kenneth Burke's famous phrase, "perspective by incongruity," and argue that leisure refers precisely to those activities (or nonactivities) that are *most* constrained by moral norms. Norms may exercise moral force because they are functionally complete (genuine virtue is, after all, its own reward). Or, in some cases, they may have been so thoroughly internalized—so much a matter of con-

science and so little a matter of something objectively "out there"—
that they are felt as motives or desires freely chosen or as moral
responsibilities freely accepted.

This is a way of saying that leisure refers to those activities whose
normative content renders them most important to us, those things
that we want to do for their own sake or those things that we feel
ethically (as distinguished from expediently) constrained to do.[9]
*That these activities may empirically be found to occur most fre-
quently in time not devoted to paid occupations is significant primarily as an indication that work has lost much of its moral content*
—that work, which was once a calling from God to an earthly place,
has become "a job"; "it's a living."

This conception of work–leisure is normative. Transcending the
usual distinction between work and leisure, it represents a comprehensive cultural ideal; it is, in short, an "ideal type" only imperfectly
realized in the actual experience of individuals. At the same time,
it is not a moralistic idea, it does not preach the gospel of leisure, it
does not regard leisure as an unambiguous good under all circumstances. It is quite probable that certain social functions require
predominantly instrumental or expedient motivation; the performance
of some essential roles may very well be obstructed by deep moral
commitments. But this view of leisure gives us the beginning of a
normative concept which can be useful because it invites questions
about the conditions under which this comprehensive ideal is attained or approximated, although it does erase the usual distinction
between work and leisure.

In place of this distinction, the conception makes possible further
distinctions between leisure and such associated terms as rest, re-
laxation, or recreation, which may not have much moral content; and
by suggesting that not everything that one encounters in one's free
time qualifies as leisure, it frees the concept from its operational
identification with specific forms of, for example, games. But even if
the study of leisure turns out to be primarily the study of fun and
games, reading and gardening, hunting and fishing, watching and

---

[9]That one finds it emotionally more difficult to beg off (for phony reasons)
from a previously accepted invitation to a party given by a friend than to call
the boss to say one's sick and not coming to work, suggests that leisure
obligations are *more* thoroughly internalized than obligations to work. Where
this is true (and, of course, it is not under all circumstances), it suggests
that free time is *more* obligated precisely because it is "free": where commitments are voluntary they carry with them a felt responsibility.

hearing (as I hope it does not), this still suggests only that we are looking away from work, occupations, and careers to find what morally involves the members of our society.

Alienation from Work and the Problem of Leisure

It is perhaps an indication of how far we have come from the great days of the Protestant Ethic that the very characterization of leisure as free time contains a damning judgment on work, for it suggests that what is not leisure is not free, that is, it is for slaves—which is precisely as the Greeks would have had it. But this judgment is a disappointed one because we have not completely lost the expectation that we have some right to moral satisfaction in work; the Protestant Ethic dies hard—values always do—and leaves in us a lingering sense of betrayal when work seems meaningless.

Where work is concerned with wresting food from the earth, creating warmth and shelter for one's family, or even where, in societies undergoing industrialization, it is ideologically envisioned as the collective creation of a bright future (as it is today, for example, in the USSR and China), Protestant ethics have been eminently qualified to confer on such activities profound moral content. But where work is concerned with the manufacture of hoola hoops or mink coats for dogs or refrigerators that never need defrosting or automobiles that almost never need lubrication, and where men trained in English language and literature devote their worklives to the skillful use of the incomplete comparison in order to sell goods, even so versatile an instrument as our traditional value system learns its limitations.[10]

Lest I be misunderstood, I should make it clear that social criticism is not my intent here. The problem of leisure is not created merely by the growth of discretionary income, the reduction in the workweek, the pensioned retirement, and the lengthening span of life, just as alienation in work is not created primarily by the inherent

[10]Advertising, of course, is the great bête noire of social critics, the very model of organized cynicism. What an interesting study of reactions might be obtained if the writers of pamphlets which are published by the big advertising agencies for distribution to college majors in English and journalism and which describe the satisfactions to be achieved through careers in advertising were confronted with the novels, stories, and nonfiction written by ex-advertising men about life along James Madison's avenue!

properties of certain jobs.[11] Both problems are created when a value system is rendered apparently incapable of conferring honor on the typical situations that a social system engenders. Where inconsistencies exist between what the social system requires and what the value system prescribes, social problems are created, prominent among which are alienation from work and the problem of leisure, reverse sides of the same coin.

The social system, for example, has created longer adolescence, more years in retirement, and assembly-line jobs, but our value system contains no moral rhetoric with which to confer honor on these phenomena; the twenty-one year old college boy is still something considerably less than a man, the aged in impoverished retirement are objects of pity or patronization, and the automobile assembly-line worker is every intellectual's model of alienation from work. Our social system needs and produces "Organization Men, but the words remain offensive to us; we are all status seekers, but nobody defends status seeking. We don't know how: our value system does not provide us with the moral vocabulary to defend much of the behavior and many of the roles which the social structure requires.

In this respect, the Soviet countries have a bitter lesson to teach us. Soviet cultural rhetoric is offensive to the ears of Western intellectuals because it transparently and grossly attempts to confer moral significance on, and to create heroic images of, precisely those roles and behavior to which the Soviet social system is committed, images which to us are sometimes laughable. The muscled worker raising his sledgehammer above the rubble, the Stakhanovite overproducing his quota, the stocky, fresh-complexioned girl on the tractor, are proper topics for heroic treatment and glorious characterization. The collectivized Horatio Alger morality of Soviet rhetoric confers heroic status on those types of individuals and roles that actually represent the collective purposes of the state.

[11]See the following three articles which document the increases in leisure time and the money spent on leisure pursuits: Joseph Zeisel, "The Workweek in American Industry, 1850–1956"; Seymour Wolfbein, "The Changing Length of Working Life"; and "80 Billion for Fun," by the editors of *Fortune*. All three articles are reprinted in Eric Larrabee and Rolf Meyersohn, eds., *Mass Leisure* (Glencoe, Ill.: Free Press, 1958). See also, Sebastian DeGrazia, "Tomorrow's Good Life," *Teacher's College Record*, 61 (April 1960), for an argument regarding why such statistics may be misleading; and Ida Craven, "Leisure," in Larrabee and Meyersohn, op. cit., and Harold Wilensky. "The Uneven Distribution of Leisure," *Social Problems*, 9 (Summer 1961) for evidence on the large number of holy days and feast days in the ancient and medieval worlds.

Consider the strain on our moral vocabulary if it were asked to produce heroic myths of accountants, computer programmers, and personnel executives. We prefer cowboys, detectives, bull fighters, and sports-car racers, because these types embody the virtues which our moral vocabulary is equipped to celebrate: individual achievement, exploits, and prowess. Again, I should make clear that this is *not* a criticism of what we have become and certainly not a celebration of the harmony between Soviet society and culture; it is, rather, an analysis of why we are uneasy about what we have become. A culture which has not learned to honor what it is actually committed to produce creates an uneasy population.[12]

The problems of leisure and of alienation in work, then, are problems created by the inconsistencies between normative and social systems. Two adaptive responses to these problems are typical. The more common response, where certain jobs are not honored, is to withdraw emotion from work, to accept work as something one has to do in order to make possible the things one really cares about. Though the Protestant Ethic is by no means in its grave, there is clearly a growing consensus (more apparent, of course, on the lower levels of the occupational ladder than on the higher) that the major moral satisfactions in life are to be sought through leisure, not work. Or, in my own terms, leisure is to be sought through activities unconnected with occupations. The withdrawal of motivation may thus be replaced, for workers, by emotional involvement in the bowling league, the bridge club, the philatelist society, the golf score, the sports-car rally, or various kinds of spectator activities. For adolescents, there is "youth culture"; for the elderly, Golden Age Clubs.

Another kind of adaptation to alienation from work is much subtler. Manual workers can cope with alienation on the job by the invention of all sorts of factory games and status play. On professional and executive levels, one notes a surprising degree of sophisticated candor about alienation. It is, of course, true that job satisfaction studies[13] generally reveal that professionals and executives are much

[12]The plethora of television heroes who bear no relation to anyone in real life may not be due to the cynicism of sponsors and network executives. Such people might be only too pleased to present dramatic shows about accountants, IBM technicians, and junior executives, if only writers knew how to write them.
[13]See the very able summary and analysis of these studies by Robert Blauner, "Work Satisfaction and Industrial Trends in Modern Society," in Walter Galenson and Seymour M. Lipset, eds., *Labor and Trade Unionism* (New York: John Wiley, 1960).

more satisfied with their jobs than factory workers, but "job satisfaction" does not necessarily tell us much about alienation. In several professional and executive milieux it has become fashionable, almost de rigueur, to be cynical about one's work. The point is that the sophistication and the subtlety of one's cynicism can be highly rewarding, thus creating a situation in which one can be quite alienated from work but quite satisfied with one's job.

The metaphor of the "rat race," so common in highly competitive occupations, suggests that work on higher occupational levels is hardly a sanctified, self-justifying thing. Even in academic life, that former citadel of self-justifying work, the phrase "publish or perish" and the utter cynicism with which scholars (frequently successful ones) typically speak of the mysterious science of grant-getting bear testimony not only to an incipient alienation from work but also to new patterns of sophisticated disaffection, the elegance of which may be granted considerable honor. For these folkways are frequently models of duplicity; functionally, they constitute the conversational equipment to deal with the psychological dimensions of success and failure. The successful contestant in a "rat race" may be all the more highly admired for his success, given the arduous nature of the competition. Thus when successful men characterize their occupational milieu as a "rat race," the characterization may well contain the not-too-well-hidden motive of self-congratulation. When, on the other hand, the characterization is made by the unsuccessful, the metaphor of the "rat race" functions as a "cooling" device;[14] it renders failure honorable, for losing in a race of four-legged rodents is testimony to one's two-legged humanity. To be sure, norms are operating here, and they may acount in large part for much of the job satisfaction on higher levels, but these norms bear little resemblance to what we have in mind when we speak of our value system. Sociologists refer to such milieux as "deviant subcultures," and effective participation in them is in itself evidence of one's alienation from the dominant value system as applied to work.

In either case, whether it is the relatively simple alienation so characteristic of assembly-line work in factories or the highly sophisticated kind of alienation we find in the folkways of higher occupations, one thing is clear; the disengagement of self from occupational role not only is more common that it once was but is increasingly

---

[14]The expert here is Erving Goffman, "Cooling the Mark Out: Some Aspects of Adaptation to Failure," *Psychiatry*, 15 (November 1952) 451–63.

regarded as *proper*. Alienation would seem almost complete when one can say with honesty and moral conviction, "I am not what I do; do not judge me by what I do for a living," and when one turns to nonworking life for values and identity.

It may be objected that this analysis ignores important counter-tendencies in the nature and organization of work. Some cause for optimism regarding the problem of alienation has been sought, for example, in the fact that, of all occupational categories, highly skilled professional and technical occupations show the highest rates of growth. And since job satisfaction tends to be highest in the highly skilled manual classifications and in the nonmanual professional and technical classifications, the future should look somewhat brighter.

While there is clearly some basis for optimism in these occupational trends, there are at the same time several factors latent in them that should considerably temper that optimism. On blue-collar levels, for example, the newest automated types of skills are frequently the kind for which no readily available standards of approbation exist within the peer groups of skilled workers. The skills of a maintenance man in an automated plant, for example, are not the manual skills traditionally accorded honor by blue-collar workers. Moreover, to the extent that progressive refinements in the division of labor represent ever greater specialization of functions, occupational skills tend to become what Wilensky has called "status-invisible": "Ask a 'hindleg toenail remover' what he does and he will tell you he works at Swift's . . . the white-collar 'console operator,' too, will name the company, [but] not the job, because nobody has heard of this latest example of automation."[15] Where such conditions exist, the tendency of highly skilled jobs to command the moral identity of men is compromised; personal ties to work are weakened, and the relevance of working to nonworking life is obscured.

Regarding professional occupations, bureaucratic organization continues increasingly to define the conditions of professional work. These conditions render such work less and less akin to the traditional model of the liberal professions, with their emphasis on responsibility, personal service, and creativity, and more and more akin to the bureaucratic model of professional and managerial skills organized in a "functionally rational" manner—a type of organization

[15]Harold Wilensky, "Work Careers, and Social Integration," p. 19. On the ambiguous status of automated skills, see Robert Blauner, *Alienation and Freedom* (Chicago, Ill.: University of Chicago Press, 1964).

to which traditional professional norms can only be applied with great difficulty. To the extent that such skills can be routinized, managers and professionals, as Wilensky and others have noted, are themselves increasingly subject to "Taylorization," which tends to weaken further a moral commitment to work. Witness the complex, rather panicky response of many teachers to the prospect of automatic teaching devices. There are, of course, professional and technical milieux which are relatively insulated from these tendencies, but to the extent that work is subject to rationalization these will decrease, and unless norms can be found within our value system to celebrate bureaucratization, the withdrawal of motivation and the disengagement of self from work is likely to continue.

As work loses its power to command the moral identifications and loyalties of men, as men look away from work to find moral experience, society loses an important source of normative integration. Widespread belief in the inherent value of work gives economic institutions the power to perform certain necessary integrative functions, and the withdrawal of motivation from work seriously strains the network of bonds which relate the world of work to the world of nonwork, and the individual to both.

In such a situation we may expect, if the functionalist view of society as a self-balancing system has any merit, the transfer of functions formerly performed by the institutions of work to the "leisure institutions," and this, it seems to me, is precisely the significance of the enormous increase in attention which the problem of leisure has received in recent years.[16] In much the same sense that functions formerly performed by the family and the church are increasingly shifted to the schools, which are reluctant and in many respects ill-equipped to handle them, "free time" is increasingly burdened with moral functions formerly performed by the institutions of work. Where public concern over leisure is not merely an attempt by moralistic busybodies to impose their own ideas of "wholesome" use of time on others, and where it is not professional or semi-professional mourning over the vulgarity of mass culture, it is a concern with the sources of moral solidarity. For with the weakening of the

[16]Edward Gross assures us that leisure performs important functions in solving all four of the "system problems" of Parsons and his collaborators, but he does not suggest why this discovery was not made until very recently. See "A Functional Approach to Leisure Analysis," *Social Problems* 9, (Summer 1961). This issue of *Social Problems* is wholly devoted to articles on leisure.

moral link which binds men to the institutions of work—and religion too—the major institutional sources of social cohesion become problematic.

The Task of a Sociology of Leisure

To my mind, the problem of leisure is a problem of finding, in the norms which exercise constraint in specific situations, the values which command moral identity and assent. The frequent appeals to individuals to use leisure "creatively" and to participate in local community institutions and voluntary associations are not likely to aid much in the solution of the problem because they beg the important questions of whether these activities actually do have moral force and whether the social structure actually does provide access to the goals which the culture recommends. Many of the recommended solutions to the problem of leisure, in short, would be viable only if there were no problem of leisure to begin with. The problem of leisure is exacerbated when men are asked to use their free time for activities beyond their means or for activities whose value they do not recognize.

The problem of leisure is difficult to treat intelligently because it lies in an area that is not amenable to our genius for organized solutions. The problem is a poignant one in a democratic industrial society because it is a Frankenstein's monster: it confronts the society with the spectre of an enormous amount of free time which is created by the society, but over which the society admits that it should, in principle, have little or no conscious influence or control. If leisure is time free of merely instrumental obligations, it is not subject to the criteria of efficiency and hence is immune to the power of rationality and organization. And if the great gift of unbeholden time and discretionary income creates a leisure whose dominant motifs are boredom, violence, and escape, the monster turns on its creator and challenges the viability of the democratic ideal.[17]

But if the values sought through leisure are difficut to find because

[17]The great success of the motion picture *Marty*—with its recurrent refrain of "what'll we do tonight?"—suggests the dramatic appeal of the attempt to overcome ennui. Having no ready answer to the question of "what'll we do tonight?" provokes great anxiety because having "nothing to do" is cause for shame in a society burdened by the old view that idleness is vice and the new view that great demands on one's time are evidence of high estate.

of changes in the nature and organization of work and the receding horizons of aspiration, they are nevertheless there, both in traditional and in new forms (which is only to say that men have culture). The task of a sociology of leisure is to discover what these values are, the patterns of activity through which they are sought, and the features of social structure which tend to change or sustain them.[18] The sociology of leisure is that part of the sociology of culture which attempts to discover the moral character of a style of life by studying the behavior of groups under conditions where that behavior is least constrained by exclusively instrumental considerations. Increasingly, these conditions are found outside of occupations, and where they are, the "problem" is not too *much* time and money, but too *little*. Leisure styles are created by the kinds of leisure activities that, empirically, tend to cluster together; these are not random, and the sociological analysis of them is the study of how social structure facilitates or obstructs the efforts of men to find in their freest time the moral satisfactions which value systems must provide.

[18]What, for example, is it about our social structure that accounts for the transformation of the bowling alley from a haunt of thieves, murderers, and con men, into an eminently respectable place to take the family for an evening of wholesome fun, whereas the poolroom has been unable to lose its unsavory reputation?

Black Culture

1967

Behind much of the recent trouble within the civil rights movement there lurks the seldom asked question about the reality of a distinctive Negro culture, and the split in the movement over the black power slogan reveals publicly for the first time just how profound that question is. The NAACP and other moderate civil rights groups have emphasized the use of the law to achieve for individual Negroes their full rights as ordinary citizens, but they have shown little interest in affirming the ethnic distinctiveness of Negro group life. The recent emphasis of the more militant sectors of the Negro revolution has been to claim for Negroes more than just their rights as individual citizens of a United States whose laws do not generally recognize subcultures. What we are now seeing in the Negro revolution, with its growing emphasis on racial or ethnic "pride" and "identity" (as well as on voting, housing, and job rights) is an attempt to *legitimate* black culture and to claim for it full parity with the rest of America's ethnic styles.

If this development has raised the spectre of "racism in reverse,"

A review of *Urban Blues*, by Charles Keil (Chicago, Ill.: University of Chicago Press, 1966). Reprinted from *Trans-action* (June 1967).

it is partly, of course, because of intentional distortions by those who, for whatever reason, wish to obstruct Negro gains. But it is partly, too, a result of the apparent reticence the leaders of the black Left have shown so far in stating concretely what patterns of black American culture they are affirming and wish preserved. For if the affirmation of black culture carries with it no clear specification of the *culture* being affirmed, it is less than surprising that middle class and other Whites (already full of anxieties and apprehensions) should fear that it is simply blackness (or its mystique) which is being celebrated. Black culture and its political slogan, black power, is a troublesome perspective for the Negro movement, then, not only because it may alienate white liberals, and not only because it may lose for the movement the support of the middle classes, white and black, but also because once the radicals invoke the perspective and the rhetoric of black culture, they place themselves under the intellectual obligation to clarify precisely *what* patterns of Negro culture they are affirming, *what* sources of institutional support for these patterns they see in Negro social organization, and *how* those patterns may be expected to provide bases of "racial pride" and "ethnic identity" sufficient to motivate the black masses to claim both their full rights as Americans *and* the nation's respect for their ethnicity.

The importance of Charles Keil's *Urban Blues is* that it is the best of very few books to attempt some answers to these questions. Keil sketches the history and structure of the blues as a musical form, describes its relevance to the social role of the blues singer, or "bluesman," in Negro society, and analyzes the relation of black culture to the problems that Negroes face in American society. It seems to me that the questions to which Keil addresses himself are so crucial—particularly to the present problems of the civil rights movement and the future of Negroes in the United States—that it is more important to say that he has made a brilliant start than to say that his book has important flaws which prevent one from praising it wholeheartedly.

Keil's basic thesis, emblazoned by his publisher on the dust jacket of the book, is that Negroes are "the only substantial minority group in America who really have a culture to guard and protect . . . and a unique perspective by incongruity on American society that may well be this nation's outstanding and redeeming virtue." The distinctiveness of black culture extends, according to Keil, from its religious institutions (the ecstatic character of the storefront

churches), to its kinship institutions (the female based household and the elusive, uncertain character of the Negro male role in it), to its distinctive sense of time and history (drift, living in the present), to its distinctive modes of perception and expression (auditory and tactile rather than visual and literary). This culture is manifest in the lyrics of the blues, in the status of the bluesman and other hustlers (preachers, comedians, entertainers—anybody, as Keil puts it, talented enough and clever enough to be financially well off without working) who "tell it like it is," and in the emergence of the "soul" ideology as the expression of a nativist, revitalization movement.

Keil traces the blues to its African sources, but goes much further than the usual romanticizers of "earthy" Negro music to an analysis of the blues in terms of its textures (instrumentation, tonality, etc.), structures (rhythmic and verbal patterns), lyrics, and contexts (the geographical circumstances in which these are shaped). From these concepts he develops a typology of blues styles, ranging in an ascending order of sophistication from "country" to "city" to "urban" to a contemporary mixed style of "soul" music. In doing this, he does not bother to conceal his contempt for the "moldy fig" mentality of blues historians (usually white) whose image of a "real" blues singer demands that he be aged, blind, arthritic, and toothless, that he has lived most of his life sharecropping, coaxing mules, and picking cotton, and preferably that he has not performed in public or made a record in twenty years. His contempt extends not only to this image, which he sees as a liberal's version of the white man's burden, but also to the overly genteel blues historian for whom "a coarse lyric of thirty years ago has poetic qualities and historical interest," but for whom the same sort of contemporary lyric is "frivolous and not worthy of scholarly attention."

Learned in ethnography as well as musicology, Keil makes a genuine *research* contribution to the understanding of these matters not just through his historical command of the sources, but through chapters which describe the business context in which a blues singer gets his start, through depth interviews with blues singers and their audience, through a marvelous blow by blow report of the intensifying development of rapport and solidarity betwen audience and performers at a large blues dance-concert in Chicago (the center of the contemporary blues renaissance), and through the use of a radio call-in show on a Negro station to evoke responses from listeners regarding the meanings they ascribe to the concept of "soul." But

impressive and original as this research is, his conclusions about the blues are less important than the inferences he makes from them about the character of black culture and the role of bluesmen in it.

"If we are ever to understand what urban Negro culture is all about, we had best view entertainers and hustlers as culture heroes." For Keil, bluesmen (and, to an extent, other hustlers, especially preachers) are *ritual* performers whose audiences are mostly "committed" rather than "appreciative" (as they are, say, in the *art* music that modern jazz has become). What these audiences want most from their ritual performers is what they call "soul," that is, the projection of authenticity of feeling about a subject matter that concerns them all (salvation and other religious matters in the preacher's case; sex, prison, gambling, whiskey, and the rest of the common coin of ghetto life in the case of the bluesman), and which permits a sort of vicarious identification and collective catharsis. These performers function as culture or opinion leaders whose talent it is to tell it, if not quite like it is, then like their inarticulate audiences feel it to be—a function, incidentally, which links the bluesman and his audience to the rock and roll groups and their audience.

In the context of black culture, it is this quasi-sacred, expressive role which relates the bluesman to the preacher and even to some extent to the political leader; they are all, as Keil says, "identity experts," whose performances are significant less for any objective technical or esthetic merit they may possess (although they may possess plenty) than for their common function of stirring collective response in their audiences and reminding them of their common identity as a people. Keil makes brilliant observations about the *stylistic* parallels, many rooted in African traditions, between bluesmen and preachers (observations whose validity extends even to the political rhetoric of leaders like Malcolm X and Stokeley Carmichael), for example, the repetition of phrases, the incantatory quality of utterance, and the use of shouts and falsettoes. And he makes these observations without at the same time losing sight of the important cultural differences between bluesmen and preachers. For of all hustlers, the preacher is just about the only role model of a "good" man black culture contains. The preacher is good because in addition to soul he's got responsibility, whereas the bluesman and other hustlers more directly involved in entertainment represent the "no-good man," that model of Negro masculinity with a strong sex-role identity as stud, rogue, or lady-killer, the exigencies and uncertainties

of whose work render him possibly here today but perhaps gone tomorrow. In short, the bluesman is a good lover but a bad husband and provider. But his functional kinship with the preacher helps explain what Keil reports as an empirical tendency for bluesmen to *become* preachers when their careers in show business are over.

It is Keil's involvement with and affirmation of the blues culture which leads him to see these things so clearly. But his involvement and affirmation begin to mislead him, I think, when he ascribes not simply a diffuse emotional charisma but a specifically political charisma to urban bluesmen who, he says, sense broader and deeper obligations to their people than country and city bluesmen. He cites plenty of evidence, for example, for his suggestion that the style and lyrics of urban blues state common problems clearly and concisely, but cites none at all for his assertion that they also take steps toward the analysis and solution of these problems, except, perhaps, for his assertion that the ritual aspects of blues performance contribute to the establishment of racial solidarity—which the left wing of the civil rights movement apparently regards as essential to any further political gains.

Borrowing an idea from LeRoi Jones, Keil sees Negro music becoming more "reactionary" (i.e. more African) in recent years: as white America appropriates and commercializes more and more Negro music, the "black community" generates a "new" music it can call its own—as Keil puts it, a black equivalent of white backlash: ". . . the soul brothers seem to be saying: 'let us fight for our rights . . . because we value our cultural identity and wish to be able to develop it without fearing punishment from the white majority.' " There is a strong nativistic quality to this black revitalization movement, but it is very complex, too, and Keil recognizes this all too well. For while he understands that the affirmation of black experience (from Africa through the slavery and ghetto experience) can function as something to fall back on if the civil rights movement fails and American realities become too grim to cope with, Keil sees, too, that many of the most militant spokesmen for black culture may be less interested in integration than in freedom and self-respect because they have vested ethnic interests in that culture (as black barbers, undertakers, and insurance men have vested economic interests in segregation) which may make them reluctant to risk disappearance in the white mainstream.

But in spite of this sophistication, Keil is misled by the sort of

faith and commitment which, although they honor him as a man, distort his intellectual judgement. He gives himself away, for example, when, in a book characterized most of the way by close observation and careful reason, he says that even after ghetto conditions are remedied "Negroes will cherish their cultural identity and see in their 'entertainers' the carriers of an irreplaceable tradition which they will be unwilling to cast aside for middle class anonymity." The statement looks at first glance as if it might be a reasoned prediction when it is actually nothing more than a statement of faith and hope which flies in the face of what is by now persuasive evidence to the contrary. It seems clear enough, indeed Keil has helped *make* it clear enough, that the blues culture emerged out of slavery and the ghetto experience that followed and that the blues have changed in response to changing conditions. And if they are likely to survive the ghetto very long, Keil gives one no grounds for believing in the probability of that survival—other than his observation that because they deal with conflict between the sexes, the blues are not likely to disappear. Even if the ghetto remains, it is not likely to remain as a homogenous slum but as a complexly stratified subsociety in which even urban blues are likely *not* to reflect the experience of a substantial part of that society as different segments of it begin to move, at varying rates, out of leaden-eyed poverty into the discontents of ordinary citizenship.

Keil is misled on this point by what I think is a desire to affirm solidarity with black people. And this desire blunts the force of his own considerable analytical powers—ironically, because I think those powers are released by his actual detachment, perhaps even alienation. Thus he is led to overcompensate with rhetorical flourishes such as "I will continue to dispute those who insist that Negroes have no worthwhile culture," a statement which, like the one quoted in the previous paragraph, is nothing more than platform oratory to which the only plausible responses are a cheer or a shrug. The important issue, with respect to the civil rights movement and the future of Negroes in the United States, is less whether he or I or you dig black culture than it is for us to understand the quality of that culture, its function in the lives of the black masses who affirm it (to the *extent* that they do—itself an unanswered question), and appraise the prospects of its survival when the conditions which generated it and sustain it are no longer present.

The essential quality of that culture is summarized by the concept

of soul, which Chicago Negroes defined for Keil and his disc-jockey collaborator with phrases such as: strong emotions and feelings, especially when shared with others; something pure, non-machined; staying power and wisdom through suffering; telling it like it is, being what you are, and believing in what you do. The concept suggests further a tight intermingling of sex, love, and reciprocal responsiveness which constitute the pattern of Negro Dyonisianism, manifest in the swing of the blues–jazz–gospel musical milieu and in the brilliant, moving, linguistic innovations which spring from it. The pattern emphasizes the erotic, the frenetic, and the ecstatic, a pattern, which when made ideological, constitutes a claim to emotional depth and authenticity—the special cultural heritage possessed by black Americans, and by those few whites, like Tony Bennett and Frank Sinatra, or Joe Cocker and Van Morrison, who come by the gift mysteriously.

This idea is a stereotype which, like all stereotypes, is founded in fact and, like some stereotypes, seems to flatter the group supposedly characterized by it. But it is hard for any group, particularly an oppressed one, to resist the stereotypes which apparently flatter it, especially when, for reasons one is never fully able to anticipate, such stereotypes not only serve the interests of the flatterers but also mollify the people stereotyped, who may be unaware that such mollification may confirm them in the cultural patterns which help perpetuate their oppression. So now to the cleverness of the Jews and the blarney-charm of the Irish and the fire of the Latins we are asked to add the soul of the Negroes.

As an attribute of "race," such a stereotype is of course nonsense. To the extent that the soul idea is founded in fact, it may be partly African in origin; it is certainly partly southern rural and probably partly evangelical Christian, but it is mostly lower class. As ideology, it is part of a venerable intellectual tradition which has characterized the lower class (and some other oppressed groups) in terms not very different from those emotionally hot-cool terms in which Keil describes black culture. Since the eighteenth century (if not earlier) those relegated to the bottom of the social heap have been heir to an ideology (created by their exploiters) which contrasted the vitality and earthy authenticity of the "simpler folk" who lived closer to nature, with the boredom and alienation of the elevated who sought "reality" by occasionally "going among" them. This ascription of a

deeper, more wholesome humanity to the oppressed and the exploited than to their decadent exploiters was one of the few small comforts granted the downtrodden, serving them as a palliative for their actual discontents, and serving their intellectual spokesmen as a symbol of their redemptive potential.

This celebration of Negro "soul"—so attractive even to people who should know better—is troubling not only because it reminds one too easily of earlier attempts to burden an oppressed class with redemptive functions for a whole society (as if it didn't have burdens enough), but because of its kinship with similar responses, apparently genuine, to other stereotyped cultural images which touch something sensitive in the collective psyche. In northern New England you can still find those tall, spare, leather-necked, white-haired old men still nodding a flat-voiced good morning to perfect strangers on a New Hampshire street. And in the West you can still find men who look very much like those raw-boned, lean-hipped, rough-textured visions in buckskin and denim who populate the Marlboro commercials. The trouble, of course, is that however spontaneous and immediate one's emotional response to these living traditional symbols, that response is in fact obsolete, sentimental, and mostly irrelevant to one's real commitments. And this outpouring of real vicarious feeling is an expression of the homage exacted by one's own complicity in perpetuating the dissociation between the images which evoke feeling and the real constraints which evoke action. Such irrelevance cheapens feeling and corrupts the very value of its authenticity. Under these conditions, culture becomes absurd and feeling decadent, the more so the more authentic it is.

Well, I think the celebration of soul contains analogous dangers. Black people are said to have soul, a quality of culture idealized in the blues, and of personality idealized in the style and demeanor of the bluesman, a quality developed under conditions of severe poverty, degradation, and ghetto imprisonment. But if soul enables those trapped in the black ghetto to soar temporarily out of their prisons, it is also the quality of culture and personality that helps keep them out of the middle class; if the development of "soul" is testimony to the capacity of the human spirit to create authentic culture under almost any conditions, it is also testimony to the fact that authentic culture is adaptive: it helps people come to terms with the conditions under which they must live—and in the case of black Americans,

impedes their social mobility at the same time as it provides, as Keil himself suggests, important compensatory satisfactions. The soul ideology, then, suits the bitter and the despairing in the ghetto who can find in it some small celebration and rationale of what they are in fact stuck with, and it suits those Negro ideologists, black and white, who can use the theory of pluralism or separatism (in this case black culture) as an intellectual hook on which to hang their attack on middle-class society.

But the soul ideology does not suit that probably enormous number of Negroes who would gladly trade a piece of their abundant emotionality for a piece of American affluence, and who care less about having an "authentic" and "worthwhile" culture than about having a good job and a house in the suburbs. To those Negroes who already have these or are on the verge of getting them, "soul" may be experienced as a symbol of a sort of old country culture (Yankee independence; buckskin and denim) to which they are constrained to respond with real feeling when in fact it may be losing or already have lost much of its meaning for them. The danger is that having or not having "soul" may be invoked as a sort of test of ethnic loyalty, and used as a weapon in a campaign of slander against those guilty of the crime of mobility. By whom? By those Negro leaders who, having given priority to the political goals of racial pride and ethnic identity over the goal of integration, might be tempted to seek support for these priorities by characterizing the already integrated or the almost integrated as having sold their souls for a piece of the American pie, or, as Keil puts it, for "middle class anonymity."

Keil's ambivalence shows here, for he says he actually hopes the revitalization of black culture will produce a race of marginal men (like Marx, Freud, or Einstein) whose grapplings with conflicting identities shape a mind which is skeptical and inquiring instead of one which, having suppressed conflict, assimilates, and then is helpless when the bigots march. But Keil has not shown how racial solidarity will contribute to this goal. Of all ideologies, racial and ethnic ones tend to be intolerant of marginality or of anything less than full commitment. Moreover any political gains to be had from "racial solidarity" must be balanced against losses in support—not simply from white liberals, but from those Negroes who still hope for a comfortable place in an integrated, middle-class America. For stripped of its mystique, black culture is basically an American Negro version of *lower-class culture*, and, race prejudice aside, can expect *on*

this ground alone to meet strong resistance from the majority of the American population, which will see in the attempt to legitimate it an attempt to strike at the heart of the ethic of success and mobility, which is as close as this country comes to having any really sacred values. No lower-class culture has ever been fully legitimated in the United States because the basic right of members of the lower class has been to rise out of it, not to celebrate its style of life.

Racist Plastic Uptight

Criticisms of Middle-Class America **1969**

For as long as I can remember reading books and laughing at co-medians, and long before that, the middle class and its morality, indeed, the whole style of life usually called "bourgeois" have been favorite whipping-boys of the intellectual and esthetic avant-garde in both the high and low arts. From Denis Diderot to Lenny Bruce, from Gustave Flaubert to Groucho Marx, from D. H. Lawrence to W. C. Fields, most of modern art has been dominated by antibour-geois feelings; the peculiar combination of aristocratic and vulgar motifs with which the highest and lowest classes expressed their antagonism to the spirit of calculation, industriousness, rationaliza-tion, and routine in middle-class life, can be traced far back into European history.

In the United States, which is one of the few historical societies which has conferred great power and prestige on businessmen for no better reason than their ability to make money, the traditional combination of elite and egalitarian themes contained in the attack on the culture of commerce was carried on the one hand by artists, writers, and other intellectuals who adopted European aristocratic perspectives in derogating the vulgarity and the spiritual emptiness of a life devoted to money-making, and on the other hand by popu-

listic satirists who attacked from below the stuffiness and the pomposities of the middle class.

But although satirical or otherwise disdainful attitudes toward middle-class style are in this sense traditional, the most recent attacks, for example by black militants on middle-class Whites, and by hippies on "plastic, uptight (read: middle class) America," have come with a radical new twist. Those who formerly attacked middle-class values (as well as those who, though not attacking them, made little pretense of living by them) rarely did so with the serious political aim of substituting their own values and cultural style for the dominant middle-class ethos, or even with the more modest aims of publicly defending the honor and the autonomy of their own cultural style and claiming legitimacy for it. The most recent attacks, however, are challenging the traditional practice of identifying "American" culture with white, Protestant, middle-class patterns, and it is the character of this new challenge which makes the current attacks interesting and important.

To speak of an "attack" implies the existence of an enemy, but despite the formal ideological doctrines of Marxist groups like SDS, the enemy is less frequently characterized as a specific social stratum definable in terms of its oppressive political and economic functions than as a diffuse cultural ethos, the accumulation of 300 years of white, Protestant domination of American society. The rhetoric of the attack, therefore, is carried less in traditional political terms against "the middle class" (too large and heterogeneous a group to make simple sense of) or even against specific segments of it (such as capitalists, Organization Men, or Chambers of Commerce) than against the mentality perceived as common to most of these groups, a mentality symbolized for militant Negroes by the word "racism" and for the hippies and the student activists by the words "plastic" and "uptight."

For black militants, the enemy is "this racist society" which victimizes Negroes not only through the more familiar forms of discrimination in employment, schooling, and housing, but by a racism which goes culturally deeper to matters of linguistic usage (black equals evil), esthetics (negroid equals ugly), and questions of pride or shame in ethnic heritage and "manhood" (the modal skin color of American Negroes represents centuries of rape and other sexual exploitation of Negro women by white men which black men were powerless to prevent). Thus, even remedial legislation with respect

to jobs, schools, housing, and voting (difficult as these are to achieve) only begins to scratch the proverbial surface of American racism. Even at its most successful, such legislation still leaves American Negroes seriously disadvantaged in psychological terms, for no legislation presently envisaged can possibly reduce their stigmatization by largely unconscious English usage and by centuries of esthetic conventions.

For black militants, then, the enemy is the racist *system*, and its participants who blandly and unconsciously profit from the system's unequal distribution of access to favorable self-conceptions, and who cannot or will not understand what all the agitation and resentment is about. Under such conditions, access to the "mainstream" of American life (promised by liberal legislation) may seem like a cruel irony, less desirable at the present time than "black power" which, by controlling black communities, can more effectively exercise a corporate or collective effort at modifying these subtler aspects of American racism by encouraging pride in blackness. Surely this is what the "soul" ideology is all about, and what the Black Panther Party (the name itself is a source of pride) intends by its campaigns emphasizing that "Black is Beautiful."

For the hippies, the enemy is more complex although perhaps less formidable. Partly, their enemy is traditional (and still influential) lower middle-class, Protestant asceticism which moralizes about their hair, their filth, their libertinism, and their high rates of VD and "needle hepatitis" (though tolerating, of course, rats and high rates of less ecstatic diseases among the *traditional* poverty stricken groups in the urban ghettoes and the rural South where squalor is more routine), but prefers to ignore the very enterprising manner in which the hippies have, within a startling short period of time, wrought a small cultural revolution with their innovations in popular music, dress, and graphic art. A more elusive enemy, however, is the emptiness they sense in the complacent images of the good life which underlie the exhortations they get from their liberal middle-class parents and from the mass media to stay in school, to get good grades, to get trained in a salable skill or profession, to sell it and get ahead with the organizations which have bought it; to get married (not on impulse) and to raise a family in a suburban home (a modest one is OK to start) with at least one sliding glass door and a garage (preferably heated, and wired 220) big enough to contain two cars, a washer, a dryer, and a freezer, all the while being circumspect

about one's opinions and heedful of one's reputation: to become, in short, a good commuter-consumer in pursuit of comfort and fun through the acquisition of the products of American technology, through "plastic."

Well, it's better than what the Vietnamese have got, but large numbers of the thoughtful middle-class, American young, sheltered for so long from what their parents like to call "the real world" (one would think that if adults were pleased with their world they'd want to introduce their children to it as early as possible rather than postpone the introduction as long as they could), and brought up to believe in "ideals" rather than comparative judgments, may be heard to murmur with existential discontent, "Is that all? Is *that* all there is?"

Whence cometh the discontent? Why the disdain of plastic? It may be, as T. S. Eliot once warned, and as Emile Durkheim anticipated, that they have not learned to avoid excessive expectation. But that's hard to avoid in America (the young are urged to be "idealistic"). Moreover, many of them have already "had" suburbia (they call it "Endsville") and, no doubt, suburban life is hard on restless adolescents; it's where the action isn't; and where if it was, it would be hard to get to. But beyond the disaffection of the hip young with suburbia (affluence's residential face), American ideas have failed to keep pace with the profound social changes induced by industrial growth and the movements of population. Despite the efforts of Time, Inc., there has been a serious failure of American rhetoric to ennoble the domestic goals of affluence (for example, more is better) to which the society is in fact oriented, and a corresponding failure to inspire the young to believe that in reaching for these goals they are engaging in anything transcendent of mundane self-interest. A culture which does not sanctify its objective goals creates a furtive and uneasy population, and the idea machines of the American culture industries have somehow failed to sanctify plastic, which remains, quite literally, synthetic.

To be locked into a life course aimed at the acquisition of plastic for which the culture provides no genuine sanctification is likely to promote a certain anxiety. And from the perspective of the disaffected young, to be middle class these days means to have your achievements and your aspirations so adjusted that you always want or need a little more than you've got, but are so dependent upon what you *have* got (and so vulnerable to it being taken away) that

threats to it compound your anxiety, and put you, in the parlance of the young, uptight.

From the point of view of its severest critics, then, white, middle-class America is racist, plastic, and uptight; and despite the many differences that divide them, the black militants and the bohemian and politically disaffected young have in common their rejection of the traditional Protestant verities that have helped make it and keep it that way. Nevertheless, American moral rhetoric is still rooted largely in "The Protestant Ethic": in the affirmation of the virtues of hard work and occupational achievement (rather than in an aristo-cratic commitment to dilettantism, leisure, and contemplation); in the virtues of self-control and self-denial, particularly the repression of erotic feelings (rather than in the emotional self-expressiveness and in the indulgence of appetites emphasized in many aristocratic and peasant milieux); in the belief that planning ahead is morally more elevated than living for the present moment; in preferring order and predictability to untidy spontaneity, piety and euphemism to candor and irreverence, and feeling cleanliness second only to God-liness.

Now in addition to the substantial numbers of Americans who, although espousing these values, did not always live up to them, there have always been, long before the advent of contemporary black militance and youthful activism, plenty of Americans who never even espoused them. But they were not often in a position to defend publicly the propriety of the values they did share, or to resist suc-cessfully the power of the middle-class consensus to define these values as in some sense indecent, disreputable, or "deviant." Great wealth and abject poverty, for example, each promote distinctive subcultures, and important sectors of the upper class and the lower class are in fact governed by values different in important respects from those expressed in the middle-class consensus. But these dif-ferences, although tolerated by the Protestant, middle-class majority, have been the object of mild or severe stigmatization which rein-forced the domination of middle-class norms.

The distinctive cultures of poverty in the United States could be neutralized in the case of native "old American" poor (in Appalachia, for example) by identifying them as "failures" and by attributing disreputable status to them in the Protestant tradition which identi-fied poverty with sin. The distinctive peasant cultures of the ethnic poor could be neutralized by attributing transitional status to recent

immigrants: they were on their way to being Americanized, i.e. bour-geoisified. The culture of the black poor could be explained away by a series of stereotypes (savage, playful, lazy, rhythmic, etc.) which stigmatized Negroes as barely, if at all, human and which justified keeping them "in their place." The Dionysian subculture of bohe-mians could be tolerated because their numbers were never large, their turnover was rapid (attractive mostly to the young, bohemianism was something most of them rapidly "grew out of"), and even if they weren't indifferent to politics, they could provide no real political threat, although they could and did supply color, romance, and exotica to urban "quarters" which served the commerce of these districts by attracting tourists.

Even certain aspects of upper-class style despite the power of the very wealthy, can be stigmatized somewhat. An upper-class sub-culture has sufficient institutional power to maintain itself in a rela-tively hostile middle-class environment. But toleration of those qualities of aristocratic style offensive to middle-class morality (ar-rogance, aloofness, luxurious self-indulgence) is promoted by an ecology which allows upper-class life to be lived in places others generally can't afford to enter, making it largely inaccesible to public view, and therefore only occasionally (when inadvertently exposed) outrageous of public (i.e. middle class) morality. That it can be out-rageous is indicated by the fact that an aristocratic style is generally a severe liability in a candidate for public office—which makes es-pecially interesting and courageous the refusal of former candidates like William Buckley and Gore Vidal to disguise or compromise theirs.

The old rich, the old poor, the Negroes, the Jews, the peasant immigrants, and the bohemians have made the United States in fact a culturally plural society for a very long time, but for most of Ameri-can history "minority" groups were either unable or unwilling to resist the efforts of the white, Protestant, middle-class majority to neutralize the political impact of their subcultures on the common life by labeling them as "deviant"—as sinful–corrupt, as deprived–disadvantaged, as decadent–snobbish, as ethnic–transitional, in short as un-American in the sense that although their members might, as *individuals*, be potentially "as good as anybody else," their sub-cultures were not as wholesome, not as honorable as the culture rooted in the secularized version of the Protestant Ethic.

But although deviance from middle-class proprieties has always involved large numbers of Americans, the dissent has never been as

loud, there has never been so many dissenters, they have never been so concentrated (in central cities and on college campuses), and they have never had as much political weight as their militance reveals they have developed in recent years. Twenty million American Negroes have going for them not only the justice of their cause (they've always had that) but their ability to destroy American cities as well. Seven million American students have going for them their demonstration that they actually can bring American universities to the proverbial grinding halt. This knowledge gives them a certain leverage, not only in pressing their claims but in pressing them in a manner that affirms their own cultural style.

It is always difficult to say just how many people are involved in revolutions like these. No doubt, the black militants do not speak for large majorities of Negroes, just as the hippies and the student activists do not speak for large majorities of the young. But like attitudes to the Vietnam war, the number of people for whom the activists speak is rapidly shifted by events. At Columbia, as at Berkeley, sympathy for the demonstrators rose sharply after frightened responses by administrators brought on brutal police treatment. Sympathy for the black militants rises sharply both in and out of black communities as evidence of the depths of American racism accumulates—as, for example, it becomes clearer that the Oakland police are in fact out to destroy the leadership of the Black Panthers.

It is true that the black ghettoes are filled with people who want a piece of American affluence more than they want a revolution, and that the universities are filled with moderate and liberal students who would like to go quietly about becoming -ologists of one kind or another. But it seems increasingly clear that they would like to do these things without, in the case of blacks, sacrificing their ethnic pride (without, as Floyd McKissick put it, "becoming white"), and in the case of the students, without having to suppress their views about sex, marihuana, and the Vietnam war. The moderate black middle class is very reluctant to put down their more militant brothers; it would give aid and comfort to the common enemy. For the same reason, liberal students and professors are reluctant to put down their more radical colleagues.

The numbers of committed militants at a given moment are, then, less significant than the extent to which their claims are being heard by not entirely unsympathetic ears. Militant Negroes are claiming

public honor and recognition for black heroes, the beauty of black women, the vital authenticity of black culture, and claiming political and economic autonomy for black communities. Bearded anti-Vietnam war demonstrators chant, "We *are* the people"; student militants claim a voice in the government of the university which, it is clear, they envisage not as an elite training institution, but as a political community; and the hippies want to turn everybody on (it seems sometimes that they have almost succeeded) and to found new communities in which everybody is turned on.

These claims have brought on a strange crisis of legitimacy in the land. Briefly stated, that crisis is constituted by the apparent incapacity of the nation's political institutions to contain, with some semblance of civil peace and order, the claims of its minorities for the public recognition and legitimacy of their subcultures, and hence for a greater voice in the formulation and administration of the policies they must live by within their social enclaves, whether ghetto, Bohemia, or academic grove. This incapacity reflects the tradition of ambivalence in American history regarding cultural unity and diversity, between the melting pot idea and the pluralist idea. While free, compulsory education was expressing the desire to Americanize the immigrants, the ghetto was expressing the impulse to cultural self-preservation (both by the natives who excluded and the immigrants who segregated themselves). While Fourth of July patriotism was expressing the gropings toward a national identity, provincial hostility to "the guvmunt" and to centers of cosmopolitan influence were expressing the affirmation of narrow local autonomies.

The ambivalence was really a double ambivalence; each pole was itself ambivalent: to be authentic, a pluralist perspective must accord equal legitimacy to diverse life styles, and this it has never completely done. The salient features of deviant subcultural styles have more often than not been regarded, even by liberal pluralists, as evidence of cultural deprivation—at best as quaint, colorful ethnicity, at worst as simple stigmata—tolerable so long as they were transitory to something approaching the dominant style. On the other hand, the attempts of provincial, nativist groups to maintain the domination of the traditional style as *the* American style stopped short of supporting the emergence of broadly inclusive *national* institutions which, by bringing the deviants into the cultural mainstream, would have supported that style and passed it down the generations. The most

enthusiastic celebrators of "Americanism" were precisely those groups most suspicious of or overtly hostile to integrating the varieties of the national political community into a unified culture.

Societies that span such substantial dissensus over the fundamental proprieties of social life but must nevertheless make laws which in theory apply to all the people, whatever, their fundamental sense of propriety, are faced with severe tensions and latent violence which continually threaten to fracture whatever brittle or fragile solidarity such a society has. In the past (and still) America has coped with its culturally plural reality in a variety of ways which maintained the official or legal domination of middle-class values: by ecological arrangements which segregated both its deviant groups, neutralizing their cultural traditions, and the deviant or illicit functions and facilities required by members of dominant groups (in a whole state like Nevada, in cities like Las Vegas, Cicero, Illinois, and Miami Beach, and in sections of cities called red light districts, tenderloins, and so forth). Most commonly, our society has attempted to cope with the discrepancies between law and custom, and between expressed values and illicit appetites, by what sociologists call "institutionalized evasion," a social process prevalent in modern, plural societies, in which the dominant social institutions, including those of law enforcement, permit or actively collaborate in the support of the evasion of their own rules in order to ameliorate the tensions engendered by these discrepancies.

Examples? The Volstead Act was blandly and openly violated by all sorts of people, respectable and not, very often with the cooperation of local officials, until Prohibition was repealed. Crew chiefs in migrant labor camps regularly sell liquor to their Negro, Mexican, and Puerto Rican workers, without a license and at outrageous prices, usually with the full knowledge of local officials who tolerate it in order to keep the undesirables out of town. Pious ladies can play Bingo in the church basement without any fear of being arrested for gambling by the cop on the beat; he might even stop in for tea and cookies. Fornication is still a crime in many states, but the highway patrol does not typically roust motel sleepers looking for evidence of legal violation, although much could be found. The fraternity boy picked up for wobbling down Main Street with a bellyfull of beer is not usually tossed into the tank with other drunks, but turned over gently to the Dean of Students, who may give him a ritual lecture

which will be ritually uh-huh'd. Everybody who knew the old New York divorce law knows that New York divorces were often elaborate staged charades in which judge, lawyers, policemen, photographers, hotel detectives, professional correspondents, and parties of the first and second part cooperated in making a farce of the law, but in getting people divorced.

My final example is the best one, reported to me by a former colleague, a Mississippi gentleman born and bred. Until just a few years ago Mississippi was officially a dry state in which anyone could get a drink. This by itself does not constitute *institutionalized* evasion. But until the law was changed recently, the state of Mississippi collected a tax on liquor illegally imported into the state. *That's* institutionalized evasion! When, as a young man sensitized to the perception of phoniness in his elders, my colleague discovered this, he confronted his mother with this evidence of adult duplicity and asked if she didn't think this was appalling. She answered no, she didn't think so, since there was actually a severe split in the state between the fundamentalist Baptists, who were dry, and the people who wanted their whiskey when they wanted it. She thought the arrangement was comfy: the Baptists had the law on their side, which made them feel righteous, which was what they wanted, and the wets could get their drinks, which was what they wanted, and the state got *its* cut too. This seemed to satisfy everybody except budding young intellectuals like her son, who demanded Moral Consistency. I don't know whether this was his first lesson in sophistication, but he hasn't been innocent since. My point is that moral consistency may be neither possible nor desirable where plural cultural constituencies must live cheek by jowl as one nation under one law.

Reflecting middle-class morality generally, the law yields to and cooperates with such institutionalized evasion when those who demand the illicit goods and services have sufficient weight to create a serious political problem if enforcement practices don't bend just a bit to the pressures exercised by local customs. But for the most part, the system of institutionalized evasion rendered most of its benefits to the periodic illegal aims and illicit appetites of respectable members of the middle class, not to the deviant groups for whose way of life the more erotic, "expressive," or Dionysian cultural style (immoral in terms of the Protestant Ethic) was central and continual rather than peripheral or occasional.

This system has been weakening for a long time, partly because the very success of institutionalized evasion fostered disrespect for the law among the increasing number of those who understood how it operated, and because this understanding made society and its establishments increasingly vulnerable to allegations of hypocrisy, that favorite indictment by the young of the old. But the tolerance for and visibility of erotic music and dance, sex, liquor, gambling, and the rest of the "dirty secrets" of American life have been accelerating for more than a generation. Fifty years ago, if you offered a man a drink, he might well have replied with pride and disdain that he never touched the stuff, fully expecting you to feel put down by his refusal; today, such a response would be regarded in most circles as absurd, and this is a measure of the downward mobility of those whose prestige lay at least partly in their abstinence. Social dancing (with bodies touching) was once similarly regarded by large numbers of influential people as sinful, and "leading to" only God knows what depths of degradation.

But these changes would not have occurred, nor would the contemporary claims to respectability by the erotic and expressive minorities have achieved their current strength without the long term decline of the Protestant Ethic, which began around the time of the first World War with the attack on the Puritanism of "The Genteel Tradition." This attack, largely uninterrupted for the past fifty years, has been part of a pattern permitting the defection of large sections of the middle class, particularly the professional, metropolitan, better educated parts of it (the so-called *upper* middle class, or *new* middle class) from Protestant asceticism to a pattern of life emphasizing leisure and the consumption of material goods. Over the past thirty years, this defection has been documented again and again. From Leo Lowenthal's work studying shifts from "idols of production" to "idols of consumption" in the character of biographies in popular magazines, to David Riesman's documentation of the shift from "inner-directedness" to "other-directedness," to William Whyte's work on the triumph of Organization Man over the old Protestant Ethic, to John Kenneth Galbraith's anatomy of private affluence, to the latest reports on family discussions over whether to get a third car or a boat, a cabin in the mountains or a house at the beach, the more prosperous sectors of American society have been learning to give up the asceticism of their ancestors to become consumers, players, and vacationers.

The defection of this major segment of support for Protestant asceticism has occurred, as I pointed out earlier, without being accompanied by a corresponding ideology which justifies and ennobles the substitution of comfort and fun for piety and thrift. But the weakening of the Protestant Ethic and the ideological vacuum of upper middle-class affluence have helped prepare the ground for the more radical demands for recognition by hippies, militant blacks, and others claiming legitimacy for their expressive subcultures.

Revolutions in cultural style like these are not ultimately successful without prior changes in technology and economic and social structure which render them viable by strengthening the hand of innovators and weakening the hand of their opponents. The revolution against asceticism would not have been as successful as it has been so far without the development of an economy dependent upon high levels of consumption for its sustenance (and without the invidious understanding of asceticism Freud helped provide). The Negro Revolution would not have met with what limited success it has had without changes in the need for rural labor, which pushed Negroes out of the South, the absence of unskilled white immigrant labor from Europe, which pulled them into Northern ghettoes, and cold war politics which made "The Negro Problem" an increasing embarrassment in the conduct of American foreign affairs. The ascendance of a new ethic with respect to sexual behaviour (love sanctifies premarital intercourse) would not have occurred without a birth control technology rendering the risk of pregnancy potentially negligible, and without changes in social structure (urbanization, employment, hence the independence of women, the decline of certain family functions) rendering even the unlikely illegitimate pregnancy an inconvenience, and perhaps even an embarrassment, but certainly not a fact which need "ruin" anyone's life, in that old sense in which we used to speak of illicit intercourse as ruination for a young girl.

Like Bernard Shaw's dustman, the blacks can't afford middle-class morality, and like Huck Finn, the hippies can't stand it and light out for the territory ahead. The blacks reject it because, in *systematically* victimizing them, it renders highly improbable their chances of achieving the good life through it, and the young reject it because they've had it and found it ideologically and emotionally wanting. The hippies have seen its failure to provide satisfaction in

the lives of their own parents, and the student activists are going further down the liberated road their liberal parents started down. And in each case their rejection of middle-class values is not a mere expression of esthetic disdain but a serious political claim for the public recognition of their own authentic life styles. In this view, it is not enough that Marian Anderson and Leontyne Price may be invited to a White House musicale; Aretha Franklin and James Brown should be too. If Fred Waring's Pennsylvanians are welcome in the White House, the Jefferson Airplane should be too. For these artists express the culture of Americans, and they have a right to expect that culture to be honored by those institutions which, in symbolizing the whole nation, must contain its variety.

In any case, the conflict is no longer simply over the provision of equal opportunities to bring America's "deprived" and "deviant" groups into the mainstream of American life; the mainstream is itself being questioned in a way that challenges not only its direction but the social composition of its waters. The hippies and the student activists have already swum in them and found them less than invigorating. But the major challenge comes from the militant spokesmen for the black ghetto. To break out of the ghetto may have once required middle-class speech, middle-class manners, and middle-class clothing. No longer. The emphasis of these spokesmen now is not on breaking out of the ghetto, but on gaining the autonomy of their people within the ghetto, and on claiming for its culture equal legitimacy with the other cultures of America. The major function of the mushrooming black student organizations on campuses across the country is to ensure that Negro access to white institutions of higher learning is not won at the cost of the black man's deracination from his own traditions. The accents and the argot of the black ghetto are increasingly heard on college campuses, intentionally used and lovingly cultivated by people who "know better." I have sat in university lecture halls and listened to black American professors clothed in imitation leopard spots turn on a ghetto style and palpably *thrill* plump, middle-class Negro matrons in the audience— as if a lovely illicit experience were finally being rendered real for them by virtue of its daring disclosure in an historically inappropriate context. And if it happens in the universities, can Madison Avenue be far behind?

The Avenue has already begun to fall in behind the hippies in

certain superficial respects, while the hippies (fulfilling the traditional avant-garde functions of bohemians) preoccupy themselves now with their experiments in the creation of erotic communities, although seriously harassed by public health officials and others in the rural counties in which they are attempting to operate. But the major point is that one of the conceivable consequences of persistent attempts by deviant groups to legitimize their subcultures would be the disappearance of many of the "middle-class" requirements for social respectability, because the success of these attempts would mean important changes in the styles and demeanor of public life, for example, changes in the norms governing dress, polite speech, and the very meaning of "education." A schoolteacher might talk and dress like a swinger, a postman like a hippie, and a black Olympic athlete might wear his hair conked, natural, or whatever way he pleases other than all-American short.

The major significance of current attacks on the middle class, then, is that the nation is being called upon to confront the fact of its plural cultural reality, and to adapt to the claims for legitimacy being made by its dispossessed, dependent, and formerly relatively quiescent groups. These claims require a reexamination of the nation's sources of solidarity because they raise the question of the point in the proliferation of legitimate pluralisms at which a threat is presented to a society's moral viability as a single social entity. If one envisions the United States as a mosaic of equally legitimate subcultures largely insulated from one another despite occasional points of contact and areas of cooperation, and someone asks where, then, lies our moral unity as a nation?, one could, I suppose, answer "in ruins." Or, one can observe that there is or seems to be very little that all or nearly all Americans share: the disposition to accommodate or bargain away our differences, to prefer disingenuousness to conflict, a few constitutional principles, perhaps not even these— which may help explain why frequent opinion polls are becoming so essential to the formulation of public policy.

But the problematic character of national solidarity is disturbing primarily to those who think of *society* as identical with *community*, that is, as a social organization governed by a deep consensus about values of a very fundamental kind. There is a sense, however, in which a community is exactly what the typical modern large scale social organization is not and, perhaps, cannot be, given its de-

pendence on differentiation. It may, for example, be said of big cities that they represent that form of social organization not governed by basic common values but by a series of perpetually *ad hoc* accommodations and temporary agreements (that is what the proverbial urban "corruption" is mostly about) which make it possible for what communal life there is to go on in the subcultures which make it up.

But the representatives of the traditional "American" consensus do not yield their hegemony easily. Ill at ease in the affluent, permissive, and erotic society which the application of their ethics to industrial productivity helped create, and allied now with that part of the blue collar work force most threatened by the claims for black power, they know who their enemies are: black militance ("crime in the streets"), student activism ("defiance of authority"), the not-so-new culture of the hippies ("immorality, obscenity, sex, drugs, and treason"), and the liberals who defend, condone, or otherwise resist repressing them. In the areas of their greatest strength (the small cities of the Midwest, the rural South, Texas, and southern California) and in the Congres of the United States they have been able to slow the decline of the Protestant Ethic. And over the past two years, as the conflict intensifies and polarizes, they have been able to put together conservative majorities and win several key elections they were not expected to win.

The grievances, however, will not disappear. Black protest will continue to grow, becoming more desperate and violent as resistance to it stiffens. The protest of the young, student and nonstudent alike, will continue as it becomes clearer that this country has no serious, honorable role for its youth except to hurl them against the Vietnamese, who kill them with bullets, or to store them in the universities, which bore them to death.

Like all major historical confrontations between established order and the claims of previously powerless groups, this conflict has at least the merit of being a real one. But "law and order" is a fragile slogan in a society which depends upon "institutionalized evasion" for civil peace; and frugality, sobriety, piety, and hard work will be increasingly hard to celebrate convincingly in a society which has distributed voluptuousness and luxury as broadly among its population as ours has.

The pessimism and apprehensiveness of liberals in 1969, however, rests on the apparently well founded belief that the conservatives have no program, other than forceful repression, for coping with the

American crisis of legitimacy. The two reasonable and viable alternatives for coping with the legitimate demands of the black and the young for recognition are those that envision either integrating them into the nation as individual first class citizens, or recognizing their corporate reality as distinctive American groups, and hence honoring their subcultures as authentic expressions of the pluralistic American experience. In 1969, the country's conservative majority seems ready to do neither.

On Sociology and Sociologists

Introduction

This section of the book contains some of my views on the theory and practice of sociology, and on its significance in contemporary intellectual discourse. **Sociology and the Intellectuals** is the essay with which I broke into professional print (I had published an essay on W. H. Auden some years earlier in my college literary magazine). In retrospect, it seems to have been my way of "committing" myself to becoming a sociologist (when I was a graduate student, there was much talk—and some anxiety—among the professors in my department about whether we students were sufficiently "committed to sociology").

In my years as a graduate student in Berkeley many of my friends were either students in humanities departments, or students not at all, or only occasionally (Berkeley had lots of "nonstudents" then too, although their position had not yet been elevated into a Social Status). The milieu I moved in bridged the academic and bohemian subcultures of the Bay Area, and in much of the former and most of the latter sociology was something close to an intellectual's dirty word, suggesting either a gross insensitivity or an antihuman sort of Machiavellian malevolence. Philosophers could and did (still do) disdain it as a naive and debased kind of pseudo-philosophizing;

historians, for its ignorance of the documented past which contained the time-bound data on which its so-called timeless principles and generalizations were said to rest; and literary people had only contempt for the prose ("barbarous" was the favorite adjective) behind whose technical vocabulary ("jargon") its lack of substantive human insight could hide[1]

But I liked being a sociologist, liked reading the books and writing the papers and staying up all night arguing with friends, and I was more or less continually faced with responding to digs, remarks, and other intellectual challenges which ranged in nobility of conception from Malcolm Cowley's careful analysis of sociology's poverty of transitive verbs to the remark of the wife of a philosopher friend of mine after a particularly heated discussion. "Shit on sociology!" is what she said.

So, like many people in the social sciences, I went ahead and tried to make intellectual work out of what was a personal problem. I had passed my qualifying examinations for the doctorate in 1955 and thought I would try out as a dissertation topic the problem of humanistic attitudes toward sociology. I was actually planning to go out and interview samples of philosophers, historians, poets, critics, and so on, to test some of my ideas, but the plans never got off the ground. My dissertation supervisor, Reinhard Bendix, wisely counseled me that one ought to learn something from one's research. He thought that my proposal indicated that I knew enough about the subject already, and that the dissertation I might produce was not likely to be much better than the proposal itself. It was his suggestion that I revise the proposal for publication, and find another dissertation subject.

Where to send the essay, though, became the kind of problem I would face repeatedly in the future, for it was too "technical" for general publication, too speculative or discursive for the sociology journals. Bendix knew one of the editors of *The Antioch Review*, and sent the manuscript to Yellow Springs for advice. The editors' remarks suggested there had been a lively editorial conference about the essay, but the magazine ran it as their lead article in the Autumn of 1957.

The publication of the article did several things for me. The con-

---

[1]Thirteen years after its publication *Sociology and the Intellectuals* has "historical" interest; my impression is that sociology and sociologists have far more prestige today among intellectuals than they did in 1957.

gratulations of several prominent sociologists indicated that I was far from alone in smarting at some of the more ignorant hostility directed at sociology by other intellectuals. Moreover, an article in effect defending sociology and sociologists in a *general magazine* of good reputation gave sociology another spokesman to the intellectual community. Bennett Berger is one sociologist who knows how to use the English language, went the comment—both from those who meant it generously and from those who wanted only to damn with faint praise. (There is a self-serving view among some social scientists that writing well is a way of cheating by seducing readers, a view—whose roots in Protestant asceticism seem clear— which suggests that "style" is a way of covering for failures of logic and evidence, the only two legitimate agents of persuasion.) The article also began to bring me invitations from other general magazines to review books and to comment on sociological matters for audiences composed largely of readers who were not social scientists.

In the meantime, I was having the first of my two experiences (both benign) with collaboration. I had taken a seminar in sociological theory with Reinhard Bendix, and I used some of the ideas developed there to organize a very long paper on American sociological theorists that I wrote to impress (and hence make peace with) two other professors with whom I had had some conflict. Bendix read it and suggested that we collaborate on a paper critical of the dominant school of American sociological theory. I did a version; he did a version. He reworked mine; I reworked his. This was repeated for more than two years (in the process of which Bendix was in Europe for a year, I was finishing my doctorate) until the paper was purged of almost all of its original polemical character—a purging which in retrospect I judge to have been wise, although I had my doubts then. Bendix arranged for the publication of one of the intermediate versions of **Images of Society and Problems of Concept Formation in Sociology** in a German journal before it finally appeared in English in 1959 in *Symposium on Sociological Theory,* edited by Llewellyn Gross.[2]

The article **On Talcott Parsons** began with a request by *Commentary* to review a symposium on Parsons, whose influence had become widespread enough in the academic world to convince the editors

---

[2]Bendix has since revised this essay still again for publication in a collection of his own writings.

that he was worthy of their readers' attention. *Commentary* had reviewed my book *Working-Class Suburb* (compensating, perhaps, for its failure to print "The Myth of Suburbia"), and the reviewer and I had had a vigorous exchange in that magazine's Letters columns. The exchange was apparently spirited enough to suggest to the editors that I might be useful to them as a reviewer of current books in sociology. In any case, I had a lot of manuscript on Parsons left over from the purgings of the Bendix collaboration, and, as with many book reviews, this assignment grew into a full blown essay. Given the problems of interpreting Parsons to a general audience, it was almost inevitable that it would. The version of the essay which appears here is slightly different from both the original manuscript and the version finally printed in *Commentary*, after revisions, additions, and other heavy editing, more than a year later.

I continued to receive requests from "popular" (if not "mass," although there was one abortive effort for *Life*) media, for example, from *The Nation, The New Leader*, and the *New York Times*. Reviewing books in sociology for the *Times* presented me with a new kind of problem: the problem of my own relationship to schools of thought within sociology when I was writing for an "outside" audience in influential media. My personal predispositions and style of work placed me in the camp of qualitative or "humanistic" sociologists. But such epistemology as I had bothered to develop was positivist. I believed that sociology was a "science"—or that it made more sense to work under the assumption that it was or could be, rather than on the assumption that it wasn't or couldn't. I thought that the kinds of statements and assertions that sociologists aim at should at least in principle be empirical and testable; I believed in the "separation" of facts and values—but also that the most "interesting" facts were the ones directly relevant to important values. One of the great joys of research and writing for me was managing the tensions between the two: that's where the "discipline" of sociology lay. I believed also that "objectivity" and "detachment" were worthwhile goals, without ignoring either the fact that one's "biases" were in any case likely to be visible to a careful reader or the fact that one's moral feelings might be a source of strength in one's work (as they clearly were in Max Weber's) by directing one's attention to the most critical and complex social issues and by sensitizing one to the power of that directive capacity.

My reviews of **Sociology on Trial** (which, from the perspective of

1969, seems to foreshadow the burgeoning contemporary movement for a more "engaged" sociology), one version of which appeared in *The New York Times Book Review*, was regarded by some activist sociologists as a betrayal of my "humanistic" commitments. I don't think it was. What it does reveal is my belief that, as a science, sociology should be concerned primarily with the discovery of what is true (the true does not always contribute to social improvement). It reveals also my belief that sociology is not well suited to being a missionary science, and that training as a sociologist (for whatever the reasons one originally undertook it) does not equip one particularly well to function as an ideological combatant in the political arenas of the larger community. Truth seeking in society requires the increasingly precise use of language and continual shifts of perspective which enable one to get that proverbial look at a question from all of its sides. But precise language is frequently ill suited to ideological purposes, and political combatants have properly little tolerance for perhapses and on the other hands and digressions to consider the "deeper" issues raised by *ad hoc* considerations of some immediately pressing problem. Nor should scholars expect very much willing tolerance for "academic" values from those so committed to "action" that "academic" becomes very nearly a synonym for trivial and irrelevant, if not downright unmanly or worse.

It is this tension between the scientific and the political that underlies my considerations of the sociologists Parsons, Weber, Mills, Riesman, and John Seeley. Ernest Becker once told me that the trouble with many of my reviews was that they didn't "take a position." I think that this is partly true, although I do not regard it as particularly damaging. Where I don't "take a position" it is because I think that with respect to some issues a certain ambiguity is the only honorable response, particularly where the unambiguous taking of a position diminishes some dimension of the truth. In these polarized times, when one is continually pushed to say whose side one is on, and when "if you're not part of the solution you're part of the problem," I think it is important that some people insist upon their right to say neither more nor less than they actually think and feel.

But nothing I have said here indicates that sociologists should retreat into the kinds of studies in which detachment is easy to maintain because hardly anyone cares about the significance of the work. The maintenance of detachment becomes a real adventure in ideas only when the pressures against it are very strong. As human

beings, sociologists come by their emotional involvements "naturally"; as sociologists, human beings come by their scientific discipline "unnaturally," by conscious, rigorous training. Neither inheritance, it seems to me, is particularly virtuous or vicious by itself. Sociologists are continually asked either to affirm their "humanity" by demonstrating their emotional commitments or to affirm their scientific training by demonstrating their detachment. Each diminishes the whole man, and it is for this reason that I honor **Weber**, **Mills**, and **Riesman**, who refuse to make unambiguous choices, whereas Parsons has apparently opted for "science" and **Seeley** for "feeling."

Similarly, nothing I have said here indicates that detachment requires ethical neutrality or the exile of social criticism from sociology. But to practice social criticism *through* sociology requires great discipline, great "cool." An example: when a sociologist analyzes a pattern of culture or a social structure that the conventional wisdom regards as malign (E.G. Merton on political bossism), and reveals the specific "latent functions" the pattern or structure performs, such functional analysis is usually (and rightly) applauded as good sociology—regardless of the "conservative" inferences it invites us to draw. But when a sociologist takes a pattern or structure that the conventional wisdom regards as benign, and tries to demonstrate its "latent dysfunctions," such analysis is often frowned upon as "social criticism"—perhaps not sociology at all. The differential treatment, I think, is grounded partly in the fact that the latter kind of analysis is often carried out in a polemical style. It does not demonstrate, it "lays bare"; it does not show, it "exposes," hence grates, and offends the ethos of science.

Now I understand well enough why conservative sentiments are readily expressible in a toneless language and a detached style. There are well established *scholarly* traditions of dealing with controversial questions in a detached and objective style while yet conveying one's political message through the mastery of that style. The language and rhetoric of conservatism have an elective affinity to academic language and rhetoric. Radicals are not so blessed; the radical sentiments of "outsiders" are usually expressed in an aggressive language and a "committed" style which readily identify them as "ideology." But there is no good reason why they *must* be expressed that way. By creating a detailed ethnography which documents the human cost of social order or by carefully and cooly

tracing the destructive consequences of normative patterns and institutional practices, one makes valid contributions to the literature of sociology *and* performs valuably as a social critic.

Indeed, it is in matters such as these that *sociologists* are best equipped to function as social critics. There is very little evidence to suggest that the scholarly study of society makes one more effective on a soapbox; quite the contrary. A commitment to the true handcuffs one in political combat as often as it arms one with "the facts." The works of Erving Goffman, precise and deadpan, constitute a more devasting social criticism than most of the anti-establishmentarians can muster at their most militant.

Sociology
and the Intellectuals

An Analysis of a Stereotype   1957

While you and I have lips and voices which
are for kissing and to sing with,
who cares if some one eyed son of a bitch
invents an instrument to measure Spring with?

e. e. cummings*

I

For some years, humanist intellectuals have been cultivating a
hostile stereotype of sociology and sociologists. Like other stereotypes, this one has its foundation in fact; like other stereotypes too,
its exaggerations, whether expressed in the language of annihilating
wit or of earnest bludgeoning, call for some serious comment. It is
surprising therefore, that the responses of sociologists have been
anything but dispassionate. These responses range all the way from
(1) Daniel Lerner's polemical defense of sociology in his article
analyzing the book reviews of *The American Soldier,*[1] to (2) the
posture of tolerant disdain toward the "misguided" stereotype, to
(3) a sort of nervous embrace of the stereotype by sociologists
themselves (which attempts—usually unsuccessfully—to demonstrate that they do *too* have a sense of humor), often involving a
self-parody whose furtive masochism is almost startling.

There is no real need to document the stereotype with exhaustive
quotations since it is rife enough in intellectual circles for everyone

From *The Antioch Review*   17, no. 3 (Autumn 1957), 275–90.
*" Voices to Voices," *Poems 1923–1954* (Harcourt, Brace Jovanovich). Re-
printed by permission.
[1]Daniel Lerner, *"The American Soldier* and the Public". In *Continuities in
Social Research*, R. K. Merton and P. F. Lazarsfeld, eds. (Glencoe, Ill.: Free
Press, 1950), pp. 212–51.

to have had his own personal experience of it. The overt expression of the stereotype in print is the exception, and whole articles devoted to it are rare. The most common vehicle for its expression is the derisive "remark" and the parenthetical aside. Occasionally, one finds a curiously ambiguous statement like the following:

Popular images are rarely entirely wrong; and if the mass media and the popular mind today see the social scientist as a man with pencil and pad in hand, buttonholing hapless citizens on the street, the error is not in the observation—it is only in seeing the social scientist as the interviewer. . . . Today, no matter what the question put to the social scientist, he begins his answer by composing a questionnaire, which he then gets filled out by having an appropriate number of respondents interviewed.[2]

One of the interesting things in this statement is the apparent convergence of images held by the "popular mind" with those held by intellectuals like Glazer. I say "apparent" because intellectuals do not often share the stereotypes of the popular mind, and the quoted instance is not one of the exceptions. Glazer does not describe a *popular* image in his remarks, but a stereotype held by intellectuals. Anyone who has done extensive interviewing of the "popular mind" knows that ordinary people are generally naïvely interested as well as pleased and flattered to be interviewed by a social scientist; it takes considerable sophistication to feel disdainful of and superior to the poised pencil of the interviewer. But in a curiously inverted "proof by authority" Glazer attributes an image to the popular mind in order to validate his own.

Using evidence like this demands some reading between the lines. For example, nowhere in the above quotation does Glazer explicitly state that the image supposedly held by the popular mind is an invidious one; it is largely a matter of tone, created by key connotative words like "buttonholing," and "hapless," and "appropriate." Many expressions of the stereotype are of this hit-and-run kind, and depend for their meaning and effect upon one's being "in" on the current scapegoatology. For example, the poet and critic Randall Jarrell explicates a few lines from a Robert Frost poem, then says, "if you can't feel any of this, you *are* a Convention of Sociologists."[3]

[2] In an introductory note by Nathan Glazer to I. L. Peretz' "The Interviewer at Work," *Commentary* (February 1953), 195.
[3] *Poetry and the Age* (New York: Alfred A. Knopf, 1953), p. 65.

A remark like this would be meaningless to someone not "in" on the current stereotype; to those who *are* "in," and presumably a good number of readers are, it is very funny indeed. Similarly, W. H. Auden speaks to Jarrell's audience when he says:

> *Thou shalt not answer questionnaires*
> *Or quizzes upon World-Affairs,*
> *Nor with compliance*
> *Take any test. Thou shalt not sit*
> *With statisticians nor commit*
> *A social science.*[4]

There are, of course, more elaborate and heavy handed assaults, J. P. Marquand's portrait of W. Lloyd Warner in *Point of No Return* not being the only one. Still, it is the light touch of people like Auden and Jarrell that is most effective in spreading the stereotype.

Stereotypes, and hostile stereotypes especially, do injury to the group stereotyped, and it is or ought to be our responsibility to correct them. But stereotypes are not generally exorcised by pretending they do not exist; nor are they dispelled by polemic or a demonstration of innocence. Although founded in fact, stereotypes are nonrational, and flourish in spite of the preponderance of evidence against them. Thus arguing from facts to correct an emotional excrescence is vain. What we want to know are the conditions that have generated the stereotype and permitted it to grow. Knowing these we can transcend polemic and use our understanding in more effective ways.

II

The stereotype of the sociologist has two dimensions, founded in contradictory beliefs which, in turn, have their source in the structure of the intellectual professions. The image of the sociologist as a pathetically ignorant and pompous bumbler (jargon-ridden, pretentious, and without insight) is based on the conviction that sociology has no special subject matter, and is therefore no science; its technical apparatus and methodological strictures are hence not only presumptuous but futile, and result only in pretentiousness and banality. The image of the sociologist as a Machiavellian manipulator, however, clearly rests on a recognition of the efficacy of

[4]"Under Which Lyre," *Collected Shorter Poems,* 1927–1957, Random House, Inc. Copyright 1949 by W. H. Auden.

scientific, especially statistical, techniques in dealing with a human subject matter. But both of these—the perceived failure as well as the perceived success of sociology—have elicited from the intellectuals a hostile response.

A. The Problem of Subject Matter: The Sociologist as Bumbler

The tendency to specialization in the intellectual professions submits them to pressure to define specifically a subject matter uniquely their own, in order to justify their existence in a profession- and specialty-conscious culture, to establish and preserve their identities with foundations and university administrations, and to demonstrate their utility and their consequent right to public support. As new specializations develop and claim professional status, entirely reasonable questions of justification can be raised. What can you do that others not trained in your profession cannot do? What competence has your training conferred on you that is denied to others because of their lack of such training? I take it that the flourishing health of the image of the sociologist as bumbler can in part be attributed to the failure of sociologists to answer these questions satisfactorily. Any discipline which claims as its special subject matter the domain of "social relations" or "social systems" or "society" or any of the other textbook-preface definitions claims not a special subject matter but the whole gamut of human experience, a claim which thousands of scholars and intellectuals are with good reason likely to dispute.[5] Louis Wirth's definition of sociology as the study of that which is true of men by virtue of the fact that they have everywhere and at all times lived a group life, strikes the eye as somewhat better, but runs into the difficulty[6] of generally assuming that pretty nearly everything that is true of men is true by virtue of this fact.

It is in part due to this failure to meet the responsibility of defining one's professional competence simply and clearly to interested lay-

[5]At a recent meeting of the Western Branch of the American Oriental Society, a distinguished member introduced a resolution affirming the Branch's loyalty to the traditions of humanistic study, and barring from the pages of the society's journal what he called articles of the "social science type."
[6]I say "difficulty" not because I think this assumption may not be useful, but because (1) such an assumption places the sociologist in the role of "academic imperialist," and (2) the implied primacy of society, or group life, over the individual runs counter to deeply rooted Western values about "the individual."

men that sociological "jargon," for example, is met with such resistance and resentment. Laymen react with no such rancor to the technical vocabularies of mathematics, the physical and natural sciences, and engineering because by an act of faith (based, to be sure, on a common-sense understanding of what these disciplines do) they decide that behind the jargon, which they do not understand (because it is a descriptive shorthand, familiarity with which requires special training), lies a *special subject matter amenable to technical treatment* which they *could* understand *if* they took the trouble. Thus the intelligent layman feels no shame or outrage at not being able to understand a technical article in a chemistry journal—or, for that matter, in not understanding the job specifications in a newspaper want ad for engineers. No such toleration is likely toward the technical vocabulary of sociology until it is accepted as a legitimate scientific profession.

That this acceptance is not forthcoming is due partly to the belief of many intellectuals that the technical vocabulary is not a natural concomitant of scientific enterprise, but rather an attempt to disguise the banality of the results of sociological studies: sociologists "belabor the obvious"; they lack insight, and substitute in its place a barrage of carefully "proven" platitudes. Doubtless, some sociologists do, but every intellectual discipline has its share of brilliant people, as well as hacks, and there is no reason to suppose that sociology has more than a normal complement of either.[7] That the hacks are identified as *representative* of sociology is probably due more to judgments regarding the quality of sociological prose than to any analysis of the significance of its contents. Certainly, the prose of sociologists may seem clumsy when compared to the efforts of those whose business it is to write well. But whereas the results of scientific endeavor can legitimately be expected to be true and important, one cannot legitimately expect either that science be beautiful or that scientists be literary stylists.

In short, then, the hue, and cry about the jargon and turgidity of sociological prose, about the pretentiousness of its methodology and the banality of its preoccupations, is meaningful as criticism only if one assumes that sociology has no special subject matter amenable to technical treatment; if it has not, then it must be judged by the

---

[7]This feature of the stereotype asserts only that sociologists are cliché experts. What is interesting is that there is no "objective correlative" sufficient to make comprehensible the passion with which sociologists are denounced for being—innocuous.

same criteria as general essays on social and cultural topics. But as long as sociologists commit themselves to the traditions of science, and address their work not to a general literate audience, but to a community of their colleagues, these criticisms cannot seem other than beside the point. For the continuing application of aesthetic criteria of judgment to a nonaesthetic pursuit reveals only a refusal to grant to sociology the status of a science.

B. The Threat of Technique: The Sociologist as Diabolist

Sterotypes generally contain contradictory elements, and the stereotype of the sociologist is no exception. For along with his alleged gifts for the labored cliché and the clumsy, inept sentence, the sociologist is also credited with the diabolical potential of making puppets out of men, of destroying their individuality with IBM machines, of robbing them of their "individual human dignity," and of presiding, finally, over their total mechanization.[8] This image of the sociologists as diabolist[9] rests not on a conviction regarding the failure to define a specific subject matter, but on a fear regarding the success of sociological techniques, particularly statistics, which is seen by some intellectuals as *threatening* in two ways. First, the possibility of a science of society apparently implies the possibility of human behavior being controlled or manipulated by those who know its "causes" or by those with access to this knowledge. This vision, fostered by stimulus–response psychology, nourished by the "sociological perspective" which finds the source of individual behavior in group influences (and thus runs head on into the myth of the autonomous individual), and made fearful by reports of brain

---

[8] If it be pointed out that punch cards, IBM machines, and statistical techniques generally are merely tools, and that men who call themselves sociologists have been in the forefront of the battle against the "mechanization of man" and the "loss of individuality," then as likely as not the alternative elements of the stereotype will be invoked to damn them. The contradictions are legion. Those who believe that there *cannot* be a science of sociology often believe also that there *ought* not to be one, although if one says that there cannot be a science of sociology, then the dictum that there ought not to be one is meaningless; while if one says that there *ought* not to be a science of sociology, then it must be possible that there *can* be one.

[9] It is possible that the contradictory images of the sociologist as "bumbler" and the sociologist as "diabolist" can be related to the two traditions of sociology, the first stemming from the American tradition of social reform, the latter from the conservative European tradition of aristocratic privilege and the consequent right and responsibility of the aristocracy to "control" the fate of the masses.

washing and by novels like *1984* and *Brave New World*, is perhaps responsible for the peculiar ambivalence felt by some intellectuals toward the very *desirability* of a science of society. Sociology is thus seen as a potential threat to democratic society. Second, and more relevant in the present context, is the fact that the application of the techniques of science to human behavior is perceived as a threat to the viability of the most basic function of intellectuals in the Western tradition: to comment on and to interpret the meaning of contemporary experience.

III

The noun "intellectual" is one of those words which, in spite of lack of consensus regarding their meaning, continue to flourish in common usage. Attempts to define the term, to ask who the intellectuals are or what the intellectuals do, while useful, have seemed to me inconclusive. Certainly some intellectuals are "detached" or "free-floating"; surely a great number are "alienated"; doubtless "neurosis" is widespread among them; "irresponsibility," although currently out of fashion, is nevertheless affirmed by some of them. There is great magic in some of their bows; but, like Philoctetes, they often carry a corresponding wound whose stench forces them to live somewhat marginally. Finally, it is true that they create and transmit cultural values—sometimes. There are, however, two difficulties with these and similar attempts at definition. First, the relation between the key criteria of the definitions and the perspectives of the definers is generally only too transparent. Second, and for my purposes more interesting, is that although the word is part of common usage, the attempts to define it have generally ignored this fact. I propose here first to ask not who the intellectuals are or what they do, but rather who they are *thought* to be—whom do people have in mind when they use the term?—and only then to go on to the other questions.

In this connection, I was present a few years ago at a forum on "The Role of the Intellectual in Modern Society" held at the Museum of Modern Art in New York. The panel members were Granville Hicks, Clement Greenberg, W. H. Auden, and Robert Gorham Davis. Auden spoke last, and at one point in his remarks he looked around at his colleagues on the platform as if to take note of the experts chosen to talk on this topic. Hicks, he said, was a novelist and liter-

ary critic; Davis was a literary critic and English professor; Green-berg was an art critic and an editor of *Commentary*; and Auden identified himself as a poet and critic. Had this forum been held in the Middle Ages, he pointed out, we panel members would have been mostly members of the clergy; in the sixteenth and seventeenth centuries, we would have been mostly natural scientists; in the twentieth century, we are mostly literary men.[10] Auden did not at-tempt to answer the question that he had left implicit, but the question is a very leading one because the contemporary image of the intellectual *is*, I believe, essentially a literary one—and in two senses: he is conceived *as* a literary man, and this conception has been reinforced by the fact that it is literary men who have been most interested in, and who have written most on, the problem of the intellectual.

But it would be a mistake to assume that, because the intellectual is conceived in the image of the literary man, his essential property is that he is an artist or a student of literature. His identification as an intellectual rests not on the aesthetic value of his novels, plays, poems, essays, or literary criticism, but on his assumption, through them, of the role of *commentator on contemporary culture and interpreter of contemporary experience*.[11] But if the intellectuals are those who assume this role, Auden's implicit question still remains: Why, in our time, has it been typically literary men who have as-sumed the role of the intellectual? It is in attempting to answer this question that the relation between "the intellectuals" and the stereo-typing of sociologists will become clear.

In our time literary men have pre-empted the intellectual's role because of (*a*) their maximal freedom from the parochial demands of technical specialization, (*b*) their freedom (within their status as

[10]Although one's conception of who "the intellectuals" are is largely a func-tion of one's own intellectual level and preoccupations, the existence of subcultural phenomena does not prevent us from making statements about cultural worlds as wholes. Thus in spite of subcultural variations, the answer to "who are the intellectuals" is likely consistently to include: Camus, Sartre, Malraux, and de Beauvoir in France; Eliot, Auden, and the group around *Encounter* in England; Silone, Praz, Moravia, and Vittorini in Italy; and in the United States the writers associated with *Partisan Review, Commentary,* the literary quarterlies, and the "little magazines."
[11]With the publication and reception of *The Lonely Crowd,* David Riesman emancipated himself, in the eyes of the community of intellectuals, from bearing the burden of identification as a "sociologist"; that is to say, he became an intellectual.

literary men) to make large and uncompromising judgments about values, and (c) their maximal freedom from institutional restraints.

A. Specialization

Intellectuals, I have said, are commentators on contemporary culture and interpreters of contemporary experience; they are critics, liberal or conservative, radical or reactionary, of contemporary life. The range of their competence is not circumscribed; it includes nothing less than the entire cultural life of a people. If they are academic men, they may be specialists in various subjects; but their professional specialties do not generally interfere with their being intellectuals. In the humanities, and particularly in literature, a specialty usually consists of *expertise* regarding a given historical period and the figures important to one's discipline who are associated with it: Dr. Johnson and the English literature of the eighteenth century; the significance of Gide in the French literature of the twentieth century; Prince Metternich and the history of Europe after 1815; Kant, Hegel, and German Idealism 1750–1820. Specialties like these do not militate against one's assuming the role of the intellectual, because the traditions of humanistic study encourage the apprehension of cultural wholes; they encourage commentary and interpretation regarding the "backgrounds"—social, cultural, intellectual, spiritual—of the subject matter one is expert about. The humanities—and particularly literature—offer to intellectuals a professional status which impedes little if at all the fulfillment of their function as intellectuals. On the other hand, the commitment of empirical sociology to "scientific method" frequently renders it incompetent to deal with the "big problems," and often instills in sociologists a trained incapacity to say anything they cannot prove.

B. Values

In commenting on contemporary culture and in interpreting contemporary experience, intellectuals are under no seriously sanctioned injunction to be "detached" or "objective." Unlike the sociologist, who functions under the rule of strict separation between facts and values, the intellectual is expected to judge and evaluate, to praise and blame, to win adherents to his point of view and to defend his position against his intellectual enemies. In the context

of free debate among intellectuals, the exercise of this function takes the form of polemics; in an academic context, it develops into the phenomenon of "schools of thought." The point is that, whereas in sociology the existence of schools of thought is an embarrassment to everyone (since it is a constant reminder that not enough is *known*—in science, opinion is tolerated only where facts are not available), in the humanities the existence of schools of thought is accepted as normal and proper, because the humanities actively encourage evaluation, the development of point of view, and heterogeneity of interpretation.

C. Freedom from Institutional Restraints

Literary men have been able, more than members of other intellectual professions, to resist the tendencies toward the bureaucratization of intellectual life. This has been possible because of the large market for fiction in the United States, and because of the opportunities for selling critical and interpretive articles to the high- and middle-brow magazines, which, in spite of repeated protestations to the contrary, continue to flourish in this country. The ability of free lance writers to support themselves without depending upon a salary from a university or other large organization maximizes their freedom to be critics of contemporary life.[12] Such opportunities are not typically available to sociologists. In addition, major sociological research is increasingly "team" research, while literary and humanistic research in universities is still largely a matter of individual scholarship. Obviously, collective responsibility for a work restrains the commentaries and interpretations of its authors; the individual humanistic scholar, usually responsible only to himself, is free from the restraints imposed by the conditions of collective research.[13]

[12]I am aware that this assertion seems to imply a view of institutions as conservative, and a view of intellectuals as liberal or radical critics of them; this implication is not intended.

[13]The question of why the intellectuals have flocked to positions in the universities in the past ten years is an interesting one. I have asserted that free-lanceness facilitates the fulfillment of the intellectual's role, and the movement to the universities apparently contradicts this assertion. One hypothesis that seems tenable to me is that, as a well-insulated institution, the university can, to a considerable extent, successfully resist the dominant social pressures. In an age dominated by radical and rebellious sentiments among the intellectuals, as were the first forty years of this century, the universities may seem to be the source of reaction and apologetics for the *status quo*; but in the intellectual atmosphere of the last ten years, the universities seem to be a fortress (not quite impregnable) of free critical thought.

The purpose of this discussion of the intellectuals has been to highlight the fact that although sociology has arrogated to itself the right to *expertise* regarding society and culture, its commitment to the traditions of science (narrow specialization, objectivity, and team research) militates against sociologists assuming the role of the intellectual. The business of intellectuals has always been the critical discussion and evaluation of the affairs of contemporary men, or, if I may repeat it once more, to comment on contemporary culture and interpret contemporary experience. When the sociologist arrogates *expertise* regarding the affairs of contemporary men, he is perceived as saying, in effect, that he *knows* more about the affairs of contemporary men than the intellectual does; and once this implication is received into the community of intellectuals, the issue is joined. The fact of this implication becomes one more fact of contemporary experience to which the intellectuals can devote their critical faculties—and with considerable relish, because the implication seems to threaten the basis of their right to the position which, as intellectuals, they hold.

Even those intellectuals with sympathies for the goals of sociology often exhibit a fundamental underestimation of the consequences of its commitment to science. The characteristic plea of these people is an exhortation to "grapple with the *big* problems."[14] Although this advice is without doubt well intentioned, it characteristically underestimates the degree to which the mores of science and the responsibility of foundations and university research institutes can command the type of work sociologists do. I mean by this simply that the sociologist is responsible to the community of social scientists for the *scientific* value of his work, and that university research institutes are sensitive to charges of financing "biased" or "controversial" research (a possibility that is maximized when one deals with the "big problems"). And when the "big problems" *are* grappled with, for example, in books like *The American Soldier* and *The Authoritarian Personality*, or in other types of work like *The Lonely Crowd, White Collar*, and *The Power Elite*, controversy and polemic

[14]Among these intellectuals, one often finds people who, by profession, are sociologists themselves; and this fact creates an added complexity. For one sector of the sociological profession is humanistic in its intellectual traditions, its characteristic substantive interests, and its methods of investigation. These sociologists often harbor the intellectual's stereotype of "the sociologist"—but in a diluted and ambivalent form, because it involves their professional loyalties, and because they are living refutations of the accuracy of the image.

follow. For the sympathetic intellectual's exhortation to the sociologist to "grapple with the big problems" says, in effect, "don't be a scientist, be a humanist; be an intellectual." This implication is supported by the respectful (if not totally favorable) reception given by intellectuals to the works of Riesman and Mills (least encumbered with the trappings of science), and their utter hostility to works like *The American Soldier*, which fairly bristles with the method of science.[15]

There is one more source of the intellectual's hostility to sociology that I would like to examine, a source that was anticipated by Weber in his lecture on science as a vocation. For if it is true that intellectualization and rationalization, to which science commits itself and of which it is a part, means "that principally there are no mysterious incalculable forces that come into play, but rather that one can, in principle, master all things by calculation,"[16] then it is not only true, as Weber said, that "the world is disenchanted," but also true that the social scientist is perceived as challenging that tradition of humanism and art which has subsisted on the view that the world *is* enchanted, and that man is the mystery of mysteries. To the carriers of this tradition, every work of art and every poetic insight constitutes further proof that the world is enchanted and that the source of man's gift to make art and to have poetic insight is a mystery made more mysterious by each illumination. The power of this tradition should not be underestimated; it is well rooted in the thinking of modern literature, with its antiscientific temper and its faith in the recalcitrance of men to yield up their deepest secrets to the generalizations of science. From Wordsworth's "to dissect is to kill," to Mallarmé's "whatever is sacred, whatever is to remain sacred, must be clothed in mystery," to Cummings' "mysteries alone are significant," the tradition has remained strong. And surely, it

[15]As "big" books, all five of these contain something of value; the point is that the works by Riesman and Mills are clearly "intellectual" works in that they use data to illustrate a "thesis." They are clearly commentaries and interpretations of contemporary experience, and as such are grist for the intellectual's mill. It is this that makes them "interesting" and reviewable in the prominent periodicals of the intellectuals. *The American Soldier* and *The Authoritarian Personality* are less "interesting" to intellectuals because their primary intent is to report facts, not to diagnose, warn, or exhort. Nothing can kill an argument as quickly as a fact.

[16]Max Weber, *From Max Weber: Essays in Sociology*, H. H. Gerth and C. Wright Mills, eds. (Oxford University Press, 1946), p. 139.

must have reached its apotheosis when, before a Harvard audience, Cummings made the following pronouncement:

I am someone who proudly and humbly affirms that love is the mystery of mysteries, and that nothing measurable matters "a very good God damn": that "an artist, a man, a failure," is no mere whenfully accreting mechanism, but a givingly eternal complexity— neither some soulless and heartless ultra-predatory infra-animal nor any un-understandingly knowing and believing and thinking automation, but a naturally and miraculously whole human being—a feelingly illimitable individual; whose only happiness is to transcend himself, whose every agony is to grow.[17]

Intellectuals in this tradition seem to believe that the fulfillment of the goals of social science necessarily means that the creative powers of man will be "explained away," that his freedom will be denied, his "naturalness" mechanized, and his "miraculousness" made formula; that Cummings' "feelingly illimitable individual" will be shown up as a quite limited and determined "social product," whose every mystery and transcendence can be formulated, if not on a pin, then within the framework of some sociological theory.[18] It is no wonder, then, that a vision as fearsome as this can provoke the simultaneous convictions that a science of society is both impossible and evil.

IV

It is no great step from the stereotypes consequent to ethnic and racial diversity to the stereotypes consequent to the diversity of occupational specialization. In those occupations which claim tech-

---

[17]E. E. Cummings, *six nonlectures*, (Cambridge: Harvard University Press, 1962, pp. 110–11.
[18]Nowhere is this made more clear than in the hostility of artists to the sociology of knowledge, art, or intellectual life. Artists resist having their work "explained" in terms of ideology, class, milieu, spirit of the age, and so forth, even when they are assured that this explanation of its sources in no way impugns the "truth" or the "integrity" of the work; somehow, the feeling persists among artists that a sociological explanation of the sources of their work makes it, in some way, "not theirs." This, I suppose, is one of the more or less rueful consequences of the belief that man is *sui generis*.

nical, professional status—occupations in which advanced, specialized training is necessary—it is likely that occupational stereotypes should find fertile ground because those on the "outside" have only secondary, derivative "knowledge" of the occupation. It is likely to be even more true of those professions which, like sociology, are so new that the nature of their subject matter is still being discussed by their members; and *still* more true if the new profession, by arrogating to itself a field of study formerly "belonging" to someone else (or to everyone else), raises, either intentionally or unintentionally by implication, invidious questions of relative competence.

Noteworthy in this regard is the fact that the social sciences that have been most active in the "interdisciplinary" tendencies of recent years are sociology, cultural anthropology, and psychology—precisely those disciplines with the most broadly defined subject matter. Each of these claims nothing less, in effect, than the totality of man's non-physiological behavior as the field of its special competence; and it is no wonder that economics and political science, whose claims are considerably more modest (i.e., whose subject matter is relatively clearly and narrowly defined), have not found it strikingly to their interests to participate much in this convergence. For there is no doubt that common professional interest as well as theoretical clarification is behind this pooling of intellectual resources by sociologists, anthropologists, and psychologists. The satire[19] (which invokes the extant stereotype) to which social scientists are submitted is of common concern to them, for the public image of the social sciences, largely created by the commentaries of intellectuals on them, is related to the amount of public support that the social sciences receive.

The stereotype of sociology and sociologists is part of a larger configuration which stereotypes social science in general; sociology, however, is the most successfully maligned. This special vulnerability is due largely to its relative lack of the sources of prestige available to the other social sciences. Economics commands a respect consequent to its age, to the generally accepted legitimacy of its subject matter, to its demonstrated usefulness, and to the wide variety of jobs available to people trained in it. Cultural anthro-

---

[19]Apparently large numbers of people find it rather amusing to indulge fantasies of anthropologists being eaten by cannibals, to hear of a sociologist who spends $10,000 to find a brothel, and to trivialize psychology by reference now to rats, now to the couch.

pology borrows scientific prestige from physical anthropology and archeology, and gets some of its own as a result of its concern with the esoteric subject matter of primitive peoples. Political science has the prestigious correlates of law, diplomacy, and international relations. Clinical psychology has the towering figure of Freud, an affinity to medicine, and the presence of the almost mythic dimensions of The Psychiatrist. Unlike economics, sociology has no hoary past, and no long line of employers clamoring for access to its skills. Unlike clinical psychology, it has no founding figure generally recognized as seminal in the history of Western science; and the tenuousness of the concept of a "sick society" denies to sociology the status of a clinical discipline, and hence the prestige that accrues to The Healer. Unlike political science, it has neither an empirical nor an historical relation to the high concerns of nations, governments, or law; and unlike cultural anthropology, it has neither empirical roots nor an esoteric subject matter. Not only is sociology's subject matter not esoteric, but its traditional concern with such peripheral problems of social life as crime, delinquency, and divorce, and others conventionally classified under the rubric "social disorganization," quite likely tends, as Merton has suggested, to diminish its prestige.

Sociology, then, is *vulnerable* to stereotyping; its position in the contemporary structure of the intellectual professions exposes it to criticism from all sides. In numbers the weakest of the social sciences, it is the bastard son of the humanities, from which it gets its subject matter, and the sciences, from which it gets its methods. Fully acknowledged by neither parent, it finds itself in the role of *upstart*, now utilizing the existing methods of science, now improvising new scientific methods, in an attempt to make the enchanted data of the humanities yield up their mysteries.

Like ethnic stereotypes, which are fostered by segregation and reinforced by the consequent cultural isolation, intellectual stereotypes are fostered by professional specialization and reinforced by the diverse (and sometimes conflicting) perspectives developed in each.[20] The lack of an intellectual perspective that transcends the provincialism generated by the limitations of a specialized perspec-

[20]How, for example, is a social scientist to respond to literary critic Stanley Edgar Hyman, when, in an article on Freud and the psychoanalytical movement, he praises Freud because, by locating the source of the neuroses in the instincts, he *permits the possibility of dramatic tragedy in literature*, and condemns the neo-Freudians because, by locating the source of the neuroses

tive makes one susceptible to clichés and stereotypic thinking about related fields of study. In race and interethnic relations, the marginal man has, with his proverbial "one foot in each culture," provided this transcendent perspective. Humanist intellectuals can fulfill this function in intellectual life by addressing their criticisms of sociology *to sociologists*, rather than to their own colleagues; for it is the ironic fact that in writing to his own colleagues about sociology, the humanist intellectual himself tends to use obvious clichés to which his immersion in his own perspective blinds him.[21] The kind of cross-fertilization that might be achieved by having humanist intellectual perspectives critically directed at an *audience of sociologists*, perhaps *in* a sociological journal, might go a long way toward providing this transcendent perspective.

---

in culture and society, they *deny the possibility of inherent tragic flaws*? Is the worth of a psychological theory to be measured in terms of how well it supports an aesthetic theory? See "Freud and the Climate of Tragedy," *Partisan Review*   XXIII, No. 2 (Spring 1956), 198–214.

[21]Arthur Schlesinger Jr.'s review of *The American Soldier* contains a catalogue of these clichés. See his "The Statistical Soldier," *Partisan Review* XVI, No. 8 (August 1949), 852–56.

Images of Society and Problems of Concept Formation in Sociology

with Reinhard Bendix   1959

To explain the known facts of society, sociological theories require some orderly framework of concepts. But, like historians who find it necessary to "rewrite" or "reinterpret" history in each generation, sociologists are continually modifying old concepts and offering new ones because of some dissatisfaction with the vocabulary as it stands. These dissatisfactions typically arise when someone discovers that the current definitions of standard concepts neglect or omit some range of fact which he regards as important. This concern with the reformulation of concepts suggests that there is some evidence for every set of concepts but as yet no agreed upon procedure for achieving consensus.

I. Definitions of "The Social Fact"

One reason for this lack of agreement stems from the failure of many discussants to reflect on the sense of the "real" which lies

Reprinted from *Symposium on Sociological Theory*, copyright © 1959 by Harper & Row, Publishers, Incorporated, by permission of the publishers.

An earlier version of this paper was published in *Koelner Zeitschrift fuer Sociologie*. We are indebted to Llewellyn Gross, Leo Lowenthal, Philip Selznick, and Milton Singer for critical comments on that version.

behind their conflicting definitions of the "social fact." Attention to these different ideas of what is significant, or "real," ín society may help to improve the chances for reaching agreement, where this is possible. And where it is not, such attention will at least clarify the reasons why the same divergent perspectives recur in ever new guises.

Simmel's work is illuminating for the present discussion because he, more than most theorists, was explicitly concerned with delimiting the subject matter of sociology. In his effort to establish sociology as an independent discipline, Simmel began by challenging the familiar assumption that only the individual was "real" while society was "merely" an abstraction. No concept, he argued, could be more "real" than any other, since every concept presupposed an abstracting operation which distorted the facts by simplification and exaggeration. For Simmel, the realm of the "social" was as worthy of study as the realm of the "individual," and he identified this social realm with the process of interaction between individuals. Yet, in making this case for sociology as an independent discipline, Simmel also suggested that the traditional concepts of social science, such as "state," "administration," "church," and others lacked "real" social content: only if the interactions between individuals were studied could the meaning of these "official social formations" be revealed.[1] Thus, Simmel argued against the common notion that certain concepts are more "real" than others; yet inadvertently he argued in favor of the concept "interaction" as the proper focus of sociological inquiry on the ground that this was a "realistic" approach to the study of society.

Simmel's dilemma on this point was not fortuitous. One cannot argue in favor of a concept on the ground that it is more realistic than another. All concepts are based on *some* evidence which the theorist arranges in order to facilitate understanding. But when Simmel argued in favor of sociology on the ground that its interaction

---

[1] "To confine ourselves to the large social formations resembles the older science of anatomy with its limitation to the major, definitely circumscribed organs such as heart, liver, lungs, and stomach, and with its neglect of the innumerable, popularly unnamed or unknown tissues. Yet without these, the more obvious organs could never constitute a living organism. On the basis of the major social formations—the traditional subject of social science— it would be similarly impossible to piece together the real life of society as we encounter it in our experience." *The Sociology of Georg Simmel*, K. Wolff, ed. (Glencoe, Ill.: Free Press, 1950), p. 9. See also pp. 10–13 and 187–88.

approach, abstract though he knew it to be, was more realistic than the traditional concepts of social science, he revealed inadvertently that the definition of concepts is also a social act. Just as research cannot be initiated without some sense of the significant, so sociological theorizing cannot be developed without a strong sense of what is "real" in society. It is each theorist's sense of the "real" which is expressed in his definition of the "social fact."[2]

Simmel, as we have seen, was preoccupied with the process of *interaction* between individuals. On the other hand, Durkheim was especially concerned with the individual's group affiliations as a source of individual and collective morality. For Durkheim, the central social fact was the *coercive aspect* of the beliefs and practices which were imposed upon the individual from without and to which he had to conform if he were not to risk social ostracism. Max Weber, in turn, defined the central social fact as the *meaning* which individuals in society attach to their own actions and those of others. For the dominant impulse of his work was to account for the transvaluation of meaning in Western Civilization, exemplified by the disapppearance of magic and the rise of rationalism in many spheres of life. Men like Simmel, Durkheim, and Weber tended to define the "social fact" in apparent accordance with the major impulse which informed their scholarly work. Unwittingly perhaps, they used their own intellectual orientations to substantive problems as the basis for formulating the fundamental categories of sociological theory. In doing this, they tended to foster pseudocontroversies, since the differences among various theories were often due to different *purposes* of cognition rather than to differences of cognition itself.[3]

---

[2]By the phrase "sense of the 'real'" we refer not to formally stipulated assumptions but to the intuitive feeling for what is significant in society and basic for a scientific theory of society. The multiplicity of social theories is in part, attributable to this psychological involvement of the social theorists. Yet, the assessment of theories should be independent of this consideration, for the criteria by which a theorist defines "the social fact" must be abstract themselves as well as explicit, so that they may be judged by others. This theoretical level must be maintained, else theorists would merely argue about why they make statements, rather than about what they say. Nonetheless, it is important to recognize this psychological precondition of our theorizing about society, because this recognition helps us to explain, and also to take into account, the peculiar perspectivism of social theories. However, the more developed a science is, the less important these considerations are likely to become.

[3]It is partly for this reason that there is no "sociological theory" but only "sociological *theories*"; sociologists tend to choose their theoretical equip-

This tendency appears unsatisfactory, despite the eminent names associated with it, because it makes the basic categories of sociology dependent upon a purpose of cognition which is specific to the work of a given scholar.

To terminate this "war of schools," Professor Parsons undertook in his *The Structure of Social Action*, to show that Pareto, Durkheim, Marshall, and Weber were in basic agreement on certain fundamental concepts concerning the actions of men in society. During more recent years he has continued this endeavor by seeking to find a common universe of theoretical discourse among outstanding representatives of anthropology, sociology, and psychology. This effort to formulate and make internally consistent the sum total of usable concepts about the actions of men in society has been linked with the attempt to develop an inclusive theory of society as a system of action. But it is noteworthy that this work of integration employs yet another vocabulary of concepts which is based on yet another selectively perceived "reality." In this case the "definition of the social fact" appears to derive from the belief that the concept "system" is indispensable if sociological theory is to become scientific.[4]

These approaches, however, do *not* exhaust the available alternatives. The major purpose of this paper is to outline another approach to sociological theory, which may transcend these disjunctions of perspective, but which appears to have been neglected *despite the fact that every major sociological theorist has been familiar with it.*

---

ment in accord with how well it suits the kind of substantive problems which interest them, and these, in turn, are intimately connected with their sense of the "real." This tendency creates "schools of thought," whose controversies are usually due to the attempt to impose a theoretical perspective, developed on the basis of certain substantive interests, on *all* substantive interests. It is partly for this reason too, perhaps, that so much criticism of sociological theories has an undertone of emotionalism.

[4] See Talcott Parsons, *The Social System* (Glencoe, Ill.: Free Press, 1951), vii, 3; "The title, *The Social System*, goes back, more than to any other source, to the insistence of the late Professor L. J. Henderson on the extreme importance of the concept of system in scientific theory. . . .

"The fundamental starting point is the concept of social systems of action. The *interaction* of individual actors, that is, takes place under such conditions that it is possible to treat such a process of interaction as a system in the scientific sense and subject it to the same order of theoretical analysis which has been successfully applied to other types of systems in other sciences."

II. The Perspective of Dual Tendencies

The "sociological perspective" has come largely to mean the study of the ways in which group influences dictate the behavior of the individual. But the task of sociological theory should be to consider not only the social conditioning of the individual but also his capacity for independent action for which that conditioning is only the necessary basis. Dewey pointed out long ago that habits facilitate action as well as restrict it; and it hardly seems necessary to re-emphasize the fact that culture and society not only determine how others expect the individual to act, but also enable him to comply with, or to resist, these expectations. This simultaneous attention to the social and the individual aspect of behavior in society has a venerable intellectual ancestry. It involves an image of man and society (a definition of the "social fact") which views both, not as finite systems, but as capable of indefinite (though not infinite) elaboration. This insight has been variously expressed in terms of tendencies or forces which are linked and opposite at the same time. From Empedocles' view of the world divided by love and hate to Freud's theory of death and eros, from the medieval idea of a universal determinism coupled with individual freedom to Marx's view of men as partly free and partly involuntary political actors under given historical circumstances, from the Confucian concepts of Yin and Yang to Kant's idea of "unsocial sociability": the variations increase, but the theme remains.[5] At the end of his analysis of freedom and equality in American society, Alexis de Tocqueville formulated this theme as his own basic creed:

I am aware [he wrote] that many of my contemporaries maintain that nations are never their own masters here below, and that they necessarily obey some insurmountable and unintelligent power. . . . Such principles are false and cowardly. . . . Providence has not created mankind entirely dependent or entirely free. It is true that around every man a fatal circle is traced beyond which he cannot pass; but within the wide verge of that circle he is powerful and free; as it is with man, so with communities. The nations of our time cannot prevent the conditions of men from becoming equal, but it depends

[5] Cf. the related discussion of the "principle of polarity" in Morris Cohen, *Reason and Nature* (Glencoe, Ill.: Free Press, 1953), *passim.*

upon themselves whether the principle of equality is to lead them to servitude or freedom, to knowledge or barbarism, to prosperity or wretchedness.[6]

What Kant and Marx, Tocqueville and Freud expressed in philosophical, ethical, and psychological terms has also been reflected in sociological theory. In his discussion of group affiliations, Simmel emphasized the coexistence of socializing and individualizing effects.

Each new group with which [an individual] becomes affiliated circumscribes him more exactly and more unambiguously. . . . As the person becomes affiliated with a social group, he surrenders himself to it. . . . But the person also regains his individuality, because his pattern of participation is unique.[7]

The multiple group affiliations characteristic of modern society may have a double effect according to Simmel. Under certain conditions they may strengthen an individual personality and give it the capacity to sustain great internal tensions; but they may also, under other conditions, threaten the integration of the personality, far more than would be the case in a simpler society with little differentiation between groups. In carrying this idea of his teacher, Simmel, further, Robert Park combined it with the related concepts of Ferdinand Toennies. In his studies of the city, of newspapers, of the interaction between racial groups, and other topics, Park distinguished between interactions in terms of their individuating and socializing repercussions.

Competition and communication, although they perform different and uncoordinated social functions, nevertheless in the actual life of society supplement and complete each other. . . . Competition seems to be the principle of individuation in the life of the person and of society. . . . Communication, on the other hand, operates primarily as an integrating and socializing principle.[8]

[6]Alexis de Tocqueville, *Democracy in America* (New York: Vintage Books, 1945), II: p. 352.
[7]Georg Simmel, *Conflict and the Web of Group Affiliations* (Glencoe, Ill.: Free Press, 1955), pp. 140–41.
[8]Robert E. Park, *Race and Culture* (Glencoe, Ill.: Free Press, 1950), p. 42. See also Robert E. Park, *Human Communities* (Glencoe, Ill.: Free Press, 1952), pp. 258–59 and *passim.*

Another example of a somewhat different kind is contained in the social psychology of George H. Mead, who distinguished the organic actions and reactions of the individual (the "I") from the "generalized other" which the individual incorporates in his personality through his interactions with others in society (the "Me").

Again, Max Weber's work is characterized by a somewhat implicit recognition of the same perspective. In his definition of the social fact, Weber emphasized the subjective meaning which individuals in society attach to their actions.[9] This emphasis is reflected in his study of the Protestant Ethic, which eschewed all imputation of motives because "the people of that period [the Reformation] had after all very specific ideas of what awaited them in the life after death, of the means by which they could improve their chances in this respect, and they adjusted their conduct in accordance with these ideas."[10] Yet, Weber also analyzed the social structures which in part conditioned such ideas. He showed, for example, that the political and military autonomy of Occidental cities was an important precondition of bourgeois class consciousness and as such prepared the way for the ideas of the Puritan sects in particular.[11]

Apparently, this perspective is well known in sociological theory. Yet, in important respects it runs counter to the "sociological determinism" characteristic of much contemporary sociological literature. Group membership and participation in the culture are used in the literature as explanatory principles which account for the conduct of individuals in society. Such terms as culture-pattern, subculture, social role, reciprocal role-expectations, social class, status group, mores and folkways, communication, human relations, and many, many others are employed in such a way that individuals appear to act as group influences dictate. Unwittingly perhaps, this vocabulary has often had the cumulative effect of suggesting that the individual merely does what is expected of him—in the literal sense in which the actor on the medieval stage reads his text from the rolled script in his hands.[12] A case in point, admittedly flagrant but conceivably

[9]*Max Weber, The Theory of Social and Economic Organization* (New York: Oxford University Press, 1947), p. 88.
[10]Max Weber, "Kritische Bemerkungen zu den vorstehenden Kritischen Beiträgen," *Archiv für Sozialwissenschaft*, XXV (1907), 248.
[11]Max Weber, *Wirtschaft und Gesellschaft* (Tübingen: J. C. B. Mohr, 1925), II: pp. 562 ff.
[12]The term "role" was originally derived from this reference to the "roll" in the hands of the actor. Cf. David Bidney, *Theoretical Anthropology* (New

symptomatic, is Ralph Linton's attempt to formulate the relation between the individual and his culture. After describing culture as "the way of life of any society" which consists of "the normal anticipated response of *any* of the society's members to a particular situation" and which provides these members with "an indispensable guide in all the affairs of life," Linton continues:

I realize that in the foregoing discussion of society and culture emphasis has been laid mainly upon the passive role of the individual and upon the way in which he is shaped by culture and social factors. It is time now to present the other side of the picture. No matter how carefully the individual has been trained or how successful his conditioning has been, he remains a distinct organism with his own needs and with capacities for independent thought, feeling, and action. Moreover, he retains a considerable degree of individuality. His integration into society and culture goes no deeper than his learned responses, and although in the adult these include the greater part of what we call the personality, there is still a good deal of the individual left over.[13]

In this view, culture and society are used as explanatory principles, and what they fail to explain is left over as a residue, which is indeed a "good deal," since Linton himself emphasizes that no two individuals in a culture are exactly alike. The trouble with this approach is that it conceptualizes only part of the evidence, while the "remainder" is left unaccounted for. Unavoidable as this procedure is where we deal with the formulation of hypotheses in particular inquiries, it is not admissible with regard to the basic concepts of sociological theory.

III. Paired Concepts of Interactions and Institutions

The basic concepts of sociological theory should be applicable to all societies. With the aid of such concepts, we should be able to formulate propositions which are true of men by virtue of the fact that they have been members of social groups everywhere and at

---

York: Columbia University Press, 1953), for an illuminating exception to the foregoing characterization.
[13]Ralph Linton, *The Cultural Background of Personality* (New York: D. Appleton-Century Co., 1945), pp. 19, 22, and *passim*. Our italics.

all times.[14] In order to achieve such comprehensiveness, these concepts should, at their appropriate level of abstraction, encompass the full range of human experience in society rather than single out some dominant feature of that experience and thereby leave some residue aside. Yet this objective cannot be achieved by the formulation of single concepts, since each of these necessarily excludes as well as includes; as Spinoza put it, "omnis determinatio est negatio." It may be possible, however, that the desired comprehensiveness can be achieved by the *paired concepts* which are familiar in sociological theory. Examples are: socialization and individualization, primary and secondary relations, status and contract, symbiosis and cooperation, Gemeinschaft and Gesellschaft, bureaucracy and patrimonialism, and so forth. Such paired concepts are attempts to conceptualize what we know about the range of variability of social phenomena so that we are enabled to deal abstractly with their known extremes, regardless of whether we focus on the level of interactions, of institutions, or of societies as wholes. We recognize that these paired concepts of sociological theory have been developed more or less *ad hoc*, but we also believe that their theoretical utility has not been given as much attention as seems warranted. One difficulty has been that these concepts appeared to invite a dichotomous classification: interactions are either "intimate" or "impersonal," organizations are either "formal" or "informal," societies are either "folk" or "urban." A given set of facts was, then, seen as approximating one or another of these concepts, and hypotheses were formulated in order to analyze the factors associated with this degree of approximation to (or deviation from) the type. The result of this procedure has frequently been that at the end of the investigation the concept appeared much less serviceable than at the beginning, for "urban" elements are found in folk societies, informal relations are present in formally rational bureaucracies, and so forth. Accordingly, the dichotomous classifications are actually misleading or inappropriate; and this may be one reason why a number of sociologists have tended to discard paired concepts altogether.

A second difficulty has been that the formulation of paired concepts has not been clearly distinguished from the formulation of testable hypotheses. As Redfield has shown, communities may be distinguished in terms of whether they are more or less isolated,

[14]This is the formulation of the late Louis Wirth.

more or less heterogeneous, more or less literate, and so forth. In using the terms "folk" and "urban" society, he sought to indicate that these traits *tend* to vary together, e.g., as isolation increases so does homogeneity. But it is clearly an empirical question whether or not and to what extent this tendency occurs in fact; and explanatory hypotheses concerning social and psychological processes are needed to explain this covariation or its absence.[15]

Finally, there is the difficulty that many of these paired concepts have not been fully analyzed. Instead, social theorists have frequently produced new paired concepts which in part overlap with, and in part differ from, analogous formulations of the past. The most familiar example is the similarity of Sir Henry Maine's distinction between societies of status and societies of contract to Durkheim's contrast between organic and mechanical solidarity, to Toennies' contrast between Gemeinschaft and Gesellschaft, to MacIver's contrast between culture and civilization, to Redfield's contrast between folk and urban societies, and still others.[16] Admittedly, these broad contrasts have had many drawbacks. But these should not be allowed to obscure their potential utility, for it might well be a good rule of

[15]Within this conceptual framework it is quite feasible to handle the fact that a relatively isolated community is found which is individualistic, lacking in solidarity and secularized, for such a finding does not disprove the utility of the variables which are subsumed under the concept "folk-society." Cf. the questionable criticism of Redfield in Oscar Lewis, *Life in a Mexican Village* (Urbana: University of Illinois Press, 1951), pp. 427–40. Much the same criticism has been leveled at Weber's concept of "bureaucracy," because administrators were found to engage in actions which are out of keeping with the formally stipulated conditions of their work. Cf. Alvin Gouldner, "On Weber's Analysis of Bureaucratic Rules," in *Reader in Bureaucracy*, R. K. Merton et al., eds. (Glencoe, Ill.: Free Press, 1952), pp. 48–51 and Peter Blau, *Bureaucracy in Modern Society* (New York: Random House, 1956), pp. 35–36. The trouble with these critiques is that they do not distinguish between concept formation and the formulation and testing of hypotheses. In cases where such critiques are justified, it would be necessary to replace the discarded with a new concept, which is more serviceable. As it is, a concept is sometimes criticized and then used anyway.
[16]As Redfield has shown in his *Folkculture of Yucatan*, these comprehensive terms are in fact composites of many paired concepts. To subsume a number of these (like isolation, homogeneity, predominance of the sacred) under one ideal type like "folk society" may suggest a closer degree of association than is useful. But not to do that also raises problems, for a concept like "competition" has many usable opposites like "communication," "cooperation," "solidarity," and others, which are in fact interrelated. There is need for a further refinement of such paired concepts, and the choice among them depends, of course, upon the purpose of inquiry, for which one set of terms will be more useful than another.

thumb to search for the missing and, perhaps, hidden opposite when a single concept is proposed.[17]

The frequent formulation of paired concepts in sociology may be seen as an intellectual response to the "perspective of dual tendencies" mentioned above. We believe that the empirical foundation of this perspective lies in the fact that concrete human relationships are ambiguous, and that this ambiguity is manifest in social action and its consequences. This is another way of saying that mankind is neither entirely dependent nor entirely free, that social interaction is partly communicative and partly competitive, that *both* the I and the Me participate in every social transaction, and so forth. This insight, however, is often lost somewhere between the point at which concepts are formulated and that at which testable hypotheses are developed.

Paired Concepts of Interactions

To say, for example, that primary relations are personal and intimate, that they "involve responses to whole persons rather than to segments," that in them "communication . . . is deep and extensive," and that "personal satisfactions are paramount"[18] is to formulate a concept. But to say that "the family" (defined independently of the quality of the relationships among its members) is the classical locus of primary relations is an empirical statement which is only partly true because it neglects such facts as formal arrangements for property settlements in a family, and the hard-headed attitude of families toward the marriages of its members—even though primary relations may remain dominant in the family. Secondary rela-

---

[17]An example may make this clearer. Robert Bierstedt noted that Weber's concepts of traditional and rational authority differ from his concept of charisma in the sense that the latter refers to leadership, not to authority. Implicitly, Weber appears to have acknowledged this point since he referred to charismatic leaders under conditions of traditional and of rational authority. But then the question may be asked what concept we should use for leadership which is noncharismatic, an eventuality for which Weber employed the phrase "routinization of charisma" though he did not explicitly formulate this idea as a contrast-conception. Cf. Robert Bierstedt, "The Problem of Authority," in *Freedom and Control in Modern Society*, Morroe Berger, Theodore Abel, and Charles Page, eds. (New York: Van Nostrand Co., Inc., 1954), pp. 67–81. It may be added that the absence of an opposite term is often due to the linguistic difficulty of finding an equally appropriate word for both concepts. "Routinization of charisma" is not as neat as "charisma."
[18]Leonard Broom and Philip Selznick, *Sociology* (Evanston, Ill.: Row, Peterson and Company, 1958), pp. 124–26.

tions, on the other hand, are impersonal and instrumental by definition. Yet, people engaged in such relations tend to impart to them some personal and emotional qualities which contrast with the dominant character of the relationship. Accordingly, these two concepts may be formulated as a universal proposition: all relations between men in society are both intimate and impersonal.[19] Such a proposition has a double utility.[20]

First: It is based on generalized, inductive knowledge and points to a problem with which men in all societies deal, not to the solutions which they find for this problem. It is, therefore, a guide to relevant questions which may be asked of every society.[21] For example, one might expect a highly personalized relationship of two people genuinely in love to be entirely without impersonal elements. But our knowledge of the universality of these impersonal elements would lead us to expect that significant social and personal problems will arise in a primary relationship from which they are absent. Love relationships tend to be fragile unless formal arrangements also provide them with some buttress of impersonality. Similarly, the absence of accepted ritual creates special psychological burdens for the survivor of an exclusively primary relationship. Yet such a relationship also militates against accepting the relevance of impersonal considerations: a happily married couple is likely to regard a detailed legal settlement of their obligations to each other and their respective relatives as a lack of trust and/or an intolerable, i.e., impersonal, consideration of eventual death. Related questions

[19]This formulation is identical with Redfield's statement: "In every primitive band or tribe there is civilization, in every city there is the folksociety." See Robert Redfield, "The Natural History of a Folk Society," *Social Forces*, 31 (March 1953), 225.

[20]In addition, such universal propositions can also reveal the limitations of sociological analysis. That is, their claim to universality can be refuted, when instances are found in which, for example, no impersonal qualities enter into a primary relationship.

[21]Functionalists would say here that societies must find some balance between intimacy and impersonality in human relationships, if man's basic needs are to be satisfied sufficiently for societies to survive. This formulation attributes the results of men's problem-solving activities to "the society" which is said to have properties of its own that are in some sense independent of these activities. And one of these properties is thought to consist of some given, but unknown degree of satisfaction which is indispensable for the survival of society. Thus, functional propositions will refer given attributes to "society," while propositions using paired concepts would refer such attributes to social actions with their anticipated and unanticipated consequences. Cf. also the discussion in Section V of this essay.

arise when the intrusion of intimacy in secondary relationships is considered. Personal elements in secondary relations have been widely denounced as fraudulent; the term "pseudo-Gemeinschaft" has been coined in reference, for example, to the "folksy" approach of radio advertisers. Yet this critique overlooks the fact that intimacy in impersonal relations is many-sided. Although intimacy is often faked for personal advantage, say in the relation between salesman and customer, an appeal to the implicit obligations of intimacy can also be used as a stopgap against the exploitation of the relationship. Indeed, this use of intimacy for and against the exploitation of an impersonal relation points to a major problem of hierarchical organizations in the United States. Equalitarianism together with the human-relations approach has led to highly personalized work relationships. These tendencies have forfeited the advantages of personal and social distance without which the impersonal criteria of organizational efficiency can be applied only with considerable difficulty. If intimacy in secondary relations is maximized, the social problems and psychological burdens arising from this intrusion may be as great as if it were minimized, though the two conditions will produce very different dilemmas of action. These examples may suffice as illustrations of the way in which the paired concepts may guide us in the formulation of sociological problems.[22]

Second: Universal propositions direct our attention to the fact that the very concepts we use limit our ability to see beyond them. If we know that all relations among men in society are both intimate and impersonal, then we are prompted to examine a predominantly primary relationship for its frequently hidden, secondary attributes, and vice versa. The paired concepts of interactions may be conceived of, therefore, as two ends of a scale so that the relations, say, between some brothers and sisters could be ranked in terms of their relative intimacy and impersonality. But such rankings only enable us to classify the data as a first step toward analysis. For example, the ready contact or great isolation of a community with regard to the world outside can be defined in terms of the number of communications with that world, and communities can be ranked accordingly. Yet, to measure the frequency of communications is clearly not enough. Two communities with exactly the same number

---

[22]Cf. the related comments on the "dialectic of opposites" in Robert Redfield, *The Little Community* (Chicago: University of Chicago Press, 1955), ch. 9.

of communications may possess very different degrees of contact (or isolation).[23] Hence, an accurate measure of a community's isolation is not meaningful without an analysis of the contacts involved (and vice versa), just as a primary relation cannot be fully understood apart from its impersonal attributes.

The paired concepts of sociology theory, then, must always be considered *together* when one is engaged in developing testable hypotheses because both concepts are necessary for an analysis of those universal tendencies of social action which, while pointing in opposite directions, are at the same time inextricably linked. A classic example of such an analysis is contained in Max Weber's discussion of class and status.

The term "class" refers to any group of people . . . [who have the same] typical chance for a supply of goods, external living conditions, and personal life experiences, in so far as this chance is determined by the amount and kind of power, or lack of such, to dispose of goods or skills for the sake of income in a given economic order. . . . "Class situation" is, in this sense, ultimately "market situation."

In contrast to the purely economically determined "class situation" we wish to designate as "status-situation" every typical component of the life fate of men that is determined by a specific, positive or negative, social estimation of honor. . . . In content, status honor is normally expressed by the fact that above all else a specific style of life can be expected from all those who wish to belong to the

---

[23]Karl Deutsch has suggested such a measure in his calculation of "input-output" ratios of foreign mail, showing among other things that in 1928–38 Germany and the United Kingdom had a similar excess of foreign mail sent out over foreign mail received (0.65 for Germany and 0.70 for the U.K.). But the U.K. was the center of an Empire with no restrictions on international communications, while for half this period Germany was a dictatorship whose censorship isolated the country culturally and politically, even if the volume of foreign mail remained unaffected. Cf. Karl Deutsch, "Shifts in the Balance of Communication Flows," *Public Opinion Quarterly*, 20: (1956), 147–48. Some logical techniques for handling the problems of typology which are involved here are discussed in Paul F. Lazarsfeld and Allen H. Barton, "Qualitative Measurement in the Social Sciences: Classification, Typologies, and Indices," in *The Policy Sciences*, Daniel Lerner, ed. (Stanford: Stanford University Press, 1951), pp. 155–92.

circle. . . . Besides the specific status honor, which always rests upon distance and exclusiveness, we find all sorts of material monopolies. . . .[24]

Weber thought of these two conditions of collective action as antithetical. The market knows of no personal distinctions. For example, transactions on the stock exchange are reduced to a few standardized phrases or hand symbols. The only relevant distinctions among the brokers are factual and impersonal, depending upon their respective credit rating. In principle, economic actions are oriented entirely to "a rationally motivated adjustment of interests."[25] Exactly the reverse is true of the status order, in which men are grouped in terms of their prestige and style of life. To safeguard their status, such men will oppose vigorously any and all suggestions that economic acquisition and power as such can constitute a valid claim to "status honor." Stratification based on the status order would be undermined quickly if a wealthy man could claim more "honor" than those who rest their claim upon family lineage and style of life. Thus, economic interests militate against the dominance of status distinctions, especially in periods of rapid economic change, while considerations of status "hinder the strict carrying through of the sheer market principle," especially in periods of relative economic stability.[26] But these antithetical tendencies of the economic and the social order are also linked. Actions based on economic interests frequently aim at the preservation or acquisition of "honor": Weber pointed for example to the voluntary and exclusive association among English stock brokers who safeguarded fair dealing on the market by excluding "unreliable" elements from membership in these associations. And status groups frequently use their social prestige in order to monopolize economic opportunities: thus the east German landowners (*Junkers*) used the privileges of their aristocratic status in order to maximize their economic interests as landowners. In order to understand both the linkages and the antitheses between these two orders it was necessary, according to Weber, to define each unambiguously, i.e., *as if* they were mutu-

---

[24]Max Weber, "Class Status, Party," in *From Max Weber: Essays in Sociology,* H. H. Gerth and C. Wright Mills, eds. (New York: Oxford University Press, 1946), pp. 181, 182, 186–87, 190–91.
[25]*Ibid.,* p. 183.
[26]*Ibid.,* pp. 185, 193–94.

ally exclusive and *as if* each was governed by a principle of internal consistency.[27]

Paired Concepts of Institutions

The preceding discussion of paired concepts has been concerned with the categories appropriate for the analysis of some universal patterns of interaction (e.g., primary or secondary relationships, and market-oriented or status-oriented collective actions). Many socio-logical concepts are not concepts of action, however, but of more or less permanent institutions or institutional complexes like bu-reaucracy, types of urban society, specific status groups and social movements, etc. The sociologist can only observe actions, but he is bound to develop many of his concepts in terms of the social conditions and institutional complexes underlying the actions he observes and in terms of the enduring results which these actions help to produce and sustain. He makes the assumption that these conditions and results exist only in so far as individuals can be observed to embody them in their actions. This assumption provides a useful roadblock against reification. But such a methodological caution has not prevented sociologists from developing concepts of collectivities and institutions even though their use is exposed to the danger of reification.[28] We believe that the above interpreta-tion of paired concepts can be applied to this level of analysis as well.

A case in point is Max Weber's analysis of bureaucracy. The

[27]In this connection, Parsons and Shils have stated that goal-directed actions must be analyzed by establishing "primacies among types of interests" so that "the . . . ambiguities intrinsic to the world of social objects" can be resolved. The authors accomplish this resolution of ambiguities by stipulating that the actions of the individual must be examined and classified when he makes his choice, on the knife-edge of the present at it were. The discussion of pattern-variables appears to be based on the assumption that all choices are dichotomous *in fact* if analyzed minutely enough, whereas for Weber the internal consistency of any action was a *logical* construction. See Talcott Parsons, E. A. Shils, *et al., Toward a General Theory of Action* (Cambridge: Harvard University Press, 1951), p. 91. Our view is that choices are pro-visional and interests ambivalent. Accordingly, Weber's "as if" construction appears to us less rationalistic than the assumption made by Parsons and Shils.
[28]Swanson has pointed out that Parsons and Shils have failed to derive the classic concepts of collectivities from the "action frame of reference" which they have developed. See Guy E. Swanson, "The Approach to a General Theory of Action by Parsons and Shils," *American Sociological Review*, 18 (1953), 132–33.

elements of Weber's definition are generally familiar and are repeated here in abbreviated form. A bureaucracy *tends* to be characterized by:

a. *Defined rights and duties, which are prescribed in written regulations;*
b. *Authority relations between positions which are ordered systematically;*
c. *Appointment and promotion which are regulated and are based on contractual agreement;*
d. *Technical training or equivalent experience as a formal condition of employment;*
e. *Fixed monetary salaries;*
f. *A strict separation of office and incumbent in the sense that the employee does not own the "means of administration" and cannot appropriate the position;*
g. *Administrative work as a full-time occupation.*[29]

These characteristics stand for conditions of employment which have been more or less successfully instituted in modern economic enterprises and governmental agencies in the course of recent developments of Western civilization. To understand the concept "bureaucracy" fully, it is necessary, therefore, to contrast these characteristics with the corresponding aspects of an administrative staff under traditional authority.

a. *In place of a well-defined impersonal sphere of competence, there is a shifting series of tasks and powers commissioned and granted by a chief through his arbitrary decision of the moment.*
b. *The question who shall decide a matter—which of his officials or the chief himself— . . . is treated . . . [either] traditionally, on the basis of the authority of particular received legal norms or precedents [or] entirely on the basis of the arbitrary decision of the chief.*
c. *As opposed to the bureaucratic system of free appointment, household officials and favourites are very often recruited on a purely patrimonial basis from among the slaves or serfs of the chief. If the recruitment has been extrapatrimonial, they have*

[29]Gerth and Mills, *op. cit.*, pp. 196–98.

tended to be holders of benefices which he has granted as an act of grace without being bound by any formal rules.

d. *Rational technical training as a basic qualification for office is scarcely to be found at all among household officials or the favourites of the chief.*

e. *In place of regular salaries, household officials and favourites are usually supported and equipped in the household of the chief and from his personal stores. Generally, their exclusion from the lord's own table means the creation of benefices. . . . It is easy for these to become traditionally stereotyped in amount and kind.*[30]

This conceptualization of the administrative staff under bureaucratic and traditional authority refers to the external coercions and enduring results which are embodied in historically evolved institutional complexes. These concepts also refer to linked and opposite tendencies of action of which one or the other will be more or less dominant *under given historical conditions.*

The last phrase suggests a level of abstraction which differs from that considered so far. A concept such as "primary relations" refers to a universal tendency of action. But if we say that the rights and duties of an administrative staff are defined in accordance with written regulations rather than with a chief's arbitrary decisions of the moment, then we have the first part of a contrast-conception based on historical experience.[31] Similar contrasts can be observed

[30]Max Weber, *The Theory of Social and Economic Organization* (New York: Oxford University Press, 1947), pp. 343, 344, 345. In this passage, Weber did not explicitly contrast the last two conditions of employment. It may be added, however, that under traditional authority the chief's arbitrary decisions frequently identify an office with the household official or favorite who occupies it; and the holders of benefices frequently attempt and succeed in appropriating the position. The term "full-time occupation" is not applicable to an administrative staff under traditional authority, either. Cf. also Max Weber, *Religion of China* (Glencoe, Ill.: Free Press, 1951), pp. 33–104, for an analysis of patrimonial government which shows close approximations to this concept of traditional authority.

[31]To define "primary relations," one assumes that complete intimacy prevails and all impersonal considerations are excluded. It would be possible to construct a model on this basis similar to that developed in economic theory, although the preceding emphasis on "paired concepts" suggests a reason why this has not been done in sociological theory. To define an administrative staff in terms of written regulations, on the other hand, is a statement of historical fact; either there are written regulations or there are not. An assumption or "as if" construction enters in only when these regulations are said to preclude arbitrary decisions. For a discussion of Weber's

under the other conditions enumerated above. Two caveats must be remembered, however. The conditions of bureaucratic or of traditional authority *need not actually occur together*. For example, the rights and duties of an administrative staff may be clearly defined in written regulations, while appointments and promotions are handled with personal arbitrariness, just as a chief might be arbitrary in assigning different tasks but highly rational and legalistic in his delegation of authority. Also, each of these institutional complexes is *relatively unstable*. For example, the written regulation of rights and duties may permit a great deal of alteration by personal influence, though the intent is to preclude such influence, while a chief's arbitrary assignment of tasks and of authority may permit the growth of independent power on the part of his officials and thus limit his arbitrariness, even though the intent is to preclude such a development. Yet despite this instability there is a secular tendency favoring the coincidence of the several conditions of bureaucratic and of traditional authority.

This statement of a historical tendency refers to the enduring results of collective actions and to the external coercions which are the partial causes and consequences of these actions. Hence, the statement is not primarily an "as if" proposition in the sense of the definitions cited earlier, as for example that the market knows no personal distinctions if the impersonal relations dictated entirely by economic considerations were allowed to work themselves out to their logical conclusion. The stipulation of rights and duties in accordance with written regulations or training and experience as formal conditions of employment are not definitions in that sense but descriptive statements. And the statement that these characteristics tend to develop together is likewise descriptive. (Indeed, these and related institutional arrangements are so widely accepted today that even the distribution of patronage positions by politicians involves some show of adherence to these characteristics of a bu-

---

concept of "bureaucracy" in modern society, which parallels the above contrast between administration under rational and traditional authority, cf. Reinhard Bendix, *Work and Authority in Industry* (New York: John Wiley & Sons, Inc., 1956), pp. 244–51.

This discussion deliberately avoids the term "ideal type" because of the many meanings which are associated with it. The distinction between theoretical models and historical types in Weber's treatment of this problem was analyzed in Alexander von Schelting, "Die logische Theorie der historischen Kulturwissenschaft von Max Weber und insbesondere sein Begriff des Idealtypus," *Archiv für Sozialwissenschaft*, 49 (1922), 726–31.

reaucracy.) Yet, the definitions of administrative staffs under legal, bureaucratic authority and under traditional authority also differ from mere descriptions in that they extrapolate the observed characteristics on the assumption that the actors themselves are completely consistent and successful. To say that the market knows no personal distinctions, *if* . . . involves logical considerations by the scholar. To say that bureaucracy is defined (in part) by training and experience as a condition of employment has reference to the more or less successful endeavor of the advocates of civil service reform. That is, the first conceptualizes actions in terms of the logical principles underlying them; the second conceptualizes actions in terms of the actual and the desired effects of social groups in the struggle for power.[32]

These examples suggest that concepts of institutional complexes also occur in "pairs" in the sense that they refer to manifold tendencies of action which are linked and opposite. It is necessary, therefore, to keep *both* concepts in mind for the purposes of any specific analysis, even though one *or* the other is primarily applicable to the given case. We saw, for example, that fixed monetary salaries of bureaucratic officials were contrasted with the dependence of traditional officials upon the household and/or the benefices of a chief. Although salary scales are readily fixed and administered, fringe benefits, promotion, and job classification are frequently subject to bargaining and personal influence. Conceivably, such bargaining and influence might go so far that they make a mere fiction out of the basic salary scale. Whether or not this will be the case depends in the first instance upon the conflicting efforts of those who seek to administer the scale and of those who use bargaining and influence to maximize their own advantages. If the latter were completely successful, they might re-establish a condition of traditional authority by making their remuneration primarily dependent upon the arbitrary decision of a chief. If the former were successful all the way, they would codify fringe benefits, promotions, and job classifications minutely so as to minimize the possibilities of bargaining and personal influence, and hence to arbitrary decisions. The same applies to the other contrasting characteristics of administrative staffs. Each of the concepts represents, therefore, an institutional pattern which has resulted from the successful activities

---

[32]The contrast is not absolute, therefore. Both theoretical models and historical types involve the extrapolation of given tendencies of action.

of certain social groups under given historical conditions. And the relevant universal proposition tells us that such success is never complete or permanent and that it is necessary for the analyst to consider the actual and potential forces which tend to circumscribe that success and which under favorable conditions may impose contrasting conditions of their own.[33]

IV. Culture, Society, and Group Conflict

The conditions of human existence are reflected in the fact that universal tendencies of action are linked and opposite at the same time. The problems of meaning posed by this fact lie in the province of the philosophers and theologians. However, the sociologist also becomes concerned with these problems when he considers the implications of paired concepts for an understanding of the culture and structure of whole societies. Contemporary social science tends to use the word "culture" to refer to the way of life of a people: their artifacts and their patterns of conduct, as well as their ideas and ideals. This use of the term tends to emphasize, as we noted earlier, that individuals in a culture "fit in" with that way of life, as a matter both of choice and of compulsion. And the term "subculture" has been used to conceptualize the fact that every known culture is internally differentiated. While this terminology emphasizes an important aspect of society, it also has peculiar disadvantages.[34] Each culture is made to appear as a whole which possesses different parts (subcultures) as well as an overall unity (the way of life), but in which the actions of individuals and of groups are limited to pre-established patterns and tend to re-enforce the culture of which they are a part. If formal institutions like an administrative staff may be conceptualized as the "arena" of contending groups, then it may also be useful to look upon the culture of a society in a similar way.

In lieu of the word "culture" Max Weber used the term "ethos," partly because the German equivalent "Kultur" had ethical conno-

[33]This perspective may be considered a corollary of Georg Simmel's emphasis upon the reciprocity of all social relations. But attention is focused here on collective actions and institutions rather than upon the interactions of individuals.

[34]Cf. Robert Bierstedt, "The Limitations of Anthropological Methods in Sociology," *American Journal of Sociology*, 54 (July 1948), 22–30.

tations which he sought to avoid, and partly also because he felt that terms like "culture" tended to be question begging.[35] The reasons for this choice of terms are of interest here. By using "ethos" as a general designation of different ways of life, Weber wanted to emphasize that each man's participation in his society involved a personal commitment to the behavior patterns, the ideas, and the interests of a particular status group. By virtue of their styles of life, such groups

are the specific bearers of all "conventions." In whatever way it may be manifest, all "stylization" of life either originates in status groups or is at least conserved by them.[36]

Such styles of life may become characteristics of a whole society. Thus, Weber was much concerned with the fact that the domineering patriarchal manner of the *Junkers* had influenced many aspects of German society. Again, certain ideas of ascetic Protestantism had gained widespread influence in modern capitalism; they "prowl about in our lives like the ghost of dead religious beliefs."[37] Weber, in fact, summarized one aspect of his studies in the sociology of religion by designating the status group which was in each case the principal exponent of a world religion.[38] To be sure, religious beliefs as well as other ideas and behavior patterns frequently exert a far-reaching influence beyond the status group to which they are originally or primarily related. But by relating a given idea and its corresponding style of life to a particular group from which these had spread, Weber construed the culture of a nation as an outgrowth of group power and group conflict in their historical development. Accordingly, the analysis of historical legacies is an essential part of the interpretation of culture, because the group relations and styles of life which prevail in modern society can be understood

[35]Cf. the remark that "the appeal to national character is generally a mere confession of ignorance" in Max Weber, *The Protestant Ethic and the Spirit of Capitalism* (New York: Charles Scribner's Sons, 1930), p. 88.
[36]*Gerth and Mills*, p. 191.
[37]*Protestant Ethic*, p. 182.
[38]Thus, Confucianism is the work of the world-ordering bureaucrat, Hinduism of the world-ordering magician, Buddhism of wandering mendicant monks, Islam of world-conquering warriors, Judaism of itinerant traders, Christianity of itinerant craftsmen. See Max Weber, *Wirtschaft und Gesellschaft* (Tübingen: J. C. B. Mohr, 1925), 1: 293 and the detailed discussion; of this theme on pp. 267–96. A brief summary is also contained in *From Max Weber*, pp. 268–69.

only as more or less temporary end-products of past conflicts among the ideas and behavior patterns of status groups.[39]

This formulation has the advantage of relating the concept "culture" to the phenomenon of power in society. If the "social roles" of individuals provide opportunities for action as well as limit the available alternatives, it follows that in many societies the individual is able to engage in more or less continual attempts to redefine his roles. We may think of culture as a way of life which is characterized by a more or less enduring pattern of interaction among dominant and subordinate status groups, each with a vested interest in the material and ideal aspects of its style of life. Hence, culture may be related to society and power by an analysis of the groups which struggle with, and against, other groups in their attempts to reformulate and institutionalize role defintions in their own interest. For example, the Negro in the United States occupies the status of a lower caste, and acts accordingly; or the government administrator occupies a well-defined position concerned with the execution of legislative policy. But the characterization of "status and role" in these terms obscures certain very relevant facts. Important Negro spokesmen in the Uinted States today, for example, are using the nationalistic movements of colored peoples everywhere as a weapon in their own struggle for improving the "Negro's share" at home; they say, in effect: "If you want less trouble abroad, you must improve our position at home." Or the government administrator who asks his "clientele" for their wishes with regard to services from his agency may run head-on into an irate congressman who claims that it is *his*, and not the administrator's job "to know what the public wants." These illustrations suggest that it is misleading to characterize the "status and role" of an individual or group in static terms because each is engaged in some strategy of argument and action designed to define their respective roles in a manner that appears advantageous to themselves.

It is necessary to combine this emphasis upon the more or less continual struggle among status groups and their partially conflicting styles of life with propositions that are true of an entire social structure. One way of doing so is suggested by the empirical obser-

---

[39]See E. R. Leach, *Political Systems of Highland Burma* (Cambridge: Cambridge University Press, 1954) for an anthropological field study which illustrates the usefulness of this perspective. Professor Leach's theoretical position is quite similar to the one discussed in this paper (cf. pp. 1–17 of his work).

vation that at any one time, and frequently for prolonged periods, a particular status group and its style of life are dominant in a society. Yet at best, this is only a partial answer. Any given pattern of inter- action among dominant and subordinate groups is so unstable that it is still necessary to consider the changing particulars of that interaction in relation to the more enduring characteristics of the society as a whole. Max Weber's answer to this question was his familiar assertion that it was necessary to simplify and exaggerate selected historical facts. In his earliest statement of this view, he maintained that such exaggerations were justified, if the facts selected for this purpose were indeed typical.[40] But to ascertain what was typical depended in his view upon a wide-ranging use of the comparative method. A model illustration of such an analysis is contained in the work of Alexis de Tocqueville, and it is instructive for our purposes to examine how he accomplished his results.

In the first volume of his *Democracy in America* Tocqueville had dealt with the institutions of a democratic society, principally in a descriptive manner. But in the second volume he had used

the ideas derived from American and French democracy only as data, . . . [in order] to paint the general features of democratic societies, no complete specimen of which can yet be said to exist. This is what an ordinary reader fails to appreciate. Only those who are much accustomed to searching for abstract and speculative truths, care to follow me in such an inquiry.[41]

To know how men will act tomorrow and how they will deal with coming events, one must be in a position to see continually what they are doing and what they are thinking. But to judge what the men of a society are prepared to become one must take a bird's-eye view of affairs in order to understand the "sentiments, principles, and opinions, the moral and intellectual qualities" which are given by nature and by an education that has lasted for centuries.[42]

In his second volume on America, Tocqueville was concerned with this truth for the long run. He had set himself the task of reconciling

---

[40]See Max Weber, "Die ländliche Arbeitsverfassung," *Gesammelte Aufsätze zur Sozial- und Wirtschaftsgeschichte* (Tübingen: J. C. B. Mohr, 1924), p. 446.
[41]Letter to J. St. Mill of Dec. 18, 1840, in *Memoirs, Letters and Remains of Alexis de Tocqueville* (Boston: Ticknor & Fields, 1862), 2: p. 68.
[42]Cf. *Ibid.*, 2, pp. 230–31, 237, 272.

the republican champions and the aristocratic opponents of democracy. The progressive development of democracy appeared to him inevitable. And though he favored it, he endeavored to show that it was not a brilliant and easily realized ideal, that such a government was not viable "without certain conditions of intelligence, of private morality, and of religious belief."[43] As a nation, France had not yet attained these conditions. Indeed, she provided Tocqueville with the image of a society in which the democratic revolution had gone astray, uncertainty alternating between despotism and anarchy with no signs at all as to when and how a stable social order might again be established. If he had children he would advise them to be prepared for everything and to rely on nothing that might be taken away.[44] And yet he wrote:

You suppose my view of the prospects of democracy to be more gloomy than it is. . . . I have endeavored, it is true, to describe the natural tendency of opinions and institutions in a democratic society. I have pointed out the dangers to which it exposes men. But I have never said that these tendencies, if discovered in time, might not be resisted, and these dangers, if foreseen, averted. It struck me that the republicans saw neither the good nor the evil of the condition into which they wished to bring society. . . . I therefore undertook to bring out as clearly and as strongly as I could, that we may look our enemies in the face and know against what we have to fight.[45]

Thus, the classic insights into the structure of American society arose for Tocqueville from an analysis of the dangers to a democratic society which had become manifest in France, but which were so far held in check in the United States.

In my work on America . . . though I seldom mentioned France, I did not write a page without thinking of her, and placing her as it were before me. And what I specifically tried to draw out, and to explain in the United States, was not the whole condition of that foreign society, but the points in which it differs from our own, or resembles us. It is always by noticing likenesses or contrasts that I succeeded in giving an interesting and accurate description of the

---

[43]Letter to Stoffels, dated February 21, 1835. *Ibid.*, 1, p. 376.
[44]Letter to Stoffels, dated July 21, 1848. *Ibid.*, 1, p. 400.
[45]Letter to M. de Corcelle, dated April 12, 1835. *Ibid.*, 2, pp. 13–14.

*New World. . . . I believe that this perpetual silent reference to
France was a principal cause of the book's success.*[46]

Tocqueville's remarkable insight into the despotic possibilities inherent in even the most successful democratic society arose from
this implicit extrapolation of American conditions in the light of how
analogous conditions had developed in the course of nineteenth
century French history. And French society in turn only provided
him with a picture of the "sentiments, principles, and opinions, the
moral and intellectual qualities," which might lead to a "species of
oppression unlike anything that ever before existed in the world."[47]

Tocqueville's analysis of American society does not, then, contain statements about its "whole condition," but rather *comparisons*
with analogous conditions in another society. And beyond that it
contains "speculative truths" concerning future developments which
may materialize if present tendencies are allowed to work themselves out to their logical conclusion. For Tocqueville this latter
assumption was useful only as an analytical tool so that society can
act "like a strong man who knows that [the] danger before him . . .
must be met, and is alarmed only when he cannot see clearly what
it is."[48] Yet, such knowledge of the dangers that threaten can never
be more than a knowledge of the limits and possibilities of development.

*I own, that this old world, beyond which we neither of us can see,
appears to me to be almost worn out; the vast and venerable machine seems more out of gear every day; and though I cannot look
forward, my faith in the continuance of the present is shaken. I learn
from history that not one of the men who witnessed the downfall of
religious and social organizations that have passed away was able
to guess or even to imagine what would ensue. Yet this did not prevent Christianity from succeeding to idolatry; servitude to slavery;
the barbarians from taking the place of Roman civilization, and
feudalism in turn ejecting the barbarians. Each of these changes
occurred without having been anticipated by any of the writers in
the times immediately preceding these total revolutions. Who, then,*

---

[46]Letter to Louis de Kergorlay of October 19, 1843. *Ibid.*, 1, p. 342.
[47]Alexis de Tocqueville, op. cit., 2: 336.
[48]Letter to M. de Corcelle, April 12, 1835. *Ibid.*, 2, 14.

can affirm that any one social system is essential and that another is impossible?[49]

It is apparent that this was a reasoned conviction which held the balance between overconfidence and despair. Tocqueville did not think it possible to predict the future of society because in his view it depended upon men and nations whether their drift toward equality would lead to servitude or freedom. Yet, he also believed that the possible directions of social change were limited in number and that it was feasible to foresee them by means of "speculative truths" which extrapolated observed tendencies on the fictitious assumption that nothing would interfere with their ultimate realization. In our judgment, this approach fits in well with a view of culture and social structure which regards both as more or less enduring end-products of past group conflicts.

V. Some Implications

The paired concepts discussed above appear to reflect the dichtomies characteristic of much sociological theorizing in the past. These dichotomies may be regarded as a methodoligical safeguard against the bias inherent in every conceptualization. Twenty years ago Kenneth Burke called attention to this aspect with his phrase "perspective by incongruity."

Any performance is discussible either from the standpoint of what it attains *or what it* misses. *Comprehensiveness can be discussed as superficiality, intensiveness as stricture, tolerance as uncertainty— and the poor* pedestrian *abilities of the fish are clearly explainable in terms of his excellence as a* swimmer. *A way of seeing is also a way of not seeing. . . .*[50]

The paired concepts of sociological theory may, thus, be regarded as a methodological or linguistic device.

But these paired concepts also have theoretical implications, because they are especially well adapted to the reciprocity characteristic of social life. If it be true that social isolation, strictly

[49]Letter to Mrs. Grote, July 24, 1850. *Ibid.,* 2, 104–5.
[50]Kenneth Burke, *Permanence and Change* (New York: New Republic, 1936), p. 70.

speaking, does not exist, that every action in society evokes or provokes reactions, that every action must have, therefore, manifold consequences, intended and unintended, valued and devalued, then it follows that sociological inquiry should search each social fact for what it hides as much as for what it reveals. This consideration has special relevance for all attempts to analyze the "function" or "dysfunction" of given social facts, i.e., their objective consequences which contribute to the successful adaptation or to the impairment of a society. The difficulties here are considerable. For example, frequent industrial strikes prevent maximum production. This statement of cause and effect is unsatisfactory, for the objective of sociological analysis is to arrive at generalizations. This objective would be achieved if it were possible to demonstrate a determinate relationship between given levels of strike activity and the degree of cooperation necessary for the successful adaptation of enterprises or of the society at large. To do that we would need a value-free criterion of "successful adaptation," which, since such a criterion is not available to the social scientist, is simply another term for the ideal of "social health." In its absence, he is frequently tempted to achieve the desired level of generalization by categoric statements, e.g., frequent industrial strikes impair the level of cooperation or cohesion required for the adaptation of enterprises or of the society. [51] Yet the facts are that strikes may interfere with maximum production only in the short run. In the long run, they may help to accelerate capital investment and to increase overall productivity. While these actions may be designed to forestall the hazard of strikes, their ultimate effect may be to increase cooperation as well as productivity. Apparently, societies have inherent sources of conflict and strain (e.g., political parties, civil rights, interest groups, etc.) *which help to maintain the social structure*, which are indeed

---

[51]Every social theorist recognizes the deficiencies of this procedure. The practice persists, nevertheless, presumably because sociologists are not satisfied with the unscientific character of political judgments. Yet, in the absence of agreed-on criteria of "social health" it remains a political judgment whether or not a given number of strikes impairs the desired cooperation or cohesion in society. As Merton has stated, "Embedded in every functional analysis is some conception, tacit or expressed, of functional requirements of the system under observation. . . . This remains one of the cloudiest, and empirically most debatable concepts of functional theory." See R. K. Merton, *Social Theory and Social Structure* (Glencoe, Ill.: Free Press, 1949), p. 52.

an important element of its "successful adaptation." And if it be accepted that generally societies are characterized by cooperation and conflict, conformity and deviance, socialization and individualization, etc., it appears probable that *every* social fact (minority status, crime, strikes, etc.) has some consequences *both* for the continued adaptation and for the impairment of the social structure.

The burden of this discussion is to suggest that we cannot specify the limits of what is possible in a society, even though such limits probably exist. We know that the actions of individuals in society fall within a range of tolerance, but we cannot identify the limits of this range because they are in a continual process of redefinition. The dilemma posed by this fact is best resolved, in our view, if we do not search for the attributes of society as a "system," such as a minimum of consensus or of satisfaction. In every society, efforts are repeatedly made to define the limits beyond which no member is permitted to go; yet individuals often fail to comply with what is expected of them. It is necessary that sociological theory comprehend both tendencies. And to do that attention must be focused on the boundary-extending as well as upon the boundary-maintaining activities of individuals, on the permissive aspects of culture and society which enable individuals *to experiment with what is possible* as well as upon the social controls which limit the range of tolerated behavior without defining that range clearly.[52]

The orientation to social theory presented in this paper is also based on an attitude toward the role of knowledge in society.[53] All social scientists desire to see the advance of their discipline and hope for the rational solution of pressing social problems. But it seems to us wise to adopt an attitude of hope *and* uncertainty concerning the constructive potentialities of knowledge. We do not know enough to be sure of what cannot be known, but we do not accept the tenet that man must only know enough in order to control society.

[52]This experimentation with what is possible can be identified in the boundary-extending activities of individuals, whether these consist of criminal activity and all other forms of deviance or of scientific research and all other forms of creative work. But this identification does not preclude the search for "hidden" results (say, the boundary-extending implications of boundary-maintaining actions, or vice versa), which our paired concepts suggest. Cf. Talcott Parsons, *The Social System* (Glencoe, Ill.: Free Press, 1952), for a different view of "boundary-maintenance" in a social system.
[53]Cf. Reinhard Bendix, *Social Science and the Distrust of Reason* (Berkeley: University of California Press, 1951) for a discussion of this point.

The approach presented here is obviously tentative, requires considerable elaboration, and does not stand or fall on superseding all other approaches. We candidly regard it as experimental and would like to have it read in the same spirit. As stated at the beginning, it is related to an intellectual tradition which views men and society in terms of tendencies or forces which are linked and opposite at the same time. This tradition has special relevance for contemporary sociological theory. For in the wake of the conflict between conservatism and liberalism in the nineteenth century, sociological theories have generally sided with the former by emphasizing the integration of the individual with the group, while the nonintegrative aspects of the individual were relegated to the unexplained residues of "deviation" and creative effort. The approach presented in this paper may help to emancipate sociological theory from the limitations of this intellectual heritage. But the import of these concluding remarks is not to label given theories or thinkers as conservative, liberal, or anything else. It is to make plain, rather, that the definition of the "social fact" embodies each theorist's image of society and that this image is the source of each theory's utility and unique blindness.

On Talcott Parsons

1962

Talcott Parsons is, among other things, one of those sociologists who write very badly—I would be tempted to say barbarously if the word were not already so overworked with reference to sociologists. Having made this dutiful observation, let me at once make clear that I do not consider the opaqueness of Parsons' language sufficient reason for dismissing him as an obscurantist or as otherwise not worth the attention of serious students of society. Intellectual history is full of large figures who said important, influential, and sometimes memorable things in a prose, like Parsons', so cumbersome, ponderous, and involuted as to discourage all but the most dedicated readers—and even some of them. Few readers, I suspect, actually sit down expecting to *enjoy* Hegel or Heidegger or even John Dewey as they might sit down to enjoy the articles in *Encounter* or *Commentary* or any general magazine of high intellectual quality. Reading Parsons is a burden, a duty, probably limited largely to two groups: to graduate students in the social sciences (especially sociology) who will be examined by their professors on Parsons, and to

Reprinted from *Commentary* (December 1952), by permission; Copyright © 1962 by the American Jewish Committee.

practicing social scientists who impose on themselves the responsibility of knowing what is going on "in theory." Others who come across his work probably do so as a result of hearing (perhaps through more readable sociologists) of Parsons' almost mythical dimensions as the Grand Theorist of social systems.

This he is. In an intellectual milieu dominated by empiricists, Parsons has been able to "get away with" (as he put it once, in an unusual moment of irony) Pure Theory. Without ever having done a major piece of what, today, sociologists would call "empirical research," he has reached the pinnacle of a profession which typically distributes honor primarily on the basis of achievements in research —or in interpretive syntheses of research.

The Social Theories of Talcott Parsons,[1] a collection of critical and expository essays on Parsons, is one of a long series of honors which document his eminence. The book is representative in the sense that it rehearses the complex attitudes that Parsons, his work, and his position call forth from his peers. A result of two years of interdepartmental faculty seminars and public discussions at Cornell, the book contains nine essays on general and particular aspects of Parsonian theory, and concludes with a long chapter by Parsons himself which attempts, somewhat in the manner of Toynbee responding to his critics, to "answer" the symposiasts. Unfortunately, I cannot even hope to summarize here the corpus of Parsons' theoretical work. Edward Devereux's bare bones exposition, an essentially sympathetic one, and by far the most lucid treatment of Parsons' work that I know, by itself runs over sixty pages of the book. Nevertheless, it is necessary to say enough about Parsons' work to convey some hint of its scope and complexity.

For almost thirty years Parsons has devoted himself to the construction of a systematic theory of human action at a conceptual level abstract enough to encompass the analysis of culture, society, and personality—and all of their component "parts" and interrelations. In principle, nothing in the distinctly human experience of men should be beyond the grasp of the theory's explanatory force. At the very foundation of the Parsonian theory is the idea that human action is organized into *systems*. Systems, in turn, have two basic characteristics: the functional interdependence of their parts, and a fundamental tendency to maintain equilibrium against "disturb-

[1] Edited by Max Black (Englewood Cliffs, N.J.: Prentice-Hall, 1961).

ances" from both within and without. Personalities, for example, are systems of "need-dispositions" which tend to maintain a balance of "gratification-deprivation"; societies are systems of "reciprocal role-expectations" which tend to maintain their "boundaries" against environmental forces and dissident elements within. At the apex of the hierarchical trinity[2] of systems stands culture, a system of value-patterns—or symbol-meanings—with an inherent strain toward consistency. Institutionalized in social structures, culture provides the normative content of role-expectations; internalized in personalities, it provides the motive force for seeking the particular gratification of particular needs.

Each of these major systems comprehends smaller subsystems; what is a system from one perspective becomes an "environment" of a subsystem from another perspective, and merely a "unit" of a larger system from still a third perspective. To complicate matters further, empirical systems are never *only* cultural *or* social *or* personal; these systems "interpenetrate" one another. While each is *"analytically* irreducible," any study of personality must concern itself with the social features of personality and any study of a social system must concern itself with the distinctive cultural features of that system.

In order for social systems to "survive," according to Parsons, they must "solve" four functional problems. (1) Systems have goals which to some extent must be *attained* if the system is to continue; (2) systems also have environments to which they must *adapt*; (3) at the same time, a system must solve the problem of its internal *integration* and maintain a level of cohesion among its parts sufficient to enable one to speak of it *as* a system; and finally (4), in solving these problems, a social system inevitably confronts a fourth and "latent" problem: it must maintain within its units the norms, the motives, and the values which energize these units, and it must manage the tensions which, somehow, seem to get generated. Historically speaking, as societies become more structurally differentiated, a kind of division of labor occurs, and certain complexes of roles and institutions come to be primarily associated with the solving of one particular functional problem. If one considers the whole society as a social system, for example, political institutions are primarily concerned with the first problem, economic institutions

---

[2]Parsons later added a fourth system, which he called "the organism."

with the second, and the family with the fourth. (But when the family itself, or any other subsystem, is considered as the system of reference, it then is faced with solving all four of the problems, which it does by a further differentiation of functions among its own units.)

Parsons analyzes social systems with the aid of his five pairs of "pattern-variables." These are pairs of opposing terms (affectivity/affective neutrality; specificity/diffuseness; universalism/particularism; quality/performance; self-orientation/collectivity-orientation) which characterize and classify the structural components of action systems.[3] In Parsons' view, orientations, roles, value patterns, and so on, can be characterized exhaustively—and then classified—by a combination of terms, one from each pair. For reasons he has never made entirely clear, Parsons insists that these variables (which are refinements of existing polarities in sociological thinking) are not continua, not matters of degree, but rather dichotomies of choice; as "independent dimensions," the variables force a "choice" between one term or the other; the nature of pattern-variables does not permit ambivalent turnings-in-both-directions-at-once.

This brief synopsis of the nature of systems, the four functional problems, and the pattern-variables does not even begin to suggest the weight of the conceptual baggage borne by the Parsonian freight nor the tortuous logical track down which it huffs and puffs and occasionally roars. I hope, however, that it conveys some sense of the enormous reach of the theory and the stratospheric level of abstraction at which the theory's concepts are formulated. For it is the level of abstraction at which Parsons works that is the primary source of both the high praise and the negative criticism he has received from his colleagues.

There is plenty of both in *The Social Theories of Talcott Parsons* —although as is characteristic of symposia, considerably more of the latter than the former. William Foote Whyte, professor of industrial relations at Cornell, examines the relevance of Parsonian theory

---

[3]In a later formulation, to give an example of Parsons "at work," he dropped "self-orientation/collectivity-orientation" as a "pattern-variable" and reformulated it—along with yet another set of terms, "instrumental/consummatory"—as an "axis of differentiation." This now moves the term to a level of abstraction which is higher, in Parsons' theory, than the level occupied by the four remaining "pattern-variables."

to the study of formal organizations (an area in which systematic theory should be most applicable) but finds virtually no help: "By failing to deal in any adequate way with data that are abundantly observable and measurable, Parsons has chosen to erect his theoretical scheme on quicksand." Henry Landsberger, an economist at Cornell, also writing on Parsons' organizational theory, is much more impressed than Whyte, but still he finds a vagueness in some of its basic concepts and a lack of clarity in the underlying purpose of the theory. One is left, he feels, with a set of categories and "mechanisms" but no real theory: "When judged against the goal Parsons has set for himself, one [*sic*] cannot but feel that the deficiencies at present exceed the achievement, and continued progress is by no means assured." Urie Bronfenbrenner, a psychologist, compares the Parsonian theory of identification with Freud's—and with O. H. Mowrer's revision of Freud—and finds Parsons seriously wanting: "By and large it has been difficult to discern much that is fundamentally new beyond the terminology . . . either he restates in even less precise language ideas that are already familiar . . . or he offers conceptions which, though provocative, are so diffuse that the basic tasks of theory construction have to be performed by the reader himself." Where Landsberger feels that there is no real theory in Parsons, Max Black, a logician, feels that there is, but that it is basically a theory of "statics," and he doubts whether it can generate any causal propositions. Black also raises fundamental questions about the source of the Parsonian categories, the meaning of *general* theory (which Parsons frequently italicizes), and the nature of the pattern-variables—which he doubts are either exhaustive or dichotomous. Alfred Baldwin, a Cornell psychologist, examines the Parsonian theory of personality cautiously because he thinks that any final evaluation of it "must await relevant data," and although he admires Parsons' emphasis on the interaction of personality and social systems, he nevertheless feels that Parsons' insistence on a systematic correspondence between the basic elements of personality, society, and culture—isomorphism, Baldwin calls it—inevitably "impoverishes" the concept of personality. "Need-dispositions," argues Baldwin, are not persons, and any attempt to treat them as such for theoretical purposes truncates the very idea of personality. Andrew Hacker, a political scientist, looks for the ideological taint in Parsons' scattered writings on politics, and finds it. But Parsons is not the conservative (at least in any practical

political sense) that several critics have charged him with being; as a matter of fact, Hacker states, Parsons is and has been for a long time a fairly typical liberal Democrat of the "egghead" variety. Yet in Parsons' theoretical emphasis on integration, equilibrium, and consensus, Hacker sees a built-in bias which has led Parsons to be overimpressed with the fact that democratic political systems of such enormous complexity as our own work *at all.*

If, then, as these critiques suggest, Parsons is biased, confused, evasive, turgid unoriginal, and vague, how are we to account for the almost unbroken *respect* which characterizes most of the analyses? With the exception of Whyte, who shows a tendency to get impatient with Parsons, and Bronfenbrenner, who does let go with a little disrespect, these critics consistently extend to Parsons a sustained courtesy and attention which seems remarkable in light of the damning conclusions to which their close textual analyses usually lead. I said there was praise in this book for Parsons, and so there is, but one looks through these essays in vain for an intellectual basis for it. What one finds is reviewers' clichés: Parsons is interesting, provocative, stimulating, challenging, and so on. But these adjectives do not begin to reveal the nature of his eminence, an eminence so real that one still carries away from this book a favorable impression of Parsons—in spite of the things said about his work; an eminence so palpable that many sociologists experience the visceral equivalent of a salute when Parsons passes among them.

This failure to understand the real nature of Parsons' eminence is a failure to recognize the criteria of judgment on which it depends. One of the going clichés in sociology is the view that theory is a "tool," justified insofar as it encourages and guides "fruitful" research. On this criterion, of course, the Parsonian theory is a conspicuous failure. Available in its main outlines for at least fifteen years, it has so far failed to produce a body of research of really impressive substance. In an otherwise excellent discussion of the general theory, Robin Williams, a sociologist, alone among the critics represented, chooses to defend Parsons' utility in this respect; but all he can cite are three or four research reports scattered in the professional journals, an unpublished study in Kansas City, and a much overpraised book on the anaylsis of roles. There *are* a few others, but like the ones that Williams cites, they are, curiously, not the work primarily of Parsons' impersonal readers but of his students

and collaborators. This suggests, of course, that a good part of Parsons' influence is *personal*; one is told that he is a brilliant teacher, and a substantial number of the foremost American sociologists have passed through his classes at Harvard. I think, in fact, that a really full intimacy with Parsons' thinking almost *requires* becoming a close colleague or collaborator, or else demands so heavy an investment of time and intellectual energy that the student, having made the investment, may be reluctant to conclude that his time and energy might have been rather better spent.

Parsons nonetheless remains, as the dust jacket of this book states, "America's most renowned social theorist." Virtually alone among American sociologists he tries (however imperfectly) to satisfy the hunger of serious sociologists everywhere for "a systematic theory" at a level of abstraction applicable to all human societies at any time anywhere. The fact is that for the past twenty years systematic sociological theory in the United States has been little else than a dialogue with Talcott Parsons. And this fact is both sufficient warrant for the respect with which he is currently regarded, and evidence of his profound influence on sociological thinking. By his sustained theoretical efforts, he has maintained among sociologists a sense of the great intellectual tradition—Saint-Simon, Comte, Marx, Durkheim, Max Weber—in which they stand, a sense easy to feel slipping away as one goes about one's workaday research at levels of abstraction—usually low—dictated by the positivist criterion of operational definitions of variables. And in 1937 Parsons earned his right to a place in this tradition (how important a place can only be a matter of opinion at this time) when he published *The Structure of Social Action*, still his best book, and still unmatched as a statement which places the body of ideas called sociology in the context of the history of social thought.

To suggest, as several of the critics in this book do (indulging themselves in another of sociology's clichés), that we must withhold judgment on Parsons because "all the returns are not yet in" is to be less than candid because nobody really believes that the returns will ever all be "in." For systematic theory, at the level which Parsons attempts it, is not the "heuristic" act of a toolmaker, to be judged by the quality of the goods it produces; it is the goods itself, a great synoptic vision, an expressive act of the mind, a *Ding an sich*, and it is for this that Parsons is honored, and certainly not for any tools that, inadvertently, he may have fashioned along the way. Parsons' eminence (an eminence in my view more durable than

one conferred by a set of significant correlations) is that of a man who represents, in perhaps its purest form, "the sociological perspective," a distinct way of looking at the world.[4]

Having said this, I must go on to say that, as a comprehensive, scientific theory of human behavior, Parsons' own particular vision still seems to me, as it does to most of the contributors to the symposium, seriously inadequate. Max Weber once said that when it came to matters of religion he was "unmusical." Parsons seems "unmusical" when it comes to matters of power, conflict, and disorder. One feels that, to Parsons, *anomie* is something he has read about in Emile Durkheim and hence knows exists, and that conflict is something a very important thinker like Marx wrote a great deal about and which he consequently must "take account of." I do not mean to suggest that one must eat human flesh in order to understand cannibalism, but when Parsons talks about political power and conflict, as he does (sometimes quite acutely) in occasional essays, his comments, as Hacker suggests, sound like something grafted onto the body of the theory rather than a natural outgrowth of it—analogous to Marx's "Hague Speeches" in which the man who was not a Marxist blithely tore a ragged gap in the fabric of his theory of revolution with the bland admission that under certain conditions workers can attain their ends by peaceful means. When, on the other hand, Parsons speaks of order, integration, function, the theory is not only logically impressive but *felt* as well; and this "emotion" is the source of the theory's occasional sharp insight, and even charm. His much-celebrated analysis of medical practice is a case in point. As Devereux points out, who else but Parsons would wonder why a child has two parents but a patient has only one therapist? Given the obvious parallels, the lack of "symmetry" disturbs Parsons.

Parsons' work illustrates the difficulties of trying to erect a general theory on the basis of "solving" a relatively specific problem. As several of his commentators have noted, Parsons originally set out to "solve" the problem of order—the so-called "Hobbesian Prob-

[4] I am not at all sure that Parsons would accept this as the high praise I intend it to be. He sees his work not as a contribution to the history of ideas but as a scientific theory of action in, as he would say, "a quite technical sense." He might even think it impertinent that his work be reviewed in a general magazine—reasoning that it would be no more relevant to review him here simply because his subject is society and culture than it would be to review a technical manual on computer engineering simply because computers "think."

lem." On the whole I think that Parsons' solution is a pretty good one; it is, as a matter of fact, *the* sociological answer: social order is possible because men have culture, a set of values which are in-stitutionalized in social structures, and "internalized" in personali-ties where they are experienced as motives and constraints. Cul-ture, in the final analysis, emerges from the interaction of living beings—which is the justification not only of the novel and the drama but also of the experimental study of small groups. But to appre-hend the nature of social order exhausts neither the data of society nor the powers of sociology; for "society" is not, as the Parsonians suggest it is, coterminous with processes of social cohesion, and the study of society is not circumscribed by the phrase "the struc-ture and functions of social systems." "Men, to be sure, live to-gether," wrote Ortega y Gasset, "but their living together cannot truly be called a society. It is merely an attempt or an effort toward becoming one"—an effort, he might have gone on to say, whose apparently inevitable lack of complete success suggests that the effort may be a fundamentally ambivalent one. At every point of human interaction the socially binding constraint of cultural norms may be countered and diluted by inequalities of power, opposition of interests, and even by an unleased *id* (which, as Lionel Trilling once observed ironically, may be the last stronghold of individuality in a sociological world).

Parsons has continually claimed that this kind of criticism is not only unjust but ideologically inspired. Conflict, change, unruly dis-order, *can*, he argues, be adequately "handled" within the structure of concepts he offers. In his rebuttal to Hacker here, he points out that change in the very structure of a system may be functionally necessary if the system is to cope with changes in its environment. But environments are systems too, and the source of changes in them (other than an organic, evolutionary sort) remains a theoretical mystery. Ten years ago Parsons tried to come to grips with his critics on this point by saying ". . . propositions about factors mak-ing for the maintenance of the system are at the same time propo-sitions about those making for change . . . *It is impossible to study one without the other.*" This statement has a deceptively convincing ring to it. It may be impossible to study one without the other, but it is quite possible to emphasize the conceptualization of one such that the other is reduced to the status of a residual category. Par-

sons would not accept his formulation if it were slightly rearranged by a conflict theorist to read "propositions about factors making for social change are at the same time propositions about those making for stability." Parsonian theory so sensitizes one to integration, order, and processes of self-regulation that conflict or other "disturbances" in the equilibrium of social systems can barely be discussed in other than pathological terms. When Parsons gives his attention to the phenomena of disequilibrium, it is almost always with a clinical vocabulary and with one eye on the compensatory, re-equilibrating forces that the system will bring to bear in order to restore "balance."

Parsonian theory, in short, conceptualizes only a part of the evidence. It is one thing to see a society's subtle patterns of integration and reciprocity and the powerful armory of "mechanisms" it has at its disposal for dealing with potential threats of disorder (sometimes repressively but usually co-optively); it is quite another thing to characterize these processes of stabilization as "the fundamental tendency of interaction." Societies have "tendencies" all over the place, and I find it no more nor less useful to assume that they have an inherent tendency toward equilibrium than to assume that they have an inherent logic of contradiction (as the Marxists do) which will be the source of their final downfall. There is, I think, considerable evidence to support both assumptions. As a matter of fact, I find it surprising that Parsons, who has taken over so much of Freudian theory at the sociological level, has not found it germane to introduce into his theory a sociological equivalent of the Thanatos concept. It is certainly no more mysterious than the logic of equilibrium, and, given the present direction of world politics, perhaps even more believable.

I have been suggesting that a thoroughgoing duality is necessary in the conceptual structure of a theory which claims to be applicable to the total range of human behavior, a duality which reflects both the ultimate opposition and the inextricable linkage between self and others, individual and the society.[5] Parsons claims that "the most ultimate principle" of the theory is precisely that of duality, and it is true that his work is full of paired concepts. But the duality in Parsons does not extend to his most fundamental assumptions; coercion does not have status equal to normative control. The tend-

[5] Reinhard Bendix and I have written on this more extensively. See "Images of Society and Problems of Concept Formation in Sociology" on pp. 258–87.

ency to disequilibrium does not have equal status with the tendency to equilibrium.

Robin Williams, as sympathetic a critic as Parsons could want, points out that "for the concept of equilibrium to have descriptive, predictive, or explanatory value, it must be possible to state a set of defining conditions specifying what 'balance of forces' is to be 'equilibrium' and what 'movements' will constitute disequilibrium. This, we submit, Parsons has not done." Until it *is* done, I do not see how one can speak meaningfully of empirical "systems." And there is considerable doubt that, at the level of analysis usual for Parsons, it can be done at all; for the very concepts (i.e., roles) which constitute the units of Parsonian social systems are themselves abstractions from behavior which is constantly changing—and not always within a readily identifiable "range of tolerance." On the other hand, it may very well be done at lower levels of analysis; not at all surprisingly some of the best work done in systematic functional analysis has been done on kinship systems—because of all roles, kinship roles are probably the most stable and orderly.

Without Freud's lucidity and Veblen's bite, the virtually unreadable character of the prose in Parsons' major books will probably prevent them from ever circulating very widely beyond the boundaries of academic social science.[6] In fact, I would hazard the guess that fully half of Persons' fellow sociologists do not know what he is about. But like Freud and Veblen, Parsons has that distinctive mark of a major social theorist: the capacity to corrupt the innocence with which we view those parts of the world that the theory touches. Having read Veblen, we can never again look at circular driveways and high heels and college gothic with quite the same innocence as we did before; having read Freud, we see mannerisms as mechanisms, predispositions and aversions as syndromes, and we think twice about letting our three-year-old daughter slip into bed with us on Sunday mornings. Parsons, even more than Edmund Burke and T. S. Eliot (in his prose writings), gives to one a sense of the essential orderliness of society and culture with their profound resources for containing and absorbing disruptive forces, a sense of

---

[6]In a superb example of understatement, Parsons says "I am not at all prepared to discount entirely the view that there are peculiar and unnecessary obscurities in my writing," and upon occasion he has apologized to his readers for what he once called his "terminological cumbersomeness."

the adaptive genius, the "wisdom," inherent in the organization of social and cultural systems.

Certainly these are "conservative" insights; and, like most insights, they contain important half-truths the appreciation of which, it seems to me, can only strengthen more dialetically founded theory. But Parsons' half-truths have frequently been met by a hostility from radical sociologists not unlike the impotent rage evoked from anxious, aggressive people by the smug disdain and patronization exercised toward them by the psychonalyzed. Radical sociologists blast away at Parsons, and he goes his bland way seeing "functions" everywhere. Fortunately, it is not necessary for the general reader to endure Parsons' attempts at formal system-building in order to appreciate the distinctive Parsonian sense of fit. We get this best not in his tomes but in his occasional essays on specific topics, most notably in the essays on age and sex grading, on the medical and legal professions, on McCarthyism, and perhaps especially in his critiques of David Riesman and C. Wright Mills—essays in which, unlike in his "serious" work, he is often as not quite lucid—lucid enough, in any case, to reveal the strengths and limitations of his theory.[7]

Parsons apparently prefers to be regarded not as a writer of occasional essays which, by virtue of his distinctive vision, illuminate specific problems, but rather as the creator of a scientific theory of action at the highest possible level of abstraction. And in his concluding essay in this symposium he polemicizes against fellow sociologists who doubt that the idea of "system" and its corollary, the principle of "equilibrium," are indispensable. Parsons' remarks here are revealing. Parsons believes that the attitude which denies the centrality of "equilibrium" is "symptomatic of the denial that social science itself is legitimate, or realistically possible." Now, if the model of what Parsons means by "science" is physics or even physiology, then he may be quite right in taking his colleagues to task. But if he is attempting to discredit sociologists who simply hold back from making any specific judgments about the ultimate shape of sociology as science, then Parsons is on much weaker ground. The eventual recognition of sociology's claim to the status of a science will depend upon the bulk and the importance of what

[7]All but the piece on Riesman can be found in one or the other of Parsons' two volumes of collected essays: *Essays in Sociological Theory: Pure and Applied*, rev. ed. (Glencoe, Ill.: Free Press, 1954); and *Structure and Process in Modern Society*, (Glencoe, Ill.: Free Press, 1960).

it convincingly tells us about social life. "Convincingly," of course, begs the important methodological questions, but I think that those who are more enamored of the existing forms of theoretical and empirical science than they are of understanding social life contribute less to this eventual recognition than do those sociologists (and Parsons is sometimes among them) who, while not insensitive to theoretical and methodological problems, plainly manifest by significant assertions, tested or testable, the enormous promise of "the sociological enterprise."

A diffidence about the ultimate shape of sociology as science need not make one an inveterate debunker of sociological "pretentiousness." It does imply—and here I write as a "practicing" sociologist—what I hope is neither a false modesty nor an easy piety before the complexity of the task, and also a view which is more temperate than that of either the omniscient pessimists who think a science of sociology impossible or the omniscient optimists who think it is a science already.

Sociology on Trial

1965

When only six years ago, in a highly favorable review of C. Wright Mills' *The Sociological Imagination*, Dennis Wrong referred to the "Humanistic Underground" of sociology, he could hardly have known that a part of that militant, clandestine group would shortly rise up into the bright glare of day to produce, of all things, an anthology. *Sociology on Trial* is a collection of essays critical of the dominant figures and schools of thought in sociology, and is almost on this ground alone a welcome sight. But in their brief introduction the editors work hard at wearing out that welcome for they adopt a holier than thou conception of themselves and their authors as the "conscience" of sociology, despised and rejected by the careerists in the discipline who have been "unable to resist society's affluent blandishments." If the editors are right about the kind of tight, guild control exercised by those who dominate the American Sociological Association, then no mere collection of essays, more than half of them published before, will loosen that grip. But they are very likely

A review of *Sociology on Trial*, edited by Maurice Stein and Arthur Vidich Englewood Cliffs, N.J.: Prentice-Hall, Inc. 1963). Reprinted from the *American Journal of Sociology* (May 1965) copyright the University of Chicago Press with the permission of the publisher.

wrong; the intellectual stance which these essays represent (a stance, by the way, which has never been adequately characterized —"humanistic," "impressionistic" and, as the editors term it, "critical" are all far from satisfactory) is an increasingly important influence in contemporary sociology. The melodramatic manner in which the editors conceive their alleged embattlement, therefore, seems to me to be without justification. In any case it is a small irony, as well as a tribute to the subtle influence of the academic life, that this moralist minority, these promoters of a *sociologie engagé* should be conducting their intellectual struggles through something that looks suspiciously like a textbook of "readings"— that most academic of literary artifacts.

Because some of the essays are very good while others are very bad, it is difficult to say anthing generally evaluative that characterizes the entire book, which is exactly what one wants to do with a volume so self-consciously and dramatically titled, wishing so much to stand *for* something collectively. At first glance, it seems fair to say that on the whole the book stands for an ethically relevant sociology and ethically involved sociologists, for attention to the large questions which command that involvement, and for the proposition that objectivity does not require ethical neutrality. Although I share these sentiments, their affirmation does not necessarily a good book make; and beyond this minimum common ground the authors go their separate ways with varying degrees of cogency, eloquence, and wit.

The best things in the book are very good indeed. Reprinted from *Social Problems* is Alvin Gouldner's critique of Max Weber, which dares to understand the complex ambivalences behind that tortured figure's influential ideas about the "separation" of facts and values. An essay of permanent value, it is one of those rare examples of sociological writing in which the "feltness" of the prose contributes to the clarity and persuasiveness of the exposition. It is a thoroughly brilliant job. Published here for the first time, John Seeley's essay deals very sensitively with some problems of perspective and indeterminacy in sociology, and with the moral consequences of the posture of moral indifference adopted by many sociologists. Although some of the questions that Seeley raises have been adequately answered by Ernest Nagel (see, for example, Chapter 13 of his *The Structure of Science*), Seeley raises them in such a thoughtful and original way that it is almost as good as if they were genuinely

original questions. That infamous Chapter V from *The Sociological Imagination*, containing the not so subtle attack on that Unnamed Sociologist for which Mills (to whose memory this book is dedicated) was so widely accused of "bad taste," is reprinted in full here. I do not find the taste bad. Although Mills' criticism of the sociological "statesman" certainly does *not* apply to Merton, whose reputation is as justly and securely founded as any sociologist's, it is very valuable for its almost perfect characterization of a type every sociologist knows at least one too many of. Lewis Feuer's essay on the history of the concept of alienation is a model of clear-eyed, scholarly thinking about an idea which, abandoned by its parents and relocated in a foster home in sociology, has comforted far too many less than clear-eyed sociologists.

Unfortunately, not everything in the book is up to the standard set by these essays. Reprinted from *Studies on the Left*, the essay by Hans Gerth and Saul Landau is simply one long peevish grievance against sociology for its alleged neglect of macro-historical concerns. It contains many of the routine complaints one hears about "empirical" sociology, but very little understanding of why sociologists do not engage in more historical research of a sociological character. Surely one important reason is that most sociologists (particularly American sociologists) are simply not in possession of the linguistic skills, the historiographic sophistication, and the sheer scholarly patience that it takes to do good historical and comparative sociology. That they are not is no doubt to some extent a matter of the failure of universities and other institutions which contribute to the support of research, but these are matters about which "sociology" can do very little. *Sociologists*, however, can use such influence as they have to see to it, for example, that students are well trained in historical method, that their language examinations do not become empty ritual, and that the appreciation of the historical character of social problems be encouraged. Under the best of circumstances, historical sociology is difficult to do well, but when it is done well "sociology" has been quick to recognize and reward it. If less time were devoted to mourning the absence of Webers in contemporary sociology, there would be more time to create a literature of historical sociology from which students could choose models to emulate.

If Gerth and Landau are peevish about "sociology," Maurice Stein is peevish about "systematic" sociology. Stein affirms clearly enough

his preference for "unsystematic" thinkers like Hannah Arendt, Paul Goodman, and Norman Brown over "systematic" thinkers like Merton; less than clear, however, is what Stein means by a "poetic metaphor" and by his suggestion that "drama" and "history," as poetic metaphors in sociology, are suppressed or ignored or relegated to the margins of sociology or out of the discipline altogether by the domination of "system" thinking—which is no less a poetic metaphor than the others. If he means what I think he means, he is mistaken. The American Sociological Association (whose activities we may use as criteria) has only this year for the first time seen fit to give its MacIver Award to a purely "systematic" thinker. In previous years, Erving Goffman received it for a book self-consciously "dramatistic," and Reinhard Bendix for a book self-consciously historical and comparative—and a study in the sociology of knowledge at that! Others, less eminent and too numerous to mention, have reaped corresponding rewards for works similarly "unsystematic." Moreover, when the ASA can elect *both* Paul Lazarsfeld *and* Herbert Blumer to its Presidency, when in successive years, it can elect three men of such dissimilar cast of mind as Everett Hughes, George Homans, and Pitirim Sorokin, it means that whatever group "controls" the ASA is far from monolithic; it means also that no sociologist need resign himself to living on the margins of sociology— unless that is where he wants to live. Sociology, to be sure, has its intellectual martinets, but compared with the other social sciences, it is a veritable free market of ideas and intellectual styles in which it is still more than possible for almost any crazy idea to get a sympathetic hearing so *long as an interesting book can be made of it*. And even that isn't necessary if you have access to a ditto machine and well placed friends to quote your unpublished manuscripts in the learned journals. Many sociologists are so bored with most of the things they have to read, that a really interesting book, however heretical of the received wisdom, is likely to be welcomed with at least respectful, if not uniformly good, reviews. The editors' own *The Eclipse of Community* and *Small Town in Mass Society* are cases in point. This does not mean that there is not a self-conscious elite in the ASA but only that it is neither monolithic nor powerful enough safely to ignore the superior intellectual achievements of hostile outsiders.

Fortunately, Stein's sense of persecution does not dominate most of the essays. Confidently straightforward and urbane, Robert Nisbet

reminds us that the great sociological visions which informed the life work of Durkheim, Weber, and Simmel were not come by "scientifically," but through much the same sort of inspiration that "possesses" artists, and that to forget the art in sociology is to risk trivializing the science or losing it entirely. Reprinted here also is Barrington Moore's well known article which criticizes the major research strategies of mathematical and equilibrium analysis in sociology for their formal, abstract, ahistorical character, for their loss of the critical spirit which informed an earlier sociology, and for bringing contemporary sociology to the point where it has less to say about society then it did a half century ago. Karl Mannheim is also represented here by his review-essay on Stuart Rice's *Methods in Social Science*, which originally appeared in a 1932 issue of *The American Journal of Sociology*. Mannheim used the occasion to contrast American with German sociology in terms that have since become the standard vocabulary with which partisans of "classic" sociology criticize recent American positivism: it is "methodologically ascetic"; it tends to dry up the sources of scientific inspiration; there is a glaring disproportion between the bulk of the scientific machinery employed and the thinness of the substantive results; and so on. Mannheim conducts his tour of American sociology with a kind of painful politeness which allows him to conclude on a conciliatory note: ". . . there were hardly ever two different styles of study so fit to supplement each other's shortcomings as are the German and American types of sociology." To which one is tempted to say Amen—in lieu of confronting and attempting to explain the disappointing fact that Mannheim's statement is not much less true today than it was a generation ago.

It is instructive to compare Mannheim's exquisite *politesse* on so "sensitive" an issue with the both-barrels polemical style of Daniel Foss writing on the "world view" of Talcott Parsons. I would almost be willing to bet that Foss, whose name I have not seen before, is a ferocious graduate student, the tiger of Brandeis. He stalks Parsons like a big cat, knocks him over with a heavy paw, torments him a little with rough tongue and sharp fang, then eats him. Foss alternates between pointed and relevant criticism of Parsonian theory and bitter, rancorous, contemptuous sarcasm about Parsons the man —and thereby hangs a real problem. For one of the interesting things about sociologists like Foss (and Stein—and others) is the apparently crucial role that the polemical style, the intellectual chip-on-the-

shoulder, plays in their work. Foss, for example, seems unsatisfied with merely revealing Parson's biases, misunderstandings, and inconsistencies; his work is suffused with a personal hatred. He must not simply show Parsons to be in error, but callously and maliciously and dangerously in error. What concerns me here is not primarily the "bad taste," not the offense this does to Parsons; he is quite capable of taking care of himself (he is, indeed, never better than when answering his critics). What concerns me is how to regard this kind of intellectual terrorism *when it is also the spirit which informs much that is good in a man's work*. Foss and Stein, like Mills, are at their best when using logic and evidence to slay real or imagined intellectual dragons. Ideas, after all, *are* fairly good weapons, and if one is not only forensically skilled but a battler as well, it's hard not to use what weapons one has.

But academic good manners are very important too (even at the risk of stuffiness), for to neglect them is to endanger the future of scholarly dialogue. Despite the personal vanities and ambitions of scientists, a scholarly dialogue must assume that the discussants have a common interest in arriving at the truth (unlike a political argument, whose participants, interests opposed, aim at winning). Academic good manners support scholarly dialogue by maximizing the probability that intellectual combat will focus on ideas not personalities, on issues not egos, on the puzzles of the empirical world not on the dogmatics of personal doctrine, not on the teller but on the tale. Academic manners constrain participants in scholarly dialogue (all too human) to yield a point when reason or sense suggests it, while minimizing the "loss of face" involved.

Many sociologists, however, whose spirit of inquiry is sparked primarily by the moral feeling of the involved rather than by the learned curiosity of the detached, find polite debate deadening to the moral imagination. Sociologists like these are quite understandably defending the sources of their own inspiration when, by exercising the polemical style, they try to prevent it from being exiled from sociology. Their very sociological sense tells them (correctly I think) that when a tonelessness without edge is established as the dominant prose style of sociological exposition, it is probably Established values which are being promoted by that tonelessness; hence their continuing interest in revealing the moral and ethical biases and consequences implicit in the "ethical neutrality" of the Established style. But this points up the interesting fact that it is not, then,

any ethically relevant sociology which *Sociology on Trial* is promoting (Parsons, for example, is still attacked for the "conservative bias" of his functionalism) but, roughly, one relevant to Socialist ethics. One pursues these, of course, in the classic polemical style of militant socialists, stopping occasionally for an exercise in the sociology of knowledge where this can be used to "unmask" one's opponents. To the extent, then, that Foss' valuable criticism of Parsonian theory depends upon the recharging of his emotional batteries by expressive hostility to Parsons the man, we may have to tolerate the "bad taste" to get the good analysis. On the other hand, those who believe in an ethically relevant sociology must be prepared to tolerate not only the ethical relevance of the work of the heirs of Marx and Mills but of Durkheim, Parsons, and their heirs too.

Max Weber
and the Organized Society

with Guenther Roth   1966

It is one of those historical ironies that in the very era when the sound of the German language was becoming symbolic of a brutal threat to millions of people, German writers, from philosophers to physicists, from psychoanalysts to sociologists, exerted a pervasive international influence. Whereas the influence of men like Marx, Nietzsche and Freud, who have helped make German the language of contemporary ideas, appears to have passed its apex, that of Max Weber still seems to be in the ascendancy.

Weber was born in 1864, the son of a prominent liberal member of the Reichstag. Brought up in Berlin, he studied law, practiced it for a while, and received his first academic appointment at the University of Berlin. In 1894 he became Professor of Economics at the University of Freiburg, moving to a similar position a few years later at the University of Heidelberg. A severe breakdown of his health not long after eventually forced him to resign in 1903, and until his appointment to the University of Munich in 1919, he worked as a

private scholar and as co-editor of the *Archiv für Sozialwissenschaft*, perhaps the most distinguished social science journal of its day. An outspoken critic of the policies of Kaiser Wilhelm II, he was a member of the commission that prepared a memorandum on German war guilt for the peace conference. He also helped with the first draft of the Weimar constitution. Weber died suddenly in the influenza epidemic of 1920.

His importance rests primarily on the awesome achievement of his comparative historical studies of social structure and social change, which provide the most comprehensive account of the nature of an industrialized and bureaucratized world, and of the types of men (we call them Organization Men today) who spend their lives in the shadow of giant organizations, and who feel impelled to understand their origins and to anticipate their future.

Weber lived and struggled for many years with a series of intellectual tensions that periodically exhausted him (and at one point almost destroyed him); yet he maintained a bleak, clear-eyed, undeluded stoicism without a trace either of self-pity or self-congratulation.

He was a stern moralist committed to a relativist doctrine, a man of no particular religious faith who spent a good part of his life studying the world religions. He was the major prophet of bureaucracy as the incarnation of rationality who yet saw it moving Western civilization toward a "polar night of icy darkness," whose dominant figures would be "specialists without spirit or vision and voluptuaries without heart."

Although Weber began his scholarly work in the highly specialized field of legal and economic history, he soon turned his attention to broad methodological problems, and became a vigorous and articulate spokesman for the idea of an objective, "value-free" social science. He believed that scientific knowledge offered no solution to fundamental ethical problems of conduct; he was in this sense a relativist. He also believed that factual knowledge of the probable consequences of one's action was a moral obligation, and his view that the superiority of one set of ethical imperatives to any other could never be "proved" apparently never weakened his own severe moral sense. Weber could be an intense partisan of "decency" while at the same time believing that what was decent was ultimately a matter of feeling and opinion about which men might irreconcilably disagree.

Weber's position here was based not simply on the logician's assertion that values cannot be deduced from facts. As an occupant of university chairs in law, political economy, and political science, he had the practical problems of the German university before him. He saw his colleagues using the lecturer's podium for nationalist propaganda which he felt that students needed far less than they needed the discipline of coping with inconvenient facts. But Weber's stand against politics in the classroom was not the sort of self-serving plea that might be made by a timid academician who longed for the safety of the world of facts. Personally, he was an eloquent rhetorician and an abrasive polemicist who held his own in several bitter controversies.

Academicians who professed too much were only half the problem as Weber saw it. He thought also that too many students were caught up in a romantic cult of experience through which they tried to transform even professors into political heroes and ideological leaders—anything but what most of them were suited for. Weber looked with a scholar's disdain—almost scorn—on those young persons who came to the university craving "personality" and "personal experience" as a substitute for what they perceived as the "unreal realm of artificial abstractions" which science and scholarship provided them.

In this respect, many German students who adhered to the Youth Movement before World War I and to resentment-laden paramilitary cliques afterward were not greatly different in temperament from those young intellectuals today who react against what they perceive as institutionalized duplicity and bureaucratic depersonalization. Their reactions take the forms of demands for personal authenticity and cries of Live! Get High! Break Through! Confront!—as if the world had not already had enough melancholy recent experience with these desperate calls to trust the blood or the feelings or the senses. "In the field of science," said Weber in his most severe voice, "only he who is devoted *solely* to the work at hand has 'personality'." The rest he regarded as so much pandering to the crowd.

Just as the scholar and the scientist must cope with the tensions between facts and values, so political men must face the tensions between what Weber called an "ethic of good intentions" (which might disregard the less fortunate consequences of its high-minded ideals) and an ethic of pragmatic responsibility (which attempts not only to balance the claims of ethical ideals with the possibilities of political

effectiveness, but to deal with the problem of priority among conflicting ethical ideals).

Weber was no starry-eyed innocent from the ivory tower. Having
grown up in the highly charged atmosphere of Bismarck's reckless
domestic politics and in a political household frequented by some of
the outstanding scholars and politicians of the day, he understood
that political men were properly judged neither by the purity of their
motives nor the nobility of their sentiments nor the elevation of their
rhetoric but by what collective actions they were able to accomplish.
Hence, as the proudly "class-conscious bourgeois" he liked to think
he was, Weber berated the liberal middle class for its ideological
softness, and the Social Democratic labor movement for its ideological intransigence, both of which he felt covered their political
impotence in the face of Prussian Junkerdom.

Yet there is usually an "on the other hand" with Weber: for although he accepted the idea of politics as the art of the possible,
he also knew that what was possible was affected by the character
of the impossible demands made, and that it was precisely ideologies of the instransigent sort which generated enough moral fervor
among their adherents to make such demands. For the serious political man who understands this, politics becomes a cruel and
absurd game which must nevertheless be played by good men lest
it become even crueler and more absurd. To the would-be intellec-
tual-in-politics Weber advised: "Only he has the calling for politics
who is sure that he shall not crumble when the world from his point
of view is too stupid or too base for what he wants to offer."

These observations on politics and science were contained in what
became Weber's two farewell addresses to the students of his day
and generations to come. Tens of thousands of American college
students must have by now read his two lectures on "Science as a
Vocation" and "Politics as a Vocation," which he delivered in the
winter semester of 1918-19 before some of the students who had
returned from the nightmare of the trenches to the equally unsettling
realities of civic chaos. These two masterpieces are the best intro-
ductions to Weber's work and provide a glimpse of his life's labors
to discover the constellation of unique historical circumstances that
gave rise to Western rationalism, capitalism, and democracy. Many
of Weber's contemporaries—from Spengler to Toynbee—shared
these ambitious interests, but Weber differed from most historians

and philosophers of culture in pursuing his goal through empirical comparative studies of religious ethics, economic behavior, and bureaucratic organization.

Surrounded by theologians and religious women for much of his life, Weber called himself "unmusical" in religious matters, yet he had a very sensitive "ear" for the varieties of religious experience. His two essays on "The Protestant Ethic and the Spirit of Capitalism" ("Die Protestantische Ethik und der Geist des Kapitalismus"), written before and after his visit to the United States in 1904, precipitated one of the great and continuing scholarly controversies of the century, involving men as diverse as British socialists Harold Laski and R. H. Tawney and the Roman Catholic scholar-statesman Amintore Fanfani.

Weber's thesis, stated in its barest terms, was that Calvinism, beyond the intention of its founder, had provided large numbers of believers with a religious rationale for economic gain through methodical hard work, and that the creed's moral asceticism discouraged the use of that gain for worldly pleasures, thus making it available for further capital investment.

It is now generally understood that Weber asserted not that Puritanism created capitalism but that there was an "elective affinity" between the virtues esteemed by Puritanism—self-restraint, frugality, sobriety—and the requirements of an economy undertaking industrialization, an assertion which has set contemporary scholars to search for equivalents of Puritanism in the so-called underdeveloped societies.

Weber's massive *Economy and Society*[1] and his three related volumes on Hinduism, Confucianism, and Ancient Judaism, together with his still untranslated book on the social and economic history of antiquity, constitute a vast comparative study of the ethical prescriptions of the major religions, the political and administrative organization of the great empires, and the social groups and classes linked or opposed to each by economic or ideological interests.

Rejecting both the purely materialist and the purely idealist approach to these problems, Weber tried to demonstrate the multicausal and frequently indeterminate relationships among the po-

---

[1](Wirtschaft and Gesellschaft), G. Roth and C. Wittich, eds. (Totowa, N.J.: Bedminster Press, 1968).

litical, economic and ideological forces involved. Whether his thesis about Calvinism is essentially correct is still a matter of live controversy—although given the scope of his research and the force of his logic the burden of disproof should rest with his critics. What is certain is that the question can be decided only, if at all, by scholarship based on the comparative research designs that Weber pioneered.

After Weber's death, his wife (who also wrote his biography) saved and edited the manuscript of "Economy and Society," but it was marred by its incomplete draft form, by serious editing and printing mistakes, and by a substantial number of inaccuracies and outright errors in the sections of it subsequently translated into English. If "Economy and Society" was indeed the answer of "the bourgeois Marx," as his socialist critics called Weber, to "Das Kapital," there is the further and perhaps not entirely accidental parallel that the fragmentary character of both great works has presented difficult problems of editing and interpretation to posterity.

It is not surprising, then, that Weber's influence on American social science has been uneven. "The Protestant Ethic" (already a standard part of the language of general cultural discourse) and Weber's distinction between sect and church have received much attention, but without their proper linkage to his analysis of the politically and legally autonomous city-state in the occident ("The City") and the rise of rational law.

Weber's distinction between "class" (economic position as measured by one's competitive role in an impersonal market) and "status" (social position in a community as measured by that community's estimate of one's personal or family honor) has become basic to the study of social stratification, but much of Weber's descriptions of aristocratic and bourgeois, rural and urban, political and religious "status groups" is not yet available in English.

Weber's few pages delineating the formal characteristics of bureaucracy have been ritually cited by subsequent students of this subject, to the almost total neglect of his comparative work on patriarchal, patrimonial, feudal and ecclesiastic types of administration. The same is true of his typology of legitimacy, which is now a standard part of learned discussions on the nature of authority.

In spite of this lack of focus and proportion in Weber's impact on American social scientists, his influence has been remarkable and is likely to grow still further as more of his work becomes ac-

cessible to the English reader. Weber is a formidable influence in the sense that his writings on social stratification, authority, bureaucracy and the social aspects of religion and economic development are required reading for those who would do further work in these fields. Moreover, his ideas about the relation of ideology, scholarship, and political action constitute something very much like an orthodoxy for American social scientists today.

Beyond these specific influences, Weber is a model to contemporary social scientists in three important respects. His successful research on such a broad intellectual front evokes a sense of kinship in that growing number of social scientists whose interest in substantive problems transcends conventional academic boundaries, and who hence prefer work in interdisciplinary institutes to work in specialized academic departments.

Secondly, Weber is a model for social scientists whose intellectual interests require them to use the comparative historical method in a manner disciplined enough for it to serve as an approximate equivalent of the scientific experiment, and thus to render it serviceable for historically grounded generalization.

Finally, Weber's intellectual stance finds empathy among those social scientists whose scholarly absorption in research of volatile political potential requires them to live, as he did, on the proverbial lid of a volcano, and yet believe, as he did, that "whenever the man of science introduces his personal value judgment, a full understanding of the facts *ceases*."

That Weber's liberal pragmatism and anti-ideologism should have brought him under attack by Marxists and Nazis alike was perhaps only natural; they regarded him, along with Thomas Mann, as among the last great representatives of the vanishing bourgeois era. Nor is it surprising that Weber should have been diabolized as the prototype of the relativist social scientist by spokesmen for the theory of natural right: for Leo Strauss and Erich Voegelin he was a "noble nihilist" and a "positivist with regrets."

It was perhaps even inevitable that in 1964, almost twenty years after the end of World War II and more than forty years after his death, Weber symbolically had to stand trial before a sort of intellectual denazification court at the Heidelberg meetings of the German Sociological Association, supposedly dedicated to honoring the centenary of his birth. Had he not spoken of the need for charis-

matic leadership in the face of universal bureaucratization? Had not his own refusal to undertake leadership turned students away from men like him toward "that Austrian private"? Was there not too much *furor teutonicus* in him?

Well, yes, perhaps there was. But Weber, who had more of the Lutheran than the Calvinist in him, answered these questions himself when he appealed at one time to the Lutheran "Here I stand, I can do no other," in defining the limits of man's responsibilities for the consequences of his actions. For us, then, Max Weber is a sort of hero fit for modern intellectuals because he exemplifies the way in which the moral stamina to live with some of the major existential dilemmas of an age can enrich a scholar's work and ennoble his life far more than shallower attempts to "resolve" what can only be resolved by sacrificing a considerable part of the complexity of experience.

Three American Sociologists

1963-1967

C. Wright Mills / 1963*

Each of the academic social sciences has at least one figure whose reputation among general intellectual publics is far greater than it is among his own professional colleagues. Anthopology has Margaret Mead, Economics has John Galbraith, and, until his premature death last year, Sociology had C. Wright Mills. From the point of view of his colleagues Mills' biggest professional sin was not that he was popular and read, not even that he was a radical, but that he was a political activist and a polemicist in a period when professional sociologists were more concerned with establishing their discipline as an objective science and institutionalizing it in universities than they were with saying something important about the world and making what they said effective in the arenas of political combat.

*A Review of *Power, Politics and People: The Collected Essays of C. Wright Mills*, edited by Irving Louis Horowitz (New York: Oxford University Press). From *The New York Times Book Review* (April 28, 1963) © 1963 by The New York Times Company. Reprinted by permission.

Mills was a man obsessed by power—and by powerlessness—and consumed by the belief that no man of knowledge could afford a detached, objective stance in a world in which men of power stood ready to use the skills and the products of intellectuals for ends over which intellectuals had no control. In an essay for *The British Journal of Sociology* in 1958, Mills put this as succinctly as he ever did. "If men do not make history," he wrote, "they tend increasingly to become the utensils of history-makers," and nothing made Mills more angry than seeing his own sociologist-colleagues acquiesce in what he regarded as a great betrayal of the intellectual's role. In allowing themselves to become tools of the "Establishment," Mills saw the intellectuals abdicating their own responsibility to establish "definitions of reality, judgments of value, canons of taste and beauty"—which are what Establishments establish. In allowing themselves to become the captives of men of power and by participating in the "American celebration," Mills saw them rendering social thought increasingly irrelevant or politically quiescent. His consequent attacks on his colleagues (and these could be, and frequently were, unjustly harsh) did not, of course, endear him to them.

Charles Wright Mills, however, was not just an angry polemicist; he was a sociologist too, and the posthumous publication of his periodical writing, speeches, and stray "pieces" reveals, perhaps more clearly than do any of his major books, the wide range and complex dimensions of this very representative modern intellectual. This collection gathered and rather reverently introduced by Irving Louis Horowitz, contains virtually every essay of any significance that Mills ever wrote, from his early articles in the professional journals on the sociology of knowledge to the late Mills, grown more and more desperate, bitter, and strident, scorning "the end of ideology," exposing "the higher immorality," condemning "crackpot realism," and encouraging the development of a "new Left."

His early essays were brilliant and cogent models of intellectual discipline, showing a real and rare talent for sustained abstract thought, and informed by the critical edge and the passion for clarity that always marked Mills' work. In a more placid age and for a less restless man, they could have suggested a line of research to absorb a lifetime of scholarship. But like Norman Mailer, Mills was always running for President "in the privacy of his mind." It was not enough, that is, for Mills to be merely a good sociologist, as it is apparently not enough for Mailer to be merely a fine novelist.

Plunging into the world of polemics, both tended to waste themselves on things that men with much less talent could have done just as well. Dozens of liberals and socialists can debate William Buckley effectively; none of them can write Mailer's novels. Dozens of radicals could play the ideas-are-weapons game as well as Mills; none could have written his essays on the sociology of language or the first few chapters of *The Power Elite*.

Still, even in his polemics, Mills the sociologist is evident. Attacking the most recent evidence of immorality or corruption or political fatuousness, he is seldom concerned merely or only with the single event, but usually with its typicality, its expectability, given the presence of social conditions adequate to engender it. Mills liked to say that "private troubles" occurring often enough and systematically enough were evidence of "public issues," and that as a sociologist he was concerned with biography and with history and with their relation in society. And even his most ephemeral effort, an article on fancy call girls for, of all things, the New York *Journal-American*, is informed by his clear understanding of the relation of sensational "news" to social structure. " . . . wherever attractive, ambitious girls meet men with the money or power to realize their ambitions, sex will be available at a price."

Mills was an intellectual hero to many left-wing students in the social sciences because he was a model of the man of knowledge *engagé*, who fit none of the stereotypes about "professors" and "academics" which have become institutionalized among nonuniversity intellectuals since Nietzsche and Schopenhauer made them the butt of scorn and satire. No sallow intellectual was Mills; a horny-handed man, a builder of houses, a thunderer, an Ernest Hemingway among sociologists. Throughout his life he continually struggled with the contradictory demands of scholarship and effectiveness in the political world; he tried to have the best of both worlds. I think he failed—each of his major books contains serious flaws; but his failure is certainly no disgrace. The scholar and the intellectual man of action, a Lenin, a Trotsky, a Malraux, are only very rarely combined in the same person, and even where they are, one is likely to suffer from the influence of the other. Mills' *necessary* failure is, in a sense, a triumph, for what he tried to be is something eminently worth being, and despite his failures as both scholar and man of action, he may well be remembered longer than those who were better at either. This book is fitting tribute to that memory.

David Riesman / 1965*

David Riesman's interests remain what they were fourteen years ago—when *The Lonely Crowd* was published. He is a student of culture and social character—what used to be called *Zeitgeist*—and in this, his second collection of essays, the topics through which he pursues this permanently elusive subject are resonant with the spirit of the age: careers and consumption, youth and suburbia, mobility and sociability, workers in blue, white, and button down collars, players in plaid, striped, and no collars at all. Riesman's work is unified by his preoccupation with the problems of the affluent future, and even his several papers on the cold war (which he sees as a way of evading a confrontation with the problems of abundance) are concerned less with matters of political power and strategy than they are with the cultural consequences of permanent political and military crisis.

The vehicle of David Riesman's mind is the essay. There are thirty plus prefaces in this book, and it makes little sense to try to summarize in a short space even a few of them for an audience already familiar with his elliptical style. Riesman regards the tendency of his senses to have impressions and his reason to make judgments as sources of strength for his sociology rather than as a mortal coil of self-deception to be shuffled off for the sake of greater objectivity. He still believes in the importance of his own observations and in the analytic relevance of the feelings these observations evoke. A cordial and diffident ethnographer of milieux, Riesman's style invites his readers to observe and reason together with him. Such intellectual charm is difficult to resist and is resisted mostly by those (e.g., certain literary men—and ladies—who cannot forgive him for being a sociologist and certain positivists who cannot forgive him for not being one) whose special intellectual interests he threatens.

Yet in spite of his affinity for the personal essay, Riesman has a peculiar sort of objectivity which rests, paradoxically, on two important personal characteristics. First, he has the self-discipline never to use his studies for irrelevant projective purposes. He can, for example, actually report on a study of cocktail parties without

*A review of *Abundance for What? and Other Essays* (Garden City, N.Y.: Doubleday, 1965). From the *American Sociological Review* (February 1965).

yielding to the temptation to be merely smart, arch, or smugly ironic. Second, despite his personal style, Riesman's essays do not reveal a highly personal vision of society. In spite of himself, Riesman is so other-directed, his radar so well attuned to the main drift that his observations sometimes seem to carry the authority of survey data.

In some of his essays (fewer than one might expect) Riesman's own observations and his thoughts about those observations constitute the substance of the exposition. But even when he has formal data, formally gathered by orthodox methods (as he has more often than his critics think), Riesman is less interested in reporting the data and describing the methods than he is in interpreting the data and speculating on the researchers' experience. He is less interested in the definitive answer to the unambiguous question than he is in new conditions of wonder; he is less interested in settling arguments than in deepening them. It is very aristocratic of him, very un*ambitious* of him (in the sense in which Mark Antony pleaded Julius Caesar posthumously innocent of ambition) to have no apparent desire to enter arenas of controversy with fists full of fact to render further disagreement banal. And it is perhaps not surprising that Riesman's failure to work in the positivist style should irritate the tender feelings of ambitious "behavioral scientists," whose desire for empirical generalization (a good thing) is in some respects not unlike the desire of other ambitious men for a Cadillac (a good car).

Although Riesman's achievements are considerable, like all achievements, his are bought at a price. He has the humanity to have the vice of his virtues. If among these virtues are the openness of his mind and the insatiability of his eye and ear for empirical detail, his vice is to seem incapable of the mental closure that it takes to make a systematic theorist. This has consequences. Without a systematic set of concepts to guide his selection of problems and data, Riesman must rely on his liberal imagination and his sensitivity as an observer. He is brilliantly evocative and suggestive but the suggestions and evocations tend to be piled one upon the other in no readily discernible order, so that it is usually difficult concisely to summarize a Riesman essay or to reconstruct his line of argument or exposition. His eye for ethnographic detail is superb but, without a theory to distinguish the more from the less important details, the result is sometimes blurred and diffuse—however con-

tinuously interesting the details. This democracy of data, along with his impulse to interpret everything, helps account for the endlessly discussable character of Riesman's work, a feature his admirers would call seminal and his detractors inconclusive.

But Riesman's lack of sharp conclusiveness is not severely damaging to the kind of sociologist he is, and given his achievements, it is surprising that so many of his colleagues continue to regard him as only marginally a sociologist. He has the good sense to work in the style that best suits his talents, but he has never given any comfort to those who would prefer never to see sociology proceed beyond the essay to the formal theory, beyond the "sensitive interpretation" to the experimental test, beyond the concrete to the abstract. Like a beautiful librarian whose good looks require her to work twice as hard to convince anyone that she really cares about books, Riesman's intellectual chic seems to be cause for suspicion to his dowdier colleagues. This is unjust. Given the kind of question he asks, he is a sober enough scholar, a rigorous enough researcher. A voracious consumer of the sociological literature bearing upon his interests, duly cautious about generalization without comparative data, having a persistent interest in and respect for methodological problems encountered in the field, Riesman is an ornament to the discipline of sociology, and it is time that this were plainly stated.

John Seeley / 1967*

Sociologists as writers can be classified as one of two kinds: those for whom language has expressive functions, and those for whom words are poor and clumsy things, blunt instruments unfortunately necessary now and then to "wrap around a table" in order to package a point for the statistically illiterate. John Seeley belongs to the first category, and with a vengeance. He writes in a sonorous, sometimes almost incantational, structurally complex, and occasionally eloquent style, and his preoccupations are usually with important and interesting ideas. But his mind is surely one of the most tortured

*A review of *The Americanization of the Unconscious* (Philadelphia and New York: International Science Press 1967). From the *American Sociological Review* (October 1967).

in sociology, because he has no answers or solutions of real consequence to any of the important questions and problems he keeps raising. And at the points where this failure becomes most visible, the writing tends to get sentimental, even a little puffy and overblown, and does less to illuminate what he happens to be talking about than it does to reveal the cavernousness of his own mind, (an enterprise which is, finally, only exhausting).

The book takes its arresting title from the first of the thirty-three essays, mostly written over the past ten years. It is a disappointing beginning because the brilliance of the title and its placement first in the collection induce great expectations. Actually, "The Americanization of the Unconscious" is one of the weaker essays in the book, dealing in a rather conventional way with the development of Freudian theory in the United States. But instead of discussing selected essays individually, I think it would be better to emphasize a few major themes which recur throughout the book, and which reveal the daemonic fervor of Seeley's mind, as it attempts to cope with the dualities which consume him.

One of his recurrent themes is that sociology cannot be value-free; research necessarily intervenes in the social processes it attempts to study, and it irrevocably alters both the student and his subjects. Moreover, sociological research and analysis inevitably damage the objects of their study, both in the general Wordsworthian sense that dissection kills, and in the more specific sense that fragile things, used to the dark, can only be injured by exposure to the bright glare of research. Researchers who claim neutrality for their findings are either evasive or dishonest, because findings are always findings for or against someone or something. And even students of "social problems," who think their sympathies lie with the vulnerable and the downtrodden, contribute to the political status quo by implicitly accepting establishment definitions of what social problems are.

Seeley has not only a sociology of sociology but a psychology of it as well. Here the main thrust of his remarks is that each piece of sociological work is not merely ideologically and ethically complicit; it is also a necessary reflection of the psychoanalytic biography of the sociologist, and is "intimately related to, if not ultimately governed by," this biography. Like a poem, a sociological study is "the cry of a soul calling attention" to himself, and it is only the formal character of the discipline which "misleadingly inclines us

to believe we are doing something much different from singing love songs to each other."

Now were it not for the fact that American sociologists tend to be rather timid thinkers, particularly where pieties about science are concerned, there would be nothing particularly original or even unusual about these ideas coming from someone in touch with contemporary social thinking outside of academic sociology. The moral passion and the anguished urgency with which Seeley presses these ideas, however, suggest that they are significant less as criticism of dominant trends in the field which he aims to correct and more as the expressive gesturing, alternating between despair and utopian visions of change, of someone who has become really a sort of antisociologist, someone who believes that what most sociologists are doing most of the time—indeed, the very ethos of modern sociology—reflects the morally indifferent and dehumanizing tendencies characteristic of science and of postindustrial mass society in general, a situation that can hardly be corrected at all short of revolution.

Thus, that the study of society affects the conditions under which what is said of it is true, is for Seeley less a methodological problem to be soberly noted and hopefully anticipated with appropriate control devices than it is a moral problem calling the investigator to ponder his scientific and moral identity and the ethical warrant for his work. Seeley's observation that the very conception of "social problems" reflects political judgments and is biased to that extent is not an occasion for him to criticize specific empirical studies and to point out how their conclusions or findings might have been different had different conceptual categories been used; nor is it an occasion to construct a sociological theory of deviance. Instead he reminds us that we are, willy-nilly, social critics, and he calls us to search our consciences for things "not done that we ought to have done, and . . . things done that we ought not to have done, and what health is there in us?" His warnings that research damages its subjects and that findings are always findings for or against are not just assertions made without much, if any, evident empirical support; they are also assertions which call us to no remedial action which might conceivably neutralize the troublesome considerations to which he points. Seeley's strictures call us only to agonized reflection on the ethical consequences of what we do. In short, he seems to me to be a thinker intellectually paralyzed by the thought

that any act he undertakes as a sociologist is likely to have consequences which he cannot anticipate, which he may not intend, and which may do harm to the individuals involved. Now I am perfectly prepared to believe that these are considerations which might well give pause to the saintly, but evidently they also make it impossible for Seeley to function as a research sociologist.

An intimate and autobiographical writer, Seeley's ideas were heavily influenced by the research experience that went into the making of his extraordinary book, *Crestwood Heights*, an experience which was apparently traumatic for virtually everyone associated with the project. Given his candor on other matters, Seeley is surprisingly restrained about the details of the shattering involvements and the "succession of crises" through which the researchers went in their relationships with the people of Crestwood Heights, but he does tell us that practically all the senior research people showed a sharp career break, that two of the senior authors ceased being social scientists at all, while he himself was necessarily turned "to the exploration of his own inner world."

This exploration is presumably responsible for the ideas in his more recent essays. But these essays have less to say that is intellectually fresh about the state of sociology or society than they have intense *feeling* to communicate about them. Seeley is a writer, full (too full), of feeling, and it is oversimple but not inaccurate to characterize that feeling as alternating between existential anguish and apocalyptic romanticism. Because the strength of such writers lies less in the power or incisiveness of their ideas than in their sensitivity and ability to articulate the feelings of certain discontented sectors of the population, they tend to need an emotional constituency to sustain them far more than do writers whose strength lies in the power of their ideas themselves. Seeley's constituency seems to be the "new youth," or, more accurately, that small percentage of the population between fourteen and twenty-five whose aggressive feelings toward a repressive society are expressed in terms of an ideology of love. They provide him with the "comfort" that sociology does not, and at one point his implicit conception of them as a sort of redemptive class becomes explicit when, in a talk to Guidance Counselors, Seeley urges the Counselors to be Lenins to the proletariat of youth oppressed by a Czarist regime of adults.

I would not wish to be misunderstood. If my remarks are unsympathetic to the perspective Seeley presents in his essays, it is

not because I think his preoccupations trivial nor his anguish easy and fashionable. It seems to me that the very importance of the issues with which he deals and the intensity of his own response to them imposes additional responsibility on him to go beyond the poignant expression of his own feelings to provide some guidance to working sociologists disturbed by the same issues that disturb Seeley. He cannot do this because his ideas undercut the whole sociological enterprise and render it either too cruel or too irrelevant to pursue. But I am very much aware that far too few American sociologists have even begun to think about the problems that hang Seeley up. It is to them that I recommend these essays very highly.

Index

DATE DUE